Indictment
*Power and Politics
in the Construction Industry*

Indictment

Power and Politics in
the Construction Industry

DAVID MORRELL

faber and faber

LONDON · BOSTON

First published in 1987
by Faber and Faber Limited
3 Queen Square London WC1N 3AU

Typeset by Goodfellow & Egan Cambridge
Printed in Great Britain by
Mackays of Chatham Ltd Kent

British Library Cataloguing in Publication Data

Morrell, David
Indictment: Power and Politics in the Construction Industry
1. Mitchell (*Firm*)——History
I. Title
338.7'624'0941   HD9715.G74M/

ISBN 0-571-14985-5

To the next generation:
in the hope that they will do better

'People who hold positions of power or trust
and violate them are probably a more serious danger to
a democratic society than organized crime or crime in
the streets.'

Robert Morgenthau,
New York District Attorney

Contents

Acknowledgements

As this book leaves my hands, I am acutely aware of the many people to whom I am indebted and without whose help and encouragement it could not have been written. It would not be possible, or politic, to mention them all by name and in some cases there must be a fear that to do so might mean repaying service with disservice. But they will know who they are, they will recognize their contribution, and I salute them.

To certain editors and journalists in particular I am indebted. Mostly young men when this saga started, they have acted in the best traditions of their craft. Interest was reawakened when, in 1974, a year after Mitchells left the site, a number of them were invited to visit Kariba where they were given one account of what had happened. Curiosity, far from being satisfied, led to further inquiry and, for some, increased determination that the real story should be unravelled. They have persisted in this interest and been unwavering in their support – sometimes not only in the face of discouragement but at considerable personal risk. They have my gratitude and my respect.

I next think of the ex-Mitchells men whose loyalty and support survived the trauma of 1973. If I have rekindled painful memories, few have hesitated to put me at my ease. I have been too close to many of them for them not to know how grateful I am for their attitude and their help. I cannot think of them without reflecting on two who, unhappily, are no longer with us. David Harries, a superb Chief Engineer, served the company well during the most exciting periods of its growth and for me will always be identified with its image. Len Chance, having left a good job to join us, arrived just in time to become ensnared in the mayhem of Kariba. But there was no reproach and his loyalty and dedication were both instant and total. The contract made great demands upon both of them, and if ability and integrity had been enough then we would have had nothing to fear.

As regards the writing, I have referred elsewhere to the influence of

Nicholas Faith. It was with him that I first discussed its form. In the event, this was something that decided itself – the story could only be told by way of personal narrative – as it happened and retracing steps as each layer of intrigue was peeled away and new facets yielded to probing. The result was inevitably long and, with production dates looming, led to a series of visits to Fraser Harrison's home in Suffolk where, interspersed with happy interludes with his family and fortified by visits to the Pickerel Inn, major surgery was performed.

Then followed a period of post-operative intensive care in the hands of Will Sulkin, my editor at Fabers – to whom, in turn, I owe my thanks for their courage in taking on a novice and guiding him with such consideration and kindness.

If I single out Helen Whitfield from the ladies who have helped me with typing and retyping my drafts, it is not because I have not appreciated the patience and efforts of them all – but Helen it was who typed the first draft, with all its corrections, who has provided a back-up service which has bridged the arrival of two babies and who appropriately finished the task when she typed the Chronology. Her cheerful efficiency was one of the factors that helped me to get the project off the ground and that has enabled me to see it through.

Introduction

In 1973 I received a letter from the late Sir Harold Harding, a past president of the Institution of Civil Engineers and one of the wisest and most respected engineers of his generation.* My company, Mitchell Construction, had just been forced into receivership as a result of a disastrous experience at Kariba, in Central Africa, where we had been engaged on the doubling of the capacity of the huge hydro-electric project on the Zambezi river. Sir Harold, after expressing disillusionment at the way civil engineering contracts were run, finished: 'One day perhaps you might write the true story if it is not too depressing. At what point does a contractor leave the work and survive?'

It was some time later that I was a guest at the Reform Club when I saw author and journalist Nicholas Faith – described by Harold Evans as 'one of the most acute men in London'. 'I want to see you sometime,' he said. 'You have a story to tell.'

If I had thought that with receivership we would have reached the bottom of a cycle, I was to be disappointed, and in the years that followed I probed with increasing incredulity the circumstances surrounding our experiences. However, it was not until 1981, after an extraordinary 'settlement' in the utmost secrecy, of what had become the Kariba litigation, that I decided to collect my material together and to go and see Nicholas Faith at his home in Oxford. He was impressed; he thought the story an important one and that he would be prepared to write it, but unfortunately he had just embarked on his book *Safety in Numbers* (his story of Swiss banking) and it would be some time before he could start.

In order to save time I decided to get the material together and thus it was that some months later I went to him with the first draft of the

---

*1900–1986. Knighted 1968. Consultant to Channel Tunnel Study Group. Engineering Member of the Aberfan Disaster Tribunal.

Kariba story. Encouraged by his reaction I then embarked upon an account of the receivership. It was only then, when I had invested a great deal of time and effort, that Nick dropped his bombshell and in doing so displayed precisely the characteristic that Harold Evans had so succinctly described: a former investment editor of *The Economist* and subsequently industrial editor of the *Sunday Times,* he insisted that the story would not be complete unless it was set in the framework of what he described as 'Mitchells' maverick role' in the construction industry in the 1950s and 60s and the problems we presented to the construction establishment. While not regarding myself or the company as anything but conservative – after all we had done no more than try to promote competitive procedures and the public opening of tenders – I felt bound to accept his argument and thus it was back to the drawing board.

Sir Harold was interested primarily in safe, efficient and economical working practices. Kariba represented a dramatic step backwards in all these fields and it will be a long time before its evil consequences cease to influence the economic deployment of resources. There is nothing new in breaking contractors – it was done all too often when they took such tremendous risks in the nineteenth and early twentieth centuries. And it is over one hundred and fifty years since Marc Brunel (father of Isambard Kingdom Brunel) complained bitterly about those who sought to make the geology fit the plan rather than the plan fit the geology. There was nothing unique about the actions of those who sowed the seed of disaster at Kariba. But most of us might have expected that we had by now progressed far beyond that stage.

I have no doubt that it was in the disappointment of these expectations that Sir Harold Harding's disillusionment was rooted. Questions of redress apart, it is to be hoped that lessons will be learned from Kariba and that the story that I have told will assume the positive role that I am sure Harold Harding would have wished for it.

STAMFORD June 1987

I

Compete to Survive

Early influences

I was born in Wembley – then a rural area – two months after the start of the First World War. My father, who was one of a Victorian family of nine, had been forced to start work at an early age after the death of his father. He was apprenticed to his uncle who specialized in the restoration of old paintings and worked in a family firm established in the reign of George IV. My father had started his own business before his marriage in 1908 and was reasonably prosperous by the time of my arrival.

My mother was a Yorkshirewoman and one of a very close-knit family. Her father had worked in his uncle's building business until it failed as a result of the harsh application of a penalty clause. She came from one of those old Yorkshire families which managed to combine successful trading, banking and a close identification with the Methodist Church. As a young man, John Wesley was a regular visitor to her great-grandfather's home.

My mother was a woman of immense character, wisdom and unselfishness, for whose judgement I held the greatest respect. She was the main influence on my brother, my sister and myself in those early years and her influence remained strong until the time of her death at the age of eighty-nine in 1971.

My father re-established himself in business soon after returning from France and in 1922 we moved from Wembley, first to Brighton, from where my father commuted to London, and then to a small residential oasis in Shepherds Bush. A little before my ninth birthday, I started at the preparatory school in the Polytechnic in Regent Street, where I stayed until I matriculated in 1930. The 600 pupils enjoyed extraordinarily good classrooms, laboratories, workshops, and a fine gymnasium – and were taught by a first-class staff. Most of its pupils came from central London and, after the turmoil of war and the revolution in Russia, it had a fairly cosmopolitan cross-section of

3

students. While lacking the community life of a public school, it was probably more sophisticated and had a greater involvement with the outside world.

Probably the most significant aspect of this period, however, was that I established an axis between the West End of London and Shepherds Bush. I had been uprooted from a rural environment where, surrounded by friends, I had enjoyed an endless range of country activities; but now I found myself in an urban environment where such pastimes were just not available. On the other hand, we were living through a period of intense political activity, and there were endless political meetings, from Speakers' Corner at Hyde Park to the street corners of Shepherds Bush. I was drawn to them as to a magnet. I read avidly about our own system of politics and about the developments in Communist Russia and its five-year plan; and with a multinational circle of friends at school, life was filled with political debate.

It was against the background of the Great Depression that my early political convictions were formed, and they have remained unshaken ever since. I was profoundly aware of the deprivation and poverty in our society and even then could imagine no solutions which were not linked to sound economic performance in a competitive world. I entirely rejected redistribution as a long-term solution, if not a negative influence, in a world that was so full of potential. I could not accept the hypocrisy which sought to put up barriers to prevent those less fortunate than ourselves from rising from their poverty. Economic laws, and not exhortation, would solve the problem of exploitation. I had embraced fully and at an early age the market theory as the starting point for reform. It had, for me, an irresistible logic, which I was later to find had a parallel in civil engineering, where one sought to harness natural laws to work for the benefit of mankind. But, for my political and economic philosophy to work, one had to accept the corollary: corruption, waste, inefficiency and the misuse of resources were an affront to the poor and underprivileged. Nor could this principle be abandoned at the frontiers. To deny the right of the poor countries of the world to raise their standards by means of protectionism and other devices would be to indulge our greed and laziness. In these beliefs I was able to form a personal philosophy which was to set me free to find my way in the world. Right or wrong, it was, from those early years, immutable.

4

Into the world of depression

In 1929, a period of fleeting prosperity before the Great Depression, we moved back to Wembley. I left school at the end of the following year, having just passed my sixteenth birthday, and armed only with a certificate of matriculation I set about finding a career. My brother had by this time followed my father into a luxury trade: he had joined the firm of Collingwoods, the court jewellers, with which my family had some connection, and of which in time he became chairman.

In those days, when there was no inflation, the luxury businesses were the first to suffer and the last to recover in a recession. I decided I would try to escape these perpetual cycles by moving into a profession or into industry, but I soon realized that it was to be a question of whether or not I could find any job at all. Four months of letter-writing and twice-weekly visits to the Headmasters' Bureau in London eventually produced a job in a chartered surveyor's office in London, but it only lasted nine months. I applied for jobs both suitable and unsuitable, and persistence was often rewarded with a place among the fourteen applicants – it always seemed to be fourteen – put forward for interviews when a vacancy occurred. There usually followed a full day during which the fourteen were weeded out until only two were left. On the third occasion I was successful. After a period of nearly four months' unemployment, I was only too happy to accept the £45 a year, together with lunch on the premises, which was offered to me by a City warehouse.

By today's standards, working conditions then seem Dickensian. Many people, particularly the married, lived in fear of losing their jobs. It is almost unbelievable that each Christmas Eve, with the end of the seasonal rush, the telephone used to ring in one department after another summoning members of the staff to the director's offices to be dismissed. This was considered a very effective way of maintaining discipline and I shall never forget the heavy atmosphere that hung over Christmas Eve as the process dragged on into the late afternoon.

I was marking time and very fretful, and some two years later, in 1932, when the government announced that the Royal Air Force was to be expanded in response to the growing threat from the fascist countries, and that there were vacancies for young men to train for short-service commission as pilots, I seized upon a chance to escape. The response from all over the Commonwealth was immense and it was many months before I found myself before a selection panel. I was accepted – subject to a medical examination. I was extremely fit and therefore very disappointed when told at the end of a long day that I had a slight irregularity in my pulse which, though not enough to disqualify me, would require my return. For the next five weeks I was under a strict regimen with my family doctor who pronounced me fit, with a pulse that was abnormally steady, considering that I was in a doctor's surgery. In due course I presented myself for re-examination, but with the same result. Now, I was told that if only I had weighed a few pounds more they would have overlooked my pulse. Ironically, a few months later I had appendicitis which cured the irregularity in my pulse rate and ensured that I would never again be accused of being underweight! It was to be twenty-five years before I got my pilot's licence, sharing with the late Danny Kaye, I was assured, the distinction of being the only person who had at the time qualified directly on twin-engined aircraft!

Very frustrated and now quite unsettled, I entered into a scheme with a young colleague to start in business on our own. We drew up careful plans and stocklists. Then came the day for action. If a whisper got around that one of the staff was looking for another job he was immediately and automatically dismissed with pay in lieu of notice. As my friend was higher up the scale, and therefore earning slightly more than I was, we decided that he should take advantage of this situation and ask for the day off for an interview elsewhere. There must have been some slight upward move in the economy, because, for the first time on record, instead of being sacked he was offered an increase in salary! He asked to be released from his bargain and I readily agreed, but by now I was so unsettled that I gave in my notice anyway. It was a rash move because, upward turn in the economy or no, there was still no sign of a job to go to.

In those days, over three million unemployed out of a working population of ten million was roughly three times the ratio that exists today. I do not recall blaming the government – after all, successive governments had failed in the same way, and there was nothing one could do but keep trying. During the ensuing months I went back to the routine of writing endless letters, applying for every kind of job and joining endless queues. Like Mr Tebbitt's father, I got on my bike to visit outlying places, like Elstree Studios, in the vain hope of finding work. I do not claim to have suffered real hardship – that was mostly reserved for the victims in heavy industry in such places as the North-east and South Wales – but I did suffer from an immense frustration which reinforced my interest in politics and economics. With unemployment benefit, albeit measured in shillings rather than

6

in pounds, a few odd jobs, and, most importantly, an evening job on the totalizator at Wembley Stadium, I was able to get by. After months without even the offer of a serious interview, I was asked to present myself at the personnel department of the EMI Group of Companies at Hayes in Middlesex. Having arrived there at half-past eight in the morning, I found myself sitting by the desk of a young executive in the production planning department. I sat there, largely ignored, throughout the morning while he gave an exhibition of authority on the telephone for my benefit, while dealing with a procession of visitors. At lunchtime I was sent out and told to return in the early afternoon. I then sat until a quarter past four, when he was able to spare a few minutes to tell me that my lack of experience made me unsuitable for the post. As I had nothing to lose, I protested that I had been there all day, and that I was quite sure I could do the job. As a result, I was, in 1935, taken 'on trial', a trial I was destined to pass. My experience that day left a lasting impression.

I rapidly became tuned to my new industrial environment, where I was to spend the next six years. I became increasingly involved in politics, and was a very active member of the Conservative Party long before I had a vote, adding to my rejection of Communism an equal distaste for Fascism. My brother, who was five years older than I, and who was also looking for solutions, had flirted with the ideas of Oswald Mosley, and we had long and sometimes heated arguments about his proposition that a gentle rate of inflation of about three per cent would be beneficial. I recall my extreme opposition, and ever since I have been very conscious of the threat of inflation. I could remember buying a twenty million mark note in 1924 for, I believe, twopence, and I could see no benefit in having an elastic measuring rod in those areas where certainty appeared to me to be vital. Even then I was afraid of the slippery slope.

My progress at the EMI Group was steady but unexciting. 1938 saw me travelling between Hayes and Coventry, following the acquisition by EMI of the Rudge Whitworth Company – famous in those days for the manufacturer of cycles and motorcycles – and the transfer of production to a newly built factory at Hayes. Among the many lessons learned, I shall never forget the eloquence of a very frustrated works manager who, coming from Coventry, with its specialist pool of labour, roundly condemned those responsible for the move who thought that they could 'go to the labour exchange and get anything from an office boy to an archbishop!'

During the 1930s, in the face of widespread and deep-rooted

pacifism and a consequent lack of resources, the government had set up the shadow factory scheme in order to lay a network from which industrial production could be boosted in the event of hostilities. The EMI Group was heavily involved and, with the outbreak of war, it was at the centre of a web of suppliers, many of whom were not meeting their commitments. I had already been given a roving commission to visit various factories and clear log-jams, when an even higher priority intervened: the development of the first radar which would give a picture in the cockpit to enable our night fighter pilots to identify enemy aircraft. This was during the Blitz, when we often went home at night and returned to work the next morning during the same air-raid. I was one of the team assigned the task of getting the new equipment into production. I well remember the three massive cabinets full of innumerable valves, wiring and assorted electrical equipment which was the earthbound link in the radar chain – equipment which would now be accommodated in a very modest box within the aircraft itself. Its production in the time taken was counted as a considerable achievement, but for me it was followed once more by a feeling of anticlimax and restlessness.

Then an avenue of escape opened up. My association with the new factory at Hayes had aroused my interest in building and quantity surveying, and I had been studying with a view to embarking on a career as a quantity surveyor. Given the massive government programme of construction, especially airfield construction, there was a desperate need for quantity surveyors. I was offered and accepted an appointment with a quantity surveying partnership and having secured my release, I was soon driving north to take charge of a small office on the site of a new aerodrome under construction in Lincolnshire.

Aerodromes and power stations

I had expected to find a well-organized site buzzing with efficiency and industry, but was soon disillusioned. It was an organization that had expanded beyond its ability and showed little inclination to fill the gap. The chairman was a staunch supporter of the Prisoners' Aid Society (with whose raw material he was destined to make much closer personal contact before his course was run) and there seemed to be little desire or effort to steer the staff from the paths of temptation. The site was the centre of every sort of petty malpractice, while vital resources allocated to it were being diverted to other activities that certainly did not have government approval. The work that was done on the site was executed with a reckless and even dangerous disregard for the specification whenever the supervising officer from the Air Ministry had his back turned. Together with the resident engineer, I found myself coping with many different management problems in an effort to improve progress, but it was a losing battle for which the chairman's fate provided no solace.

A chance meeting created a welcome opportunity to join another quantity surveying practice, also heavily engaged on airfield construction. Its main attraction to me, however, was that it had, in addition, been extensively involved with power station work for different authorities. With my customary impatience, I had already decided that a constant succession of aerodrome work would prove tedious and unrewarding, and I readily accepted the offer.

Recently married, I returned to London with my wife; but I was almost immediately posted to an aerodrome site in the Midlands where I found a very different state of affairs. My new firm had initially declined the work because they were fully committed elsewhere, but the contract had nevertheless been assigned to them, with the result that the contractors, one of our most famous firms of civil engineers, had had a five-week start. Not only that, but they were unusually well-equipped with a large fleet of earth-moving equipment and had largely transformed the countryside before my arrival. As civil engineers, the firm had not been accustomed to having quantity surveyors on their staff, but they had some diligent engineers. Faced with a totally transformed site and the major task of measuring all the soil that had been shifted, I retreated to my office with the original survey plans prepared by the ministry and those that were presented to me by the contractors. The least I could acknowledge was that the latter gave evidence of extraordinary guile and skill, and showed that the contractors were determined not to be disadvantaged by the absence of quantity surveyors within their organization.

But despite their enterprising approach, here were people who were taking the job itself very seriously and much could be forgiven.

The contrast between those two aerodrome sites established some very definite reference points on my scale of values. The cynicism and waste on the first I found utterly repugnant, while the dedication to progress on the second certainly won my admiration.

I never did know how the discrepancy in site levels was eventually resolved, because after only a few months I was asked to go to Yorkshire to work on a new power station being constructed for the Yorkshire Electric Power Company (YEP). It was to be the beginning of over thirty years of almost unbroken association with power station contracts – thermal, nuclear and hydroelectric – which was ended only by my precipitate retirement in 1973.

During my years in Yorkshire, all my spare time was devoted to study; while at work I was engaged on a number of different power station contracts, all of them with heavy foundations, riverside works, culverts, and other deep excavations below ground-water level in what was usually very bad ground. Superstructures, administrative blocks, laboratories and control buildings completed a wide range across the construction industry. This provided an ideal training ground and one of which we in Mitchells took full advantage in later years.

In 1947, towards the end of my time in Yorkshire, the electricity supply industry was nationalized. My introduction to the new regime came while I was working on Ferrybridge power station. A big conference room was ordered to be cleared, and in due course a large number of functionaries arrived in chauffeur-driven cars. Extensive questionnaires were issued, calling for detailed returns of all the facilities available for the men, including lockers, toilet facilities, and right down to the number of dartboards! Hitherto progress meetings had for the most part been held in the office of the chief engineer of the YEP which occupied the parlour of a miner's cottage in Drighlington, while the drawing office consisted of a timber-built annexe at the back. Because the chief engineer was a very big man with a very large desk in a very small office, if there were more than four people present the rest had to stand.

I learned early that there were three cardinal factors governing the design and construction of the YEP's installations. They were to be installed at the lowest rate per unit capacity in the industry, they were to have the lowest operational costs per unit generated, and, finally, although surplus capacity was exported to the national grid, the first unit that had to be imported would cost the YEP £30,000. Constant attention to these factors was sufficient to ensure a very efficient operation.

Far away from head office, I was by now considering the next step in my career and had become attracted by the thought of going into industry. This was primarily because I missed the practical element and felt the need for direct involvement in carrying out the work. I had already made one tentative approach to the Mitchell Construction Company. At that time it was a small company – in fact, only a department of its parent company, Mitchell Engineering Limited, and originally intended to carry out civil work incidental to their major mechanical installations. It had almost withered away following the death of its general manager during the war, and had never been caught up in the mainstream of war-time contracts for aerodromes, munition works, etc., which had given so many contractors the chance to improve and expand their organizations in a way that was of such benefit in the post-war building room. I had seen the company's performance on small contracts associated with the mechanical installations of its parent, and I believed it had great potential. I felt it was an organization in which I could make a contribution, and which would offer the sort of opportunity I was seeking in order to expand my own horizons. My approach was very well received but, following the severe winter of 1946/47, the then general manager had to tell me that, although he would like me to join them, they were unfortunately not in a position to support a man of my qualifications and experience. This, I may add, was more a reflection of the financial state of the company than the very limited burden my requirements would have imposed!

I was still debating my next step when at least one part of my problem was solved for me. In a reorganization at head office the senior partner withdrew from active participation in the firm, while the other partner with whom I worked, left to take over another company. I had had no involvement with the people who took over in London and, given that the YEP was their most important client, it was not long before somebody was seconded to understudy me. The writing was on the wall. This was about the only time I can remember since the war when there was a brief dearth of work for quantity surveyors. The reason was that all Air Ministry and similar work, had dried up and London offices were having to reabsorb their scattered staff without having a compensating increase in the central work-load.

Fortunately, however, I soon found an alternative post in London with Gardner and Theobald, one of the leading practices. My position was that of 'senior taker-off', whose function is to analyse the work content of a project in a form which can then be incorporated in a bill of quantities which, when priced by the contractor, forms the basis of the contract. I was also responsible for the administration of a series of contracts, including the preparation of valuations and the agreement of final accounts. For me it was a good opportunity to study the internal organization of one of the largest Central London practices.

The firm was still run in the very best traditions of the old school, and the two senior partners, although no longer heavily involved, still had the affection and respect of the staff. The partner to whom I was responsible, though very much younger, was cast in the same mould. Their standards had not yet yielded to the commercialism that seems to have invaded the professions since. My efforts seemed to meet with approval and I enjoyed immensely my association with the firm and with my immediate colleagues. But all the time I was having to think about the future. My family – we now had three children – were still living in Doncaster and for two years I commuted there on as many weekends as I could manage. Meanwhile, I organized and supervised the rebuilding of my parents' home and two others which had been damaged beyond repair by a stick of bombs during the war. I also bought and thoroughly refurbished a very pleasant home for myself and my family.

Into the industry

Taking stock, I could see before me a steady career in a professional practice, commuting between London and the suburbs, which would permanently remove me from what had been a growing ambition to become directly involved in the challenge, excitement and companionship of contracting. I had accumulated a small amount of capital and this, together with my freedom, would be tied up in my new way of life. I did not relish the prospect, and before leaving London to spend Christmas in Yorkshire, I wrote to two contractors, one in Sheffield and one in York and arranged interviews with both of them.

Returning south after Christmas I found three letters waiting for me, one from each of the two firms I had seen, both of which offered me a post, and one, entirely unexpected, from Philip Harrison, the general manager of Mitchell Construction. He asked me if I would like to reopen the discussions we had had some two years before. I had no hesitation and immediately went to see him. The company was still fairly small, and the offices were in fact located in one-half of a large house, the other half of which he occupied as his home. (I was to sell the whole lot five years later, together with eight acres of land, for £3,500.) After some discussion, he offered me the post of chief surveyor, at the same time telling me that the firm 'would want blood for its money'. As I had never asked for or expected anything else, I assured him I had never been accused of being anaemic and the die was cast. Eighteen years after I left school, a deal had been struck that was to end my search and settle the pattern for the rest of my working life.

I joined the company in March 1949 and if I had any doubts about the wisdom of my choice they did not last long. Three months later, after a week spent on contracts in the North-west, I was crossing the Pennines via the Snake Pass on my way home to my wife and young family in Yorkshire. It had been a happy week, and I had enjoyed companionship in a team to which I now knew I could make a contribution. I was conscious of a feeling of wellbeing: I had not made a mistake, but had found a niche which I knew with certainty was going to give me the opportunity and satisfaction for which I had sought so long. Going over the pass I drove down to the Ladybower reservoir, beautiful in the early summer evening. I stopped my car at the water's edge and went for a walk, conscious only that the moment had to be savoured. That was thirty-eight years ago, and nothing has dimmed that memory or marred the recollection of the near quarter of a century that followed. During that time the company's employees increased from two or three hundred to five thousand, annual turn-over from less than £1 million to £50 million (say £250 million in today's terms) and our profits from £28,000 to an average of £1 million for the last four years before receivership. Aided by good fortune, I saw my beliefs vindicated as Mitchells went from strength to strength, breaking new ground, innovating and establishing records on its way.

When I joined it, the company's aspirations were very limited. Philip Harrison and I had had different backgrounds and training – he had started his career as a tradesman and had taken his engineering degree in studies at the Evening Institute of the Regent Street Polytechnic – but our attributes were complementary. He was a man of great energy, who believed in direct action and, when faced with a production problem, was quite likely to be waiting for the men when they arrived on site in the morning. With like spirits around him, he had a series of chindit forces on different sites, many of them sharing his energy and enthusiasm, but with little respect for central organization. As a result, cash flow was unsatisfactory, causing slow payment to suppliers and subcontractors, which was a source of unwelcome and unexpected embarrassment. My early impression of the head office was of a lot of very enthusiastic and hard-working people walking around with pieces of paper in their hands and worried looks on their faces, sorting out problems which were largely self-induced. None of this is to denigrate Harrison's performance. He had taken over a company that had been run right down during the war and with his direct approach had brought it round in a way I could never have done. My own arrival, at a time when administration was probably getting on top of him, enabled us to benefit each other. I was concerned to establish company standards and procedures and increasingly to involve engineers particularly, in the overall administration of the company, and these efforts met with a ready response.

These were good days because there was an increasing sense of belonging to a team, while as a company we were going from strength to strength. After only a few months, Harrison broached with me the question of the company's future and the need to 'establish a hierarchy' – in which he proposed I would act as his deputy. It was to be over three years before this was implemented, primarily because he was aware of the immense prejudice that engineers harboured against my profession. This prejudice is one of several factors that have inhibited the development of a unified industry able to achieve its full potential.

In 1952 there was an important development in the company's affairs. There had been a steady build-up in the programme of the North of Scotland Hydro Electric Board, but the construction of dams in particular had been severely hamstrung by the desperate and continuing shortage of carpenters to do the shuttering work, as well as by shortages of cement. These problems were greatly aggravated by the seasonal nature of the work. Tom Lawrie, the general manager, had learned of a process whereby eighty per cent of the Portland cement used in concrete could be replaced by finely-ground granulated blast furnace slag, the raw material for which was readily available from the Ravenscraig steelworks in Glasgow. He was looking for a contractor who would tender on the basis of using this material in competition with traditional concrete. Our company was well placed to do this because of our association with Mitchell Engineering Limited, who could supply all the necessary mechanical handling plant and the ball mills for preparing the cement. As a result, we secured a contract in what was to us a new and challenging field.

However, then came an unexpected twist. There were two dams at Glenmoriston, one large and one much smaller, but the scheme also included some four-and-a-half miles of tunnelling with intakes, outfalls, shafts, portals and other ancillary works, together with the first major underground power station in the United Kingdom. The tender documents had gone out together, but the work was to be let under separate contracts. Mitchells were interested in the dams only, although we tendered for the tunnels and other underground works. We were excited to learn that we were the successful tenderer for the dams and were not a bit surprised or disappointed that we had been unsuccessful with the underground works. Then we learnt that the lowest tenderer had made a considerable mistake and had withdrawn, with the result that we were to be awarded the contract, and this time we reacted with incredulity, if not dismay. Our previous experience in underground work had been limited, and indeed our appointment for the tunnelling works was greeted with scepticism and even amusement by those more experienced in the field. However, we had taken a step towards what was to become a major activity and one in which we were destined to become second to none in the world.

This new contract was obviously going to make major demands within the company, and Harrison responded by taking the whole project under his wing. He transferred a very limited number of staff to it and made his major recruitment outside. As the work progressed, demands on his time became more and more onerous, and in May 1953 I was appointed assistant general manager. During the ensuing months, the problems in Scotland became more acute, placing an ever bigger burden on Harrison, while I assumed increasing responsibility for other operations within the company.

It all happened very suddenly. In December, Harrison, who had complained of not feeling well, stayed at home and called for the doctor. Two weeks later he came to the office for just one meeting and I was shocked to see the deterioration in his health that had taken place over such a short period. Tests were made, and early in the new year he was admitted to hospital. The prognosis was bad. He was subjected to immediate and massive radiation treatment, but two weeks later he died.

Before my appointment as assistant general manager, Philip Harrison had been offered a half share in the Mitchell Construction Company on terms the parent company were prepared to adapt to his circumstances in any way that the Inland Revenue would permit. He had rejected the offer, though I had tried to persuade him to take it up. He had been concerned with the burden of debt which he would have to assume. I had made the simple if obvious point that after we had built up the company he would be able to sell a small part in order to repay his initial debts, and then be free. But he would not have it: he was discouraged, and would not accept my plans for growth – 'It provides good jobs for you and me – why should we change it?' He had, in fact, made up his mind to retire by the time he was fifty; or, rather, to take up full-time farming, for he was a very energetic man.

Although we were, as a company, shocked and saddened that a man of such great energy had been struck down at the age of forty-four, I had already given considerable thought to the future shape of Mitchells. The fact that I was now likely to be called upon to implement my

15

proposals some five or six years earlier than I had anticipated was a challenge which, not without some trepidation, I was fully prepared to meet.

What sort of company did I want?

A company is a living thing, with its own personality and its own philosophy. In our case, thanks largely to the pattern set by Harrison, our development took place against a background of fierce independence. And yet there could not have been a more close-knit family unit – though without a trace of nepotism because we had all come in 'off the street'. This spirit could only have originated from the influence and extraordinary personality of F. G. (Tiny) Mitchell, the chairman and founder of Mitchell Engineering Limited, with whom I had had one short meeting during Harrison's illness, and a further meeting after his death when I was offered the post of general manager.

Even as a department of Mitchell Engineering the Mitchell Construction Company operated very independently. Our offices were in different parts of Peterborough, we had our separate bank accounts, and indeed no common services or administration of any kind. When the operation was set up, finance was provided by Mitchell Engineering's guarantee of overdraft facilities up to £100,000 at the British Linen Bank, and as we always operated within the facility, even this was never varied or discussed. Even my own terms of engagement did not seem to be known to F. G. Mitchell, because he only proposed a slight increase in my salary and a continuation of the share of the profits which I already enjoyed. But I had great confidence in the company's future and had no hesitation in assuring him that the terms were entirely satisfactory. In view of the nature of my own commitment, however, I did need to make one condition. I had outlined the sort of company I wanted Mitchell Construction to be, and expressed my confidence in being able to do the job, but I said I would not undertake it without an assurance that I 'would have no one on my back'. This assurance was instantly forthcoming and was faithfully observed.

My relationship with F. G. Mitchell was one of the most important in my business life. Six foot four and over twenty stone, it was impossible not to respond to his personality. He had an infinite capacity to relate to all those who worked closely with him and he was rewarded – for I think it was a reward for him – with their unstinted loyalty and affection. At first, though, I was wary. Was he really going to leave me alone? Weeks went by and I heard nothing. The time came when I wanted someone to talk to. I visited him and soon gained confidence as it became clear that he had no wish to interfere, but was always there to give encouragement. He had a great capacity to share enthusiasm and, when it was present, excitement, and he opened windows on to a wider world. It was a great sadness when, nearly nine years later, he died, almost on the eve of our flotation.

There were, of course, other influences at work. I had gone into civil engineering contracting because I had been close to it for so long, and because it held, on a large scale, all the attraction that the small boy enjoys when, having given up trying to dig a hole to Australia, he sets out to control the tides on the beach. The definition of a man as a little boy with money has a certain ring of truth. I had chosen Mitchells because of its potential and because I perceived a vacuum: conditions which were ideal for a late starter. Probably the first clear-cut influence was the reaction of a friend of my father. He worked with one of the major contractors (Balfour Beatty) and was vaguely condescending, if not disparaging. The implication was that I had joined a firm that was in some way inferior. I didn't like the feeling. I needed to be proud of my firm, and what I needed, others needed too. I remember clearly when, no doubt still influenced by that initial reaction, I told F. G. Mitchell that I wanted a firm that would bend the knee to no one. It was perhaps ill-expressed. Maybe it said even more than I intended. But it remained with me and became attached to me, and through me to the company whose philosophy, for better or for worse, it helped to shape.

The next, and most important, motivating force derived in part from the frustrations I had suffered in my early days. If the company was to prosper it had to attract and retain the right staff. When I took on the company in 1954 I was thirty-nine and had been in contracting for less than five years. We had a number of practical men who had come up 'through the tools'. Skilled, resourceful and courageous, generous with their knowledge and experience, they were the very essence of the construction industry. There were also the young engineers. In what was becoming an increasingly technological age the future lay with them. Each had much to give to the other. Good management and exposure to opportunity would not only bring out this potential but would develop an appetite for management itself.

There was no problem in arousing enthusiasm as we set about widening our technological and management skills. Rather, the pressure came the other way as we sought to satisfy aspirations. The programme of training we adopted resulted in rapid growth supported by an enthusiastic staff. As our order-book grew, I devoted every Saturday to long interviews with young engineers, testing whether their philosophy and ours fitted together. And we could not afford to waste a place: every young man I interviewed was being assessed not only for the job in hand, but for future management potential. It came as something of a shock when, still in my thirties, I realized that for the most part there was a ten-year gap between us, and that I had acquired the soubriquet 'the Old Man'.

A further element in my philosophy took shape much later, in 1959. I had already realized that it was time we made a contribution to the industry at large when I accepted an invitation to join the committee of the Midland Section of the Federation of Civil Engineering Contractors. My association with the members of that committee remains one of the most rewarding experiences I had within the industry. Although some of the biggest firms were represented, we were in the main what one might call second-tier contractors, albeit substantial ones. We confronted the same problems and we worked together. With few exceptions we shared an understanding that, while we were within the Federation we were looking for a bigger cake on behalf of the industry, and when we went away we would spare no effort in competing for the biggest slice. I was to find that this was what distinguished the regional sections from the hierarchy in London. I always felt that the key to a successful operation, especially in the long term, lay in reconciling different interests. At first this meant reconciling the interests of the company, its employees and its customers, and of Mitchell Engineering Limited who owned it. As time went by, I expanded my horizons, which I now felt had to embrace the industry and ultimately the economy at large. In this I was greatly influenced by Sir Miles Thomas, one of the leading industrialists of his day, who suggested that ideally one should divide one's life between establishing oneself, working for a firm, and, finally, leaving some time to devote to the national interest.

In fact, I never did break through the establishment layer in the federation. Attractive as might have been the opportunities that would open up, the price was too high. It was not until much later when, by pure chance and in spite of some opposition, and I found myself recruited to the National Economic Development Office (NEDO), that I caught once again the earlier spirit of the Midland Section.

The brief view of the wider scene that I gained through NEDO was eminently satisfying, but it also served to convince me that the price of progress is constant vigilance.

By the time I had joined the Midland Section of the Federation in 1959 I had become convinced that there was indeed a vacuum and that the rewards for efficient organization through high output and productivity were there for the taking. We had already proved it in the field on a number of occasions and were to prove it extensively in the future. There is, in fact, an incredible flexibility of output within the industry, margins that can become multiples rather than variations of a few percentage points.

The management aim at Mitchells was to organize as efficiently as possible, to offer the men the opportunity of earning good money, and then to leave it to them. Given these conditions, they never failed to respond. It is only in conditions of inefficiency, frustration and uncertainty that morale degenerates and disaffection and unrest thrive. Unfortunately they have been generated all too often in the industry at large by management defects, for which the men are in no way responsible.

In practical terms, efficient organization amounts to the rapid transmission of effective and accurate information and the elimination of special cases. This leaves no room for intrigue, deceit, corruption or lying. There is nothing altruistic about such standards; they are practical and efficient, creating an environment which encourages confidence and allows targets to be more rapidly achieved.

Strengthening foundations: 1954–58

By the time I was appointed general manager, Glenmoriston had become a source of anxiety and was beginning to show a very serious and consistent adverse cash flow. In his closing months Harrison had not been able to give it the vigorous attention that it would normally have had and, due to the way our roles had been compartmentalized, I had not even visited the site. That had to be my first priority. It represented such a substantial proportion of our business that the health of the company was inextricably bound up with it. There was therefore an urgent need to get a wider and more balanced order-book so that our welfare could not be placed in jeopardy by a single contract.

My first visit to Glenmoriston was very worrying. In contrast to the rest of the organization, it was being run by the agent on the basis of divide and rule. Below the agent there was an extremely enthusiastic and able, albeit frustrated, echelon of young engineers, whose links with the work-force had not been properly forged. I decided to introduce on to the site a works manager to bridge the gap, a man who

19

had trained as a bricklayer and who, although he had never dealt with hydroelectric works, had proved his worth on power station and other contracts. His arrival provoked a twofold reaction. First, he became the immediate object of political intrigue, and I had to remove the agent and promote the works manager to fill his place. This was one of the very few dismissals that ever took place while I was with the company. Second, the consulting engineer informed me that he thought there should be an engineer in charge of the site. He was a very pleasant man, for whom I later developed the greatest respect, but I had to tell him such decisions were for the company to make. It was therefore a matter of great satisfaction that the site rapidly welded together. In due course, despite having to work through one of the worst winters on record, we were congratulated by the general manager of the North of Scotland Hydro Electric Board for having been the first firm of contractors who had ever completed a dam on time.

Meanwhile, in the spring of 1954, we had been awarded another hydroelectric contract at Breadalbane. This involved the construction of 22 miles of tunnel, two power stations, one of them underground, a series of intakes, outfalls and shafts, one of them over 800 feet deep, pipelines and a great number of ancillary works. The contract covered an area of approximately one hundred square miles. Profiting from earlier experience, we had appointed one agent to prepare the camp, the workshop and other amenities before the arrival of the main civil engineering force, thereby avoiding a division of effort which we had found to be counter-productive at Glenmoriston. After the completion of these preliminary works, there was a handover to a new agent who was responsible for the main underground and other civil engineering works. The man who now took charge, George Cummings, was only twenty-nine and had had no previous experience of hydroelectric works. He had, however, already been in charge of a major power station and had the ideal temperament for the task. Within twelve months the company had established British, European and finally world tunnelling records, and it was to be the first of three sites on which the company drove tunnels at the rate of over one mile a month, the only contractors in Scotland ever to achieve such outputs. These achievements were obviously a great boost to confidence and morale, but, most importantly, they endorsed the fact that our basic philosophy was right.

Chapelcross nuclear power station

Our hydroelectric work had advanced hand in hand with a number of contracts for conventional power stations, and with the arrival of nuclear power we were naturally anxious to continue a natural progression. We were indeed fortunate when, in 1954, we tendered, and by the narrowest of margins secured, the contract for the construction of the Chapelcross nuclear power station – the second nuclear station in the United Kingdom. In spite of the mystique which surrounded nuclear power stations, we insisted that this was just another civil engineering job, and this was the message we conveyed to the numerous young engineers who, attracted by the challenge and glamour, applied to us for work. To this day we have the satisfaction of knowing that Chapelcross was one of the most successful and economical projects ever carried out in the nuclear energy field.

In parallel with Chapelcross, we were awarded another contract by the United Kingdom Atomic Energy Authority (UKAEA), this time to build a series of cooling towers at the uranium enrichment plant at Capenhurst. The contract was particularly interesting from the point of view of labour relations, and one from which there were many lessons to be learned. Not only was it in the Liverpool area, and therefore vulnerable to the industrial disruption for which the district is renowned, but it was also, as an atomic energy project, a political target which received special attention from the extreme left wing. The project involved an extension of the original plant and, although we did not know it, the cooling towers had been used by UKAEA to divert attention on the first stage of construction. Following repeated disruption of the programme for the main installations, the story had been deliberately circulated that commissioning of the station was dependent upon the cooling towers and that their rate of construction was causing extreme anxiety. The ruse succeeded and the cooling towers became the focus of disruption until the station was nearing completion, when handsome payments were paid to the men in order to complete the works.

When we arrived on the site we knew nothing of these matters, which were hardly an ideal inheritance, and it was not long before we encountered trouble. Almost anything was used as an excuse for disruption. There was a dispute about the use of the term 'waterproof clothing', involving a demand that it should be called 'protective clothing', as otherwise the men would be expected to work in the rain. There was also a dispute about scaffolding. The regulations require

21

that there should be a handrail and toeboards on all external scaffolding, the first to stop men falling and the second to prevent materials
falling; but handrails and toeboards were demanded, not only on the
external face of the scaffolding, but also on the face adjacent to the
wall. After all, it was pointed out to us, the regulations did not
specifically state that these items should be erected on one side only. It
was suggested to the shop steward that, with such equipment between
the workmen and the wall, it would be impossible to build the wall, to
which he responded, 'Are you suggesting that the men don't want to
get on with the work – they wouldn't like that.'

Cooling towers are particularly vulnerable to skilfully planned
disruption, and lend themselves very well to a campaign to cause the
maximum damage with the minimum loss to the men concerned. The
massive and conspicuous shells are only 4½ or 5 inches thick and are
hollow after the first few feet above the lower ringbeam. A successful
contract depends upon creating a rhythm – raising scaffolding, placing
reinforcement, fixing shutters, and concreting – and this is basically
dependent upon the setting and curing time of the concrete. Our plans
were based on the rate of one complete ring a day, and once that
rhythm was established the whole project fell within an economic
formula. Any small disruption, however, destroys the rhythm, and
renders the whole of the work uneconomic.

It was not long before the contract attracted the attention of the
militants. The men were well organized and executed a grand strategy
worked out largely under the guidance of Leo McGree, general
secretary of the Communist Party in Liverpool and secretary of the
National Society of Woodworkers. Disruption of the work was an end
in itself, but the campaign also involved steadily escalating wage
claims. Here the strategy was simple. One contractor would be
selected as a target. Wage claims would be pressed against him and his
work stopped until he yielded in the face of catastrophic losses.
Normal work would then be resumed on his site and the campaign
would move on to another contractor, using the newly agreed rates as a
lever.

While this strategy operated on the labour side, there was no
comparable strategy on the employers' side. When a strike was called,
the majority of the men moved to other sites where they were
immediately employed, leaving only one or two men on the original
site, thereby minimizing the cost to the unions and their members.
New contractors moving into the area, who had not previously been
exposed to these tactics, offered a soft target. Not only did employers

fail to cooperate in resisting union pressure, but the local contractors tended to trade on the situation by promoting the idea that they alone knew how to handle local labour, and they were consequently less than helpful to those in difficulties. I might say there has never been any evidence that they were more successful than outsiders; in fact, many reports of major contracts in the area suggest the opposite.

Eventually there was the inevitable strike, arising in this instance out of a shop steward's refusal to repair the roof of a hut after a gale. The unions were wrong-footed on that occasion, but there was an interesting discussion following the settlement of the dispute at a meeting at the Midland Hotel, Manchester. After the meeting I had a drink in the bar with Leo McGree, who was undoubtedly behind the strikes that caused such appalling damage at Cammell Laird. I asked him if he wasn't concerned that, with so much dispute, potential employers would be frightened away from the area. He replied that there was no such danger – they had the Mersey and nobody could take that away!

Owing to our work at Chapelcross and the settlement of the Capenhurst dispute, our name became synonymous with good labour relations at the UKAEA, from whom we received a number of further contracts, including the construction of the nuclear chemical separation plant and the completion of the advanced gas-cooled reactor at Windscale (now Sellafield).

Sir Robert McAlpine: a brush with a dynasty

Not long after I assumed responsibility for the company, an incident occurred which lodged firmly in my memory, although it appeared to have no particular significance at the time. It related to the contract for the extension of Little Barford power station, near Bedford. This was only six miles from Goldington power station, which we had nearly finished, and within easy distance of our head office at Peterborough. We were naturally anxious to secure it. The first section had been built by Sir Robert McAlpine.

In the event, our tender was successful. However, the next time I met F. G. Mitchell, he told me that Sir Edwin McAlpine, whom he had met at the Dorchester Hotel, was 'very annoyed' that the contract had been awarded to us. The expression stuck in my mind. I, like other contractors, had had a great deal of experience of being 'disappointed' when we had failed to secure a contract after working very hard on the tender, but to be 'very annoyed' seemed to introduce quite another dimension. It was the first time I had been conscious of

any personal element in such matters, or even that Mitchells were sufficiently big to exercise the interest of Sir Robert McAlpine or Sir Edwin.
However, the fact was that there was a great deal of work going on in
power station construction, for which there was keen competition, and in
this particular field Mitchells were big by virtue of having specialized.

The McAlpine family and their companies are phenomena: no
review of experience in the industry is likely to be complete without
reference to them and, in view of the fact that our paths were to run so
closely together, a few notes on their extremely influential and
powerful organization are relevant.

The extraordinary growth of the McAlpine empire throughout this
century would make a fascinating story in itself, reaching its apogee
under the guiding genius of Sir Edwin.

Founded in 1869 by the legendary 'Concrete Bob', who survived a
series of financial crises before he finally got the show on the road, the
family has been showered with a profusion of knighthoods, baronetcies
and peerages. That to be a McAlpine is to be a millionaire may not be
an axiom, but the spread of wealth throughout the family must be
unique in this country, and it must compare in virility with the
Kennedys on the other side of the Atlantic.

The family is well represented in that most prestigious of organizations, the Jockey Club. A recent press report commenting on some
of its stewards designated them according to wealth: from £1 to £10
million they were designated 'R' for rich; from £10 to £100 million they
were designated 'VR', very rich. The one McAlpine member who was
mentioned was designated 'TRTC' – too rich to count.

From my early days, McAlpine had excited both my curiosity and
my admiration. Looking back over the history of the industry one
could read any number of names that had disappeared, for it has
traditionally been very dependent upon individuals. Of those who have
survived, most have abandoned contracting in a truly competitive
sense and, having acquired their stake money, have gone into the
more respectable spheres of finance; Weetman Pearson, later Lord
Cowdray, is, of course, the classic case. But the McAlpines have
continued to go from strength to strength, and while spreading their
influence through every channel of industry and finance they have
nevertheless stayed firmly rooted in their construction base. The
success of the dynasty has been truly remarkable and one looks for
some explanation. One that immediately comes to mind is, of course,
the size of the family and its capacity for producing male progeny. But
that is scarcely reason enough.

Another explanation given to me many years ago, which may be apocryphal – though such is the sagacity of the family that I doubt it – was that the first Sir Robert tied up the family fortunes in a trust, from which its members would derive their income on the one condition that they worked, in whatever capacity, in the family firm – a piece of very elementary but effective psychology. There is nothing like concentrating the mind at an early age and, if true, it must have been an effective deterrent to those who, scorning the source of the family fortunes, might feel tempted to go into the church or on to the stage! Since that time the development and preservation of these family fortunes, glimpsed only occasionally through the mystery surrounding the empire, has followed a pattern of such ingenuity and sophistication that it might even make the Vesteys green with envy. The anonymity, which is the refuge of the very rich, was largely preserved through a web of family companies, which over the years amassed immense wealth while attracting little public notice. The tradition lingered on, with two quoted companies, Newarthill and Marchwiel, the construction arms of Sir Robert McAlpine and Sir Alfred McAlpine, providing the only significant manifestation of a public profile until quite recently, when Marchwiel changed its name to Sir Alfred McAlpine Limited.

I was too busy running my own company to concern myself unduly with the affairs of others, and indeed Mitchells, located as we were in Peterborough, were outside that circle which exchanges information in London. Nevertheless I could not fail to be impressed by one short paragraph in *The Times* which announced the sale by the McAlpine family company Development Securities of its holding in Edger Investments to the Prudential in exchange for shares. As a result, Development Securities increased its share in the Prudential's now enlarged capital to 2.6 per cent.

One of the other assets of Development Securities Limited was the Dorchester Hotel, which was originally acquired by the McAlpines in 1929 as an investment following the financial difficulties of the client for whom they were building it. It was a typical example of their laudable opportunism, and one which was to lead to the Dorchester becoming the virtual centre of the construction industry. As part of the McAlpine war effort, young consulting engineers and the like, who had been on active service, were able to spend their leaves at the Dorchester Hotel with their wives, and after the war the Dorchester became the home of a series of informal high-level discussion groups and, on an official level, it became the venue of annual events, such as the dinner of the Federation of Civil Engineering Contractors. Such was the identity of McAlpine with the Dorchester and the industry that it caused occasional embarrassment; for example, I remember Julian Amery, then Minister of Housing and Construction, proposing the health of the Federation with such a long laudatory prologue about the McAlpines that some members began to shuffle in their seats.

It was from the penthouse at the Dorchester that Sir Edwin presided over an extraordinary circle of influential friends, entertaining them with an impressive programme of luncheons and dinners throughout the year, culminating in his Christmas luncheon, which was held in the ballroom. As a public relations exercise it was without parallel, being attended not only by the rich and the powerful, but also by the great and the good (though not, it may be said, by commercial rivals). To receive an invitation was the hallmark of acceptance even among the most eminent, while an invitation to the aspiring was a clear indication that they were likely to arrive. To leave the function armed with a guest list, which each guest was given, was to have a key which could open the door to almost any deal and the solution to almost any problem.

Though Sir Edwin was the very personification of the construction industry in many people's eyes, he was nevertheless something of a mystery to those who actually worked within it. I recall being one of a group of five company chairmen in the early 1970s, all of whom were very active in the industry, serving on its many councils and commit-tees, but none of whom had ever met Sir Edwin, or would recognize him. To this day he remains only a name to me, as he does to many others even at the very highest levels in the industry, but a name with astonishing connotations. One has heard repeatedly of conferences with the heads of nationalized industries and even with prime minis-ters – conferences that always appeared to take place at the Dorchester rather than at government offices or Downing Street.

The anonymity was jarred a little when the following article appeared in the industry's newspaper following Sir Edwin's Christmas luncheon in 1970.

McAlpine's beano

It's an oft heard cry in the construction industry that engineers do not enjoy enough status – that building and civil engineering are the poor relations of industrial activity.

Let any men so inclined look at the table plan for Sir Edwin McAlpine's Christmas luncheon, held last Wednesday at – guess where – The Dorchester.

CN's social correspondent writes: 'What an event! With about 700 attending, there is certainly not enough room to give everyone a mention. But on the top table I did spot on Sir Edwin's right – Edward Heath, Lord Chandos, Lord Redcliffe Maud, Sir Gerald Templer, Harold Macmillan, Sir Joseph Lockwood, Lord Thomson, Lord Inchcape, Lord Renwick, Selwyn Lloyd, Dr Finniston, Sir Ronald Leach, Lord Hall, Lord Stow Hill, Sir David Brown, J. A. Boyd-Carpenter, Lord Mancroft, among others.

Seated on his left – Sir Louis Glickstein, Sir Alec Douglas-Home, Sir Halford Reddish, Reginald Maudling, Lord Shawcross, Sir Arnold Weinstock, Duncan Sandys, Lord Hill, Sir Max Rayne, Lord Aldington, Sir Harold Samuel, John Peyton, Sir Miles Thomas, Sir Paul Chambers, Sir Roy Matthews, Sir Charles Forte, Desmond Plummer, Lord Perth, Lord Amory, Ray Gunter, Gordon Brunton, Lord Citrine, Charles Clore, Lord Hinton among others.

'And all the guests, as well as enjoying La Friand de Perdreau "True Love" washed down with a Chateau Raucan Gassies, were presented with a biography of Teddy Heath.'

Anyone who can hold a private lunch party and make it virtually impossible to get a Cabinet quorum cannot be without influence or friends. In which other industry can any personality boast such a wide and diverse circle of acquaintances? None.

At an unchecked count, the McAlpine lunch was noshed by some 31 Lords and some 92 knights.

The author might well have extended the article to include a reference to the fourth estate, because the chairmen and/or chief executives of all the major press groups and all the television services were also present. However, his efforts did not prove very popular. It was reported that fury reached boiling-point at McAlpines' following the publication of the article. As the journal, *Construction News,* was part of the Thomson Press, it was reported that Gordon Brunton, chief executive of Thomson Newspapers, who had been a guest together with his chairman, Lord Thomson of Fleet, was urged to do something about this irresponsible article that was said to be damaging to the construction industry. Exactly how the article damaged the industry was unclear, but the editor was hauled over the coals and advised to get rid of allegedly subversive elements on his staff. He was then presented with a list of editorial criteria for his guidance, with which he refused to comply. Although the matter was patched up, he subsequently resigned after more interference from the same quarter.

For anyone who has been offered assistance by one of the McAlpine family, perhaps with a problem in a nationalized industry or with a ministry, this access to power is invaluable. It was an impressive experience to arrive at the Dorchester, mention the magic name and be wafted up to a penthouse suite and, after cocktails, find oneself sitting down to luncheon with the appropriate minister or head of industry. The new arrival was bound to gain the impression that for the first time he had entered the world where the real decisions were made. He had arrived.

This exercise of power and influence, which makes Cliveden like a church tea-party, is awesome indeed, not least by virtue of its continuity. As prime ministers, politicians and the heads of national-ized industries have come and gone, Sir Edwin, indulging his fasci-nation with the manipulation of people and situations, has gone on spinning his extraordinary web.

At first I had admiration for a superb public relations operation carried out with great *élan,* but later I began to have my doubts. Was it 'sour grapes', or was it the growing conviction that the philosophy enshrined in 'What's good for General Motors . . .' was being mani-fested too effectively in Park Lane?

Following the sale of the hotel by McAlpine, the last of Sir Edwin's Dorchester Christmas luncheons was held on 7 December 1978, and the centre of McAlpine hospitality moved to the far end of Park Lane. During the early 1970s, watchers of the London scene had been mystified by the appearance of hoardings around the superb island site at Hyde Park Corner, which was bounded by Hamilton Place, Park Lane and Piccadilly and contained the architecturally notable Apsley House. McAlpines were building a new hotel on a site which, like a lot of other property in Park Lane, was substantially owned by them: this was the Inter-Continental. Some may regret that the planning applica-tions and approvals went through so smoothly, without attracting the publicity that other important London sites had provoked, because otherwise a building that, in the view of many has ruined the approach to Hyde Park Corner from Park Lane might have been modified or its building forestalled altogether. In the years that followed, the Christ-mas luncheons were replaced by an annual cocktail party at the new venue. An era ended as other McAlpines moved in to start easing the burden from Sir Edwin, now Lord McAlpine of Moffat, who had borne it with such style for so many years, and with such immense benefit to the family's ever-widening interests.

There is no denying the immense commercial benefit that accrues to the McAlpine family as a result of the influence they wield. I was once told by a member of the family that Sir Robert McAlpine had never lost money on a contract. The calculation of a contractor's risk is a very careful and thorough operation, providing for all known contingencies, and wise contractors do not take immense gambles: that sort of pastime can be far better accommodated in the casinos and in more comfort. The probability is that, once a contract is awarded and the accumulated talents of his contract staff and the planning department are concentrated upon it, the breaks will be more likely to come the contractor's way than against him.

Nevertheless, it must be said that McAlpine's experience of not losing money on contracts is not shared by many within the industry. The less affluent do not have the option of resting on vast resources and, if necessary, delaying settlement until the moment is propitious for them to get their entitlement. Slow payment within the construction industry is a national scandal, which strikes at its very heart. The effect as far as the most powerful and influential contractors are concerned is to restrict or drive out competition, and it is a widely held view that this is the reason why those with most power have never put their weight behind efforts to secure reform. It is a weapon used by the major contractors in a constant effort to restrict competition. A leading QC told me that he had a steady flow of contractors coming through his door who were literally fighting for survival, and trying to secure settlement on contracts at almost any cost, irrespective of entitlement. Not for them the luxury of being able to settle a whole list of outstanding claims with one nationalized industry by taking a huge lump sum.

It is a question of priorities. In my view, senior ministers, permanent secretaries and other government personnel, or the heads of nationalized industries, should not be involved in the settlement of purely commercial matters on an *ad hoc* basis. This is not a question of entitlement, but of even-handed treatment being meted out to competing contractors. It also raises the question of diversion of resources into channels which can be ill-afforded. Such short cuts are an admission that the procedures through which many contractors have to strive for payment are quite unsatisfactory. If all were treated equally, there would be more incentive for those who virtually control the industry to seek reform and the establishment of better practice.

In a comprehensive study made by the stockbrokers, Greene and Co., in 1971, assessing and analysing the performance of thirty-five companies with a turnover in excess of £10 million, they concluded that Sir Robert McAlpine's profit margin as a percentage of turnover was the highest in the industry, but that turnover per employee was twenty-eighth in the list. The McAlpines are entitled to the profit they make for the service they provide, but what a difference it would make to the industry and to the economy if a little more equity could be spread to those who have no political or other influence!

Reappraisal

Over the years Mitchells had gone from strength to strength, especially in the field of thermal power stations and hydroelectric and nuclear works. By 1958 we had on our staff a body of young engineers, attracted by our performance, whose enthusiasm made it a joy to visit our many sites. They were the raw material of our future management and expansion.

Other circumstances that came together in 1958, to provide an ideal opportunity for a reappraisal and to plan the years ahead, included the influence of the first very big post-war credit squeeze in the public sector, which resulted in a massive curtailment of work, making competition suicidal. We were a private company and did not have to publish our results; our turnover was therefore relatively unimportant. In an industry that had a general level of profitability of the order of three per cent, we were making fifteen per cent. In the circumstances, rather than pursue the market downwards, we decided to devote 1958 to reorganization so that we would be ready for the correction when it came.

During the year we booked very little new work, but nevertheless underwent a period of intense activity. At a meeting of the senior management we decided to give management structure and training the highest priority. At the same time we reviewed the role of the engineers and their contribution to management in an industry that should virtually be their own. Quantity surveyors were valuable administrators and frequently worked in partnership with civil engineers, but in such cases the engineer should be *primus inter pares,* and in order to make this possible it was essential that he should widen his knowledge of commercial subjects, the law, accountancy, and economics in order more effectively to harness the services of those around him. We decided that each year, irrespective of all other considerations, our most promising engineer would be detached from all other duties to undertake a management project in conjunction with management training. In the early years, this involved attachment to head office as my personal assistant for a period of twelve months to undertake a specific project. Support was available from other senior management and outside consultants, where necessary.

This was also an opportunity for reinforcing a fundamental part of my philosophy: that we should have an absolutely 'open' company with no secrets and no barriers to information. This annual appointee was given complete access to averything I was doing, attended all meetings, and was therefore able to assimilate easily and quickly the broad sweep of the business. In later years, this scheme was extended as we developed a very close association, first with the Oxford Business Summer School and then with the Oxford Centre for Management Studies, of which we were corporate members from its inception. The basic pattern, however, remained the same. In addition to those who attended particular courses, one engineer was always appointed annually to undertake a specific management project and he was sponsored jointly by the company and the Oxford Centre. We owed an immense debt to the Oxford Centre and to its director, the late Norman Leyland, and it was particularly gratifying that Colin Brooks, our first nominee for the Business Summer School in 1966, was appointed director of the summer course in 1977 and later became a member of its governing body.

A further feature of our training programme was a six-monthly report on every member of the staff, even the most junior, detailing the work they had been doing, the experience they had had, the gaps in experience and what steps were being taken to fill them. Points were allocated on attitude to work, colleagues and clients and, in fact, on all those attributes which led to an efficient and worthwhile member of the company. This report provided the basis of a review between myself, the director and the head of the department concerned, at which we would consider not only what the employees themselves had done, but what care had been taken to extend their capabilities. None of these reviews, however junior the person, was perfunctory, because the most valuable part of the exercise was the inevitable examination of their own performance by all those involved in it.

The effect of our programme was to create an intensely self-critical management. By 1972 Mitchells had some 235 employees with degrees or equivalent professional qualifications, the vast majority of whom were engineers. At that time there were thirty-two companies within our group including commercial, property and development companies, and of their seventy directors twenty-eight were engineers, fourteen had qualifications in building, nine were quantity surveyors and nineteen had accountancy, secretarial or legal qualifications. Many

31

of these people had a pleasant surprise when they had to readjust their lives following receivership, and their management skills were tested against those prevailing elsewhere in the industry. In a speech on 14 February 1983, Margaret Thatcher suggested that Britain had not produced industrial managers to match its many brilliant scientists and engineers. Testimony to the efficacy of Mitchells' management development is provided by the history of some of those who were with the company at the time of its demise in 1973. Apart from the rump still playing a very significant part in the management of Tarmac Construction Limited, at the time of writing no less than twenty-three ex-Mitchells men are now directors in other construction companies, and no less than fourteen are chief executives. In addition there is a plethora of professional practices founded by ex-Mitchells men embracing engineering, management consultancy, quantity surveying and other disciplines. In view of Margaret Thatcher's comments, it is, however, ironical that all these talents, many of them engaged directly on the Kariba project, were not enough to save the company. As will clearly emerge, there are more powerful influences at work within our economy than the mere deployment of management proficiency.

The year 1958 saw another important development: the incorporation into a separate company of the Mitchell Construction Company, which in legal terms had previously been only a department of Mitchell Engineering. This was a necessary step on the road to eventual flotation, and it afforded me the opportunity of confirming my confidence in the future of the company. In the face of grave warnings about the perils of a minority holding in a private company, I bought my first stake in Mitchell Construction Company Limited. It was a step that absorbed every penny of my available capital. The government-imposed credit squeeze was so severe at the time that the bank could not even accommodate me for 24 hours to allow my premium bonds and those of my wife to participate in the monthly draw, which took place the day after payment for the shares was due. On the principle that one should never miss an opportunity when the odds are in one's favour, I borrowed £1,000 from my brother for 24 hours and was rewarded with a £25 prize! This share purchase was the first tranche towards the twenty per cent holding in the company to which I aspired, and which I and my family hold to this day.

By 1959 we were well organized, confident of our ability to succeed in a competitive environment, and with a management structure that would allow us to take full advantage of any opportunities which the future might present. There were, however, some gathering clouds.

32

Changing the rules

The experiences of my early youth, followed by my attempts to get launched in the 1930s, left a deep impression upon me, which remains to this day. I accepted that booms and slumps were part of a natural process of correction. Their inevitability was beyond question, and it was only their intensity which could be ameliorated by politicians. The extremes of suffering owed more to ignorance or stupidity than evil intent. Through the post-war years I watched with growing apprehension the extension and distortion of Keynesian principles to meet circumstances quite different from those of his day. Time after time, when we breasted the crest of a boom and started to descend, new words and phrases were invented to justify the artificial stimulus which would set us once more on the path to spurious prosperity. I feared that we were only postponing the inevitable and I was sure that when the correction process came it might well be uncontrollable. I could only guess at how long it was likely to be delayed, how long it would take the politicians to scour out all the tremendous hidden reserves in a country that had been as wealthy as ours. I was convinced that if Mitchells were sound and competitive, in the long run there would be a place for us in the leaner economy that was bound to emerge.

But even as we planned, the scene was undergoing a change which was to prove quite fundamental. There was, however, one growing cause for concern. With the vast increase in public ownership and government and local authority expenditure, we were very dependent on the public sector for our work-load. Unfortunately, but perhaps inevitably, the public sector reacted to the first major government squeeze, in 1958, by slowing payment, rather than cutting back their immediate work-load. At first they confined themselves to delaying payments until the last date permissible under the terms of contract. This was perfectly legitimate, although the effect upon cash flow was bound to damage the economics of the industry, and ultimately its principal clients. However, the matter did not stop there. Payment in the construction industry is made upon the issue of a certificate by the engineer or the architect, the date of payment being related to the date of the issue of that certificate. It was not long before employing authorities found ways of interfering with the issue of certificates and, although engineers and architects are required to be independent in the exercise of their powers under the contract, many of them had to face the fact that if they did not succumb they would have no alternative clients.

Happily, privatization will progressively relieve the worst excesses, which are in any case affected by swings in the economy and whether one is operating in a buyers' or a sellers' market, but the influence of this immense public sector purchasing power on efficiency, economy and ethics, is a question of such importance that it merits far more study than it has so far received. Thus it was that the important issue for us at the time was that having prepared a lean and efficient company to withstand and survive any competitive situation, we now found that our limitations were not imposed by our own potential, but by the environment in which we worked.

This was all part of the background against which I accepted the invitation to join the Midland Section of the Federation of Civil Engineering Contractors.

If I hoped that through the Federation I, or the Midland Section, could make any significant impression upon the steadily deteriorating situation regarding cash flow from the public sector, the following years were to dissipate that hope. It became even more apparent that it was not a high priority among those who controlled the industry. This was confirmed at a Federation function at the Dorchester Hotel when one of the junior members of the industry's self-appointed elite, the 'Third Generation Club', commented with new-found sophistication that slow payment was a good thing because it weeded out the competition.

The fact was that within the hierarchy of the Federation, a group of major contractors were insulating themselves from the effects of slow payment, and had other fish to fry. With all the hundreds of different units which had now been nationalized in the electricity, steel, coal, gas and transport industries from whom we had hitherto gained our clients, now centralized in London, a very powerful lobby devoted itself to influencing all that immense concentration of purchasing power. Similarly there was let loose a flood of public-relations men whose function it was to become involved with and to influence those who had control of the vastly increased volume of local authority spending. Only one safeguard stood in the way of the full development of all this potential: the traditional commitment in the public sector to competitive tendering. In order to exploit the situation it was necessary to break down this resistance and widen discretion to make negotiation acceptable. If there is one concept that has been promoted relentlessly now for nearly thirty years, it is that of 'increased flexibility' in this area.

The administration of construction contracts inevitably involves a considerable amount of discretion, but the erosion of traditional safeguards long ago reached a stage where it placed an unacceptable burden on standards, which have always been difficult to maintain. It led to a two-tier industry, dominated by a vast area of cost-plus in disguise. This in turn led to inefficiency and incompetence; and the corruption which emerged in the many scandals of the 1960s and 1970s were firmly rooted here.

Any reasonable analysis of the paths that we were following over twenty years ago would have indicated clearly where they were going to lead. The indictment of those responsible lies not in the fact that they examined the circumstances and came to a different conclusion, but that every attempt, whether by government inquiry or otherwise, to take a hard look at what we were doing was obstructed.

The Banwell Committee

In October 1962 Geoffrey Rippon, then Minister of Public Building and Works, appointed a committee under the chairmanship of Sir Harold Banwell with the following terms of reference:

> To consider the practices adopted for the placing and management of contracts for building and civil engineering works; and to make recommendations with a view to promoting efficiency and economy.

These terms of reference were an indictment, if not of the industry itself, of the overall process involved in construction. The long succession of earlier committees, working parties and reports, all with similar terms of reference, was testimony to the intractability of the industry's problems.

In due course I was to learn that intractability was indeed the key characteristic, and that anyone who approached the construction industry with a genuine desire for reform had misunderstood both the industry and the powerful influences that controlled it.

An economic/political animal, I had studied all these reports and measured them against the background of my own varied experience on both the professional and contracting side of the industry. I had formed theories and I had put them to the test. Equally important, Mitchells were now operating overseas and had had the opportunity of testing these beliefs in a different environment, particularly in Canada where we were operating very successfully in open competition under North American practice.

Certain conclusions appeared to be inescapable and, as Aneurin

Bevan once said, 'Why look into the crystal ball when one can read the book?' During the whole period covered by these reports the industry had operated with a generous work-load. The Banwell report itself recorded that 'the extent of work now facing the construction industry is so great that no efficient firm can possibly have any real doubt as to its ability to obtain work'. I was convinced that the contractual procedures in this country were the most sophisticated and efficient in the world. On the other hand, there had been a steady erosion of discipline, partly as a result of the heavy work-load and partly because of the shift into a public sector which was not geared to accommodate it. This erosion of discipline had already been accelerated by inflation. The argument that any savings accruing from time spent on proper planning and preparation would be more than offset by the effects of inflation was almost impossible to refute, because rapid rises in rental values effectively eradicated the results of even the most inept budgeting. Thus the prudent use of national resources was sacrificed in a self-generating inflationary cycle. This problem has persisted and even increased during the years following the Banwell report, making it particularly difficult to reconcile the interests of the private developer, who, understandably, wants certainty even at great cost, with the public interest which demands, or should demand, the most efficient utilization of national resources of labour and materials.

Perhaps naïvely, I was both interested and excited by the prospect of the Banwell inquiry and report. By that time I was on the council of the Federation of Civil Engineering Contractors, and serving on the two committees that would be most intimately concerned with the inquiry; namely the conditions of contract committee and the wages and working conditions committee. This, then, was going to be an opportunity for my generation to attack the problems that had beset the industry in the past and to set a better course for the future.

I was aware that others held different views from my own. I saw the solution to our problems in terms of the elimination of abuse and the full utilization of our contract system in conformity with good practice, a conviction which had been fully endorsed by our Canadian experience. Others, however, were promoting proposals that envisaged more relaxation rather than less. It promised to be a good debate and, in the meantime, the protagonists of negotiation were not letting the grass grow under their feet.

Hardly a week seemed to pass without the newspapers carrying some piece of self-denigration by the construction industry. Its leaders vied with one another in describing the shortcomings of their industry, as

36

well as the alleged inefficiency or incompetence of smaller contractors, the uncertainty of final costs, and the incidence of claims. The gound was being prepared. No mention was made of the regular succession of disastrous mistakes made on major projects, nor of the fact that many of the largest contractors were the worst offenders in the matter of claims. It was well known that if they could not settle their problems over the coffee cups, they would wheel in claims by the barrow load and win the day by sheer intimidation. One of the largest and most self-righteous contractors retained virtually a whole quantity-surveying practice devoted to dealing with claims on his behalf. The lines were already being drawn for a struggle between those who saw their future in a competitive industry, and those who were determined to establish conditions of privilege.

The Federation's policy in relation to the Banwell Committee was awaited expectantly. Would it be developed through the existing committees, or would a special subcommittee be formed to report back? Neither of these things happened.

The first time the general membership became involved was when a paper incorporating all the Federation's evidence to the Banwell Committee was placed before the council for endorsement. I found this quite unacceptable, particularly since the paper placed far too little emphasis on much-needed reforms, while having all the characteristics of a promotional document for the concept of negotiated contracts, a concept that had certainly never been debated or accepted at industry level. Although only a very newly elected member of the council, I protested strongly and insisted that the paper should be referred back to the appropriate committees, and should only come before the council for ratification after consideration and revision.

There is little in the Federation which is not carefully orchestrated, and this extends to the seating arrangements in the council chamber. At the head of the room there is a long table, where the chairman, the president, the director and his senior staff and senior vice-presidents sit. From each end of this top table, two long sprigs extend down the length of the room, council members sitting on both sides, and vice-presidents sitting at each end in the immediately adjacent places. Across the top of the room away from the platform sits the Federation secretariat. The vice-presidents, who are all ex-chairmen, are permanent members and, in effect, form a self-perpetuating oligarchy. The more transient members of the council sit along the tables sandwiched between the platform party at one end and the senior vice-presidents at the other, and it takes a little time before they get used to the fact that whenever they raise anything awkward the platform's response will be instantly reflected by the other end of the room, reducing the obstreperous interloper to the status of one of Mr Bateman's famous characters. By the time the provincial members of the council, who normally only serve for two or three years, have learned to cope with this they are usually back in their regions.

My proposal that the Federation's paper to the Banwell Committee should be referred back was accorded the full treatment, but I stood my ground and fortunately found support, with the result that the paper was referred to the conditions of contract committee before submission. Had there been time, it would have been far better if the entire paper had been scrapped and a new one prepared, but in the event it was impossible to secure more than some revision and a slight change of emphasis before the paper was submitted to the committee. My disappointment over the way this matter had been treated was not dispelled. I did not think that the membership generally had had adequate opportunity to express their views, or that the views which were expressed were representative. In particular, I felt that the memorandum put undue emphasis on the views of a limited number of the larger national contractors, and that there should be an opportunity to express an alternative view where a fundamental difference of opinion existed.

Banwell was a government inquiry intended to receive evidence from individuals as well as from organizations, and in the circumstances I felt entirely justified in submitting separate evidence on my own behalf, particularly since I had found a great deal of sympathy for my views within the industry. This I did in the form of a memorandum dealing with four items which I considered were directly relevant to the committee.

The first of these, concerning negotiated contracts, stated that, while an immense promotional campaign had been initiated in support of this concept, there had been no attempt to consider the countervailing arguments. My second point related to the question of fixed price contracts *vis-à-vis* contracts which incorporated a fluctuation clause. Here I thought that a compromise should be found and that valuations for work done should be adjusted against an index which provided only a broad protection against inflation. The third point concerned the training of engineers in managerial matters, a question to which Mitchells were, of course, already giving considerable attention. The final point concerned the problems arising from interference, by employing authorities, with the engineer in carrying out his duties, which in many cases frustrated the intention of the contract. The implications of this will become clearer when considering the influence of the public sector purchaser on the industry generally.

The most controversial of these was, of course, the point concerning the negotiation of contracts. My view was that such proposals were likely to result in a drift further away from definition, discipline and good practice, that a release from genuine competition would be inflationary, and that negotiation would open the way to abuse and corruption. Time has, of course, endorsed all these arguments, but I do not claim special credit on that account. The Poulson affair was eight years away, but apart from the inevitability of abuse inherent in the whole concept, the symptoms of similar activities were there for all to see when I submitted my evidence in 1963.

I was to learn later of the depth of hostility my paper aroused in the industry's establishment. Indeed, there had even been an attempt to stop it being considered on the grounds that the Federation had submitted evidence, and that what I had to say was therefore irrelevant. This objection was overruled. However, when the Banwell report was submitted, it reflected all the promotional arguments for negotiated contracts to which I had objected and contained no reference to the countervailing arguments. Nor did it contain any warnings about the potential for corruption or abuse. This was not surprising; my ideas were unlikely to commend themselves to those industrial members of the committee, who had for the most part already embraced the concept of negotiation. Ironically, Angus Paton – senior partner in consulting engineers Sir Alexander Gibb and Partners – who was later to be so deeply involved in our misfortunes at Kariba, was a member of this committee and subsequently chaired the working party which submitted the large sites report on the placing and management of contracts for large installations. This, like the Banwell report, gave further support to those who were promoting the concept of negotiated contracts.

I have referred earlier to the philosophy of 'What's good for General Motors . . .'. I recognize that there is no reason why those who hold different views from my own should not be sincere in their conviction. It is, however, unfortunate that while full rein has been given to their theories the industry is still encumbered with the same problems that beset it twenty years ago. As for open debate, it has always remained impossible. In 1971, some eight years after I gave my evidence to Banwell, I was asked if I would give an interview to the editor of the

Consulting Engineer. I agreed and a published account of the interview appeared in August. The article, which contained a concise exposition of my views, particularly those relating to negotiation of contracts, appeared under the heading 'Compete to Survive' (see Appendix). Immediately afterwards, the editor, whom I had not met before the interview, telephoned to tell me that he had been hauled up before the publishers and instructed that no such controversial material should appear again. He was in a dilemma and he wanted to know whether I could help. I had to tell him that I knew exactly what he was up against, and that other editors had found themselves in the same position when publishing my comments, but that unfortunately I could not match the power of my opponents and could do no more than offer him my sympathy and moral support. Interestingly, the publisher in this case was again Thomson Newspapers, of which the ubiquitious Gordon Brunton was chairman.

I never tired of repeating that the solutions to our problems lay at the focal point where the true interests of all the parties to the constructional process converged, which can be defined as good practice. In my experience, by far the most significant development in the forty years following the Simon report* was the increasing influence of the public sector client. An examination of the way this influence operated is perhaps as good a place as any from which to start looking for the causes of failure.

The tyranny of the public sector

> The standard of morality in the public sector frequently does not reach the very minimum that private industry would regard as essential to its survival.
>
> Lord Chandos
Chairman of AEI, 1945–63

Lord Chandos's *cri de coeur* was uttered at a time when, as chairman of Associated Electrical Industries (now part of General Electric Company (GEC)), he was finding it impossible to extract payment from the Central Electricity Generating Board (CEGB). English Electric were more fortunate in that, although they could not secure payment, they did extract a loan from the CEGB while the latter made up its mind. It was well known that one of the very largest public

---

*The Placing and Management of Building Contracts, HMSO, 1944 (Report of the Control Council for Works and Buildings).

companies, no doubt considering that imitation was the sincerest form of flattery, adopted a similar attitude towards its suppliers, thereby acquiring what was in effect a £500 million interest-free loan. It is hardly a chain of virtue, and those who believe in the possibility of a beneficial influence from public sector purchasing might profit from studying it. Bad examples and bad practice are often more contagious than good practice, and many companies were crippled, and some ruined, by these chains.

It is not profitable for an industrialist to fall out with his principal client, and Lord Chandos must have been *in extremis* to have uttered his protest in such forthright terms; he did, after all, belong to a generation that subscribed to different standards.

It is, perhaps, appropriate to lift the cloak of self-righteous virtue with which the public sector customarily clothes itself and give some indication of how power can be used and abused.

As we have seen, from 1958 onwards, the issuing of certificates in the public sector ceased to become a contractual matter and became virtually discretionary. In this situation, the chief result of issuing a certificate was to deprive the client of an interest-free loan. In many cases, repudiation of the contract conditions became quite blatant, with the threat, sometimes implied and sometimes explicit, that either the contractor accepted the terms being imposed upon him or he would receive no more inquiries. It is enshrined in most of our standard contract documents that certificates based on valuations made by the architect or the engineer, acting independently and, so far as this function is concerned, in a quasi-judicial capacity, are a condition precedent to payment to the contractor. It cannot be emphasized too strongly that valuation and payment as the work proceeds is fundamental to the terms of nearly all conditions of contracts, and it is just as reprehensible, or dishonest, for a public servant to interfere with the process as it would be for a private client. In certain circumstances a contractor may be compelled to finance work over extended periods, particularly if unexpected conditions arise, and this is something he is used to and has to make provision for. What he cannot do is plan his business logically if payment is arbitrary and unpredictable, which was the case in the public sector throughout the 1960s. It was not only the contractor who was put under extreme pressure but also, far more seriously, the professional appointees under the terms of the contract. Consulting engineers, architects and quantity surveyors alike were put in a position where they either did as they were told in the matter of the administration or interpretation of the contract and the issue of

41

certificates, or were faced with the threat of losing the goodwill of a monopoly client.

Problems arose principally because of changes in design resulting from a lack of adequate definition and discipline before the contracts were let, and these problems were usually compounded by the lack of a cost benefit analysis. They were almost invariably swept under the carpet, only to reappear at a later date. In the process, the consequent increases in costs were all classified as 'claims', and surrounded with an emotive aura, whereas in the vast majority of cases they should properly have been dealt with under the contract. This was, of course, incredibly inefficient and wasteful, involving massive diversion of resources merely trying to get paid for work already done. Out of this emerged the two-tier industry, under which some contractors spent their time endlessly tied up with the impossibly convoluted procedures created by the employing authorities, while the more powerful and influential contractors short-circuited these procedures by getting direct settlements sponsored from above. If contractors, consultants and the heads of nationalized industries were able to arrange negotiated contracts in an atmosphere of mutual patronage, all was sweetness and light. This was not because there was less waste and disruption on the sites themselves – there was frequently more – but because there was always a glib explanation and sufficient influence to prevent further inquiry. Under the British system the key to successful contracting became not efficiency in the field, but influence at appropriate levels and, failing this, sufficient financial muscle to lay siege to the client until a satisfactory result was obtained. The powerful and rich contractor can thrive on chaos. Whereas the less affluent firm has to apply all its energies to completing its work and getting paid, others, if they so wish, can sit back quite deliberately and watch the client's liability pile up. They can be secure in the knowledge that at the end of the day they will not only be paid but will be paid generously, together with interest on any money which they have been forced to provide. It is a very expensive way of financing work, particularly in the public sector.

One of the recurring wonders of the construction world is the way that apparently sophisticated clients, who in any other field would readily accept the need to define their requirements and agree the terms with the suppliers, harbour a hope of finding a slick formula enabling them to abandon these principles and to emerge unscathed. There is, of course, no shortage of 'management contractors' who will hold their hands along the paths to disillusionment, and perhaps outrage – but since most clients only commission a few projects, experience generally comes too late. For a number of others pride, vanity and sometimes more dubious considerations lead to acceptance of a situation which by then they are powerless to alter.

Evidence of the lure of management contracting and of the difficulty in assessing its efficacy – particularly when one depends for information on those who I am tempted to call its victims – is not hard to come by. During the period 1978 to 1984 the volume of work let on the basis of management contracts increased by a multiple of six (in real terms). During that period probably one of the most prominent examples of the genre was the new Lloyd's building. As the work proceeded many encouraging accounts emerged from Lloyd's, and in 1984 its head of Corporation Services announced that all concerned were satisfied that both the budget and the programme would be met. As one who had been interested in the project from the start, and had been critical of the form of contract, I found it difficult to understand these statements. The history of the project may therefore be of interest.

The original contract cost estimate for the demolition of the old building and the construction of the new was £76 million. At an extraordinary general meeting at Lloyd's on 17 November 1982, Sir Peter Green, then chairman, in a statement leading up to the announcement of a very significant increase in Lloyd's members' subscriptions, announced delays and increased costs. These were said to be due, among other things, to obstructions in the foundations, the replacement of aluminium with stainless steel following experiences of fire in the Falklands campaign, and a substantial increase in the air conditioning capacity to meet the conditions under which it would be required to work. There were also other substantial alterations to meet ventilation and other requirements of the Building Regulations. Sir Peter then announced that it was now considered that the building cost could be contained within a new figure of £90 million to which had to be added the cost of demolition (originally said to be included in the first estimate), fees (were these not provided for in the original budget?), the cost of inflation and of furnishing. With this blanket explanation and the statement that everything was being done to contain costs, Sir Peter announced that the new estimated final cost would be an astonishing £157 million – more than double the figure projected some eighteen months earlier. With such a history behind them it was significant that having introduced a new, and some would say grossly inflated base all concerned with the project were singing with one voice and way into 1984 were expressing confidence that both the budget and the programme would be met. Nor did they seem to be particularly put out when in November 1985 Peter Miller, Peter Green's successor, announced that with the building nearing completion further factors, and in particular improvements to specification, had resulted in another increase to £163 million. These reactions reflect the sort of cosiness that disturbs many who consider that management and other forms of contract, that avoid full commitment and definition by all the parties at the outset, are almost invariably uneconomical, inefficient and all too often end up as cost-plus in disguise. Perhaps one day taxpayers, shareholders and even members of Lloyd's will rebel and demand a return to procedures that introduce more discipline and real competition in the application of their funds.*

Finance and the industry

The Banwell report provided an excellent summary of the financial provisions intended to govern contracts. It also recognized the existence of abuse and made recommendations for reform. I will quote from it:

> The procedure under which money passes from client to contractor during the progress of construction is well known and we need only say by way of description that, in general terms, payments are made to contractors at monthly or other agreed intervals on the basis of work done as certified by the appropriate officer . . .   (9.1)
> The operation of this system is not always smooth. Payments . . . are often slow and uneven . . . This has an adverse effect on the efficiency and stability of the whole industry . . .   (9.2)
> Valuation, certification, and the honouring of certificates are sometimes late, and in consequence contractors are obliged to use their own financial resources for longer than should be necessary . . . (9.4)
> Many public authorities . . . are dilatory in their payments . . . Clearly public funds must be safeguarded, but public authorities should make use of procedures which nevertheless comply with the contracts into which they have entered . . . It is the responsibility of

---

*Apparently the saga has still not ended. In his most recent statement (24 June 1987) Miller reports 'with some disappointment' a further increase of £28m – to £191m – in the, apparently still estimated, final cost. Yet in his November 1985 statement Miller recorded his belief that Lloyd's Redevelopment Committee deserved thanks for the careful way in which they had supervised the enterprise and went on to say that in the circumstances the cost overruns were reasonable!

authorities to adjust their administrative procedures to the timetable
laid down by the contract and failure to do so is no justification for
withholding payment lawfully due . . .   (9.7)
Prompt payment of certificates and measures aimed at a more rapid
flow of finance, which we have recommended, should minimize the
risk of financial difficulty . . .   (9.10)

Banwell clearly recognized the existence of considerable abuse in the
public sector. After the report was published I pressed hard within the
Federation and council meetings to have some sort of follow-up
machinery set up to implement its proposals. I found no enthusiasm
amongst the higher echelons, and in fact encountered considerable
resistance. I argued that this was our generation's opportunity to
change the pattern and see that something was accomplished for the
benefit of the industry. As the result of initiatives taken elsewhere,
there was some follow-up to the Banwell report, and a further
committee was set up under the chairmanship of Sir William Harris,*
as he was to become, but no significant progress was made except in
the area of his special concern.

Far from there being any improvement in cash flow within the
industry, following Banwell, there was a quite dramatic deterioration.
In 1963, when evidence was being submitted to Banwell, I commissioned an exercise within my own company whereby we examined
every contract in the previous fifteen years to ascertain how much
money on average had been undercertified at the time of practical
completion of the works. It was discovered that it amounted to seven
per cent. With profitability running at a reasonably high level, as in our
case, this was tolerable from a practical point of view, but it imposed
an unnecessary constraint upon cash flow, and therefore efficiency.

Assuming that Mitchells' experience was typical, and allowing that
the average profitability on turnover on contracts throughout the
industry amounted to three to four per cent, this must mean that
contractors generally were financing work from other resources, and in
any final settlement would have to secure interest on outstanding
money in order to render their work viable. On 25 June 1970, at a
conference on 'Contracting in Civil Engineering Since Banwell'
organized by NEDO, Donald Rees, chairman of the family firm
William F. Rees Ltd, gave a paper in which he referred to a recent
report which indicated that between one-fifth and one-quarter of the

---

*Director General Highways, Ministry of Transport, 1963–65.

value of work executed was tied up in financing it. This meant that somewhere between £700 and £800 million (over £4 billion in today's terms) was being held by employing authorities, most of which was in the form of a hidden or unauthorized retention.

A few firm facts may be helpful in illustrating the magnitude of the problem. On 10 May 1973 *Construction News* featured on its front page an article headlined 'Construction Group owed £11 million at time of shock collapse' and, underneath, 'Mitchell ruined by delayed payments'. The editorial for that week was devoted to an article titled 'A company killed by cash starvation'. I have never been able to find out from what internal source *Construction News* obtained all the information that was contained in that article but it was nevertheless factually correct. It was however the aftermath that was most revealing. While the Mitchell affair was still a live issue, another company – French Kier – encountered liquidity problems. Like ourselves they were one of the limited number of contractors who could be relied upon to carry out major projects for the DOE and were always prepared to tender on a competitive basis. The DOE could hardly face another scandal with one of its major contractors and obviously had to come to terms. The upshot was that after prolonged negotiations the DOE payed French Kier £9.5 million *as an ex gratia payment on account of claims* and agreed to make available a loan of up to £4.5 million subject to the right of conversion into shares. Of this only part was drawn down and subsequently redeemed – but the enormity of the figures tells its own story. Looking at Mitchells, Kier had good reason to recognize that it is an ill wind . . . French Kier's problems had been brought to crisis point by underpayment on road contracts. Mitchells' case was a little different. Until 1972 consistent underpayment had only been an appalling constraint on its development – it was only Kariba that was to introduce an uncontrollable element.

Two questions remain. How is it possible for contractors to finance the public sector to such an extent? And why is it allowed to continue? So far as the first of these questions is concerned, it might be supplemented with another question. How is it possible to provide a fair picture to the shareholders? The answer to the first question, of course, lies in the way that contractors value their work in progress. Some allow themselves more discretion than Mitchells, but generally the principle remains the same. In Mitchells we valued work in progress at cost less provision for losses and brought profits into account only on contracts that had been completed and on which all outstanding items had been agreed and settled. The result was a very large pool of untaxed surplus which was concealed in the value of the work in progress and released resources to finance further work.

At the time of the preparation of our last published accounts, Mitchells had within their United Kingdom operating companies alone approximately £125 million of orders. Of this, about £75 million represented completed work, in respect of which no profit had been taken, all overheads had been written off, and a reserve of £2,612,000 had been provided for contingencies. Thus there are three vital elements in the accounts: first, not taking any profit at all on uncompleted contracts results in an overall conservatism. This is particularly the case because a contract is not regarded as complete until the last 't' is crossed, the last 'i' dotted, and the final account settled and paid. The remaining two elements are the incorporation of the profit on finalized contracts which, of course, permits no discretion, and the provision for contingencies, which is a matter for a contractor's judgement. It is therefore possible for a contractor to accumulate a vast reserve of undisclosed profit. Alternatively, if a contractor has had a very bad time, he may widen arbitrary provisions for losses in order to give himself a good base from which to start a 'recovery'. In all these matters discretion plays a large part, but it has to be remembered that when profits do fall, tax will have to be paid on them. It may be thought that there is an element of rough justice in the fact that unpaid tax is one of the primary sources of capital to finance government work. But, on the other hand, all such financial considerations are reflected in the overall economics of the industry, and therefore in the tender price and the ultimate cost of the work. To cite Canada yet again, where the tax laws are different, and work in progress is valued realistically, what a boon it would be to have within our construction industry the same element of certainty regarding receipts and disbursements which the Canadians enjoy!

Given the method of valuing work in progress and the tremendously high incidence of post-completion payments in the form of claims, how can a public company give a fair picture to its shareholders? Knowing that it has an immense reservoir of concealed profit, does it smooth out the peaks and troughs? Does it show losses when it knows there are none? And does it thereafter show an extra £1 or £2 million windfall profit in a single year because a long outstanding account has been settled? These matters call for careful judgement, particularly when it is known that information is available, or could be available, to speculators (including, for example, the pension funds of some of the big employing authorities!). Mitchells conducted their affairs very prudently, and for us to have taken a more conservative view would have been to present a very unrealistic picture to the shareholders.

If it is accepted, as it must be, that notwithstanding Banwell there was a massive deterioration in the cash flow position in the construction industry, how and why did this come about?

The two-tier industry

The following is an extract from the paper that I submitted to Banwell in 1963:

> With the increased proportion of negotiated work concentrated in the hands of relatively few contractors, these firms are able to insulate themselves to a considerable extent from the effects of the competitive price mechanism. The situation gives rise to a double price structure in the industry, and the more the proportion of negotiated work extends, the more unhealthy will the competition for the remainder become; at the same time, those who find refuge in an increasing proportion of negotiated work can, thus subsidized, push prices in the competitive sphere down still further when they wish to maintain or inflate turnover.

I expanded upon this in my chairman's statement accompanying the 1963 accounts, with further reference to the effect upon wages:

> Tremendous efforts have been made by contractors generally to secure protection against the cold winds of competition by promoting negotiated and speculative work. I am in no doubt that this has created, at least temporarily, a double price structure in the industry and a division of interest in securing healthy contractual arrangements . . . By far the most important consequence is the undermining of the wage structure which is inevitable when the normal limitations placed on a contractor by competition no longer apply. Many arguments are put forward in favour of negotiation, valid only in a very limited number of cases, but I believe it is only competition that can create a proper price structure, and that it is only against the background of competition that we can hope to protect our wage structure . . .
>
> This is not a plea to limit wages; in fact, I think that a rationalization of our wage structure, and in particular of the hourly rate when considered in conjunction with excessive overtime working and the payment of so-called 'incentive bonuses' . . . may be long overdue, but anything that weakens the accepted and agreed structure,

weakens the unions in their efforts to establish responsible leadership, and is inflationary.

These trends which could be clearly identified before 1963 intensified throughout the decade. In the conditions created by successive governments, it was unavoidable that clients in the private sector were sometimes waiting in the anterooms of some of our biggest and most influential contractors trying to get contracts signed on almost any terms. The traditional relationship between contractors, architects, quantity surveyors and consulting engineers changed. Some climbed on a shared bandwagon and pushed their product in a joint commercial relationship that went far beyond the modest reform which was necessary to draw the industry together. By doing so they undermined the very fabric of professionalism itself. There are innumerable monuments to those days, when costs escalated in multiples rather than percentages, and the commercial viability of projects was only saved, and in some cases turned into massive profitability, by the process of inflation.

If a private client decided that, as a result of inflation, it was wise to make a very early start on a job without adequate preparation, and to shoulder the increased costs knowing that they would be absorbed in the eventual out-turn, it would be difficult under my philosophy to interfere with his judgement. There are, however, two things to be borne in mind: first, the resources that are wasted are national resources and they are lost for ever. Second – and here again there is a distinction between practices in this country and in North America – there is no sensible wage structure in Britain, and lack of competition leads to ever-widening and inflationary abuse.

The concept of entering into a contract on an ill-prepared basis, relying upon inflation to balance the eventual equation, is completely unacceptable for work in the public sector. The government's primary duty to maintain a stable currency and secure the proper use of national resources is in direct conflict with non-competitive and inefficient practices in the public sector, which fuel inflation.

My opposition and attempts to highlight inherent dangers in the false climate that was being created by the promotion of sectional interests were deeply resented by certain of the major contractors in 1963, but subsequent events showed my warnings to have been justified. In this connection a comparison of the indices for retail prices, building costs and tenders, for the years since Banwell (see graph, p. 50) confirms very clearly the validity of the arguments.

49

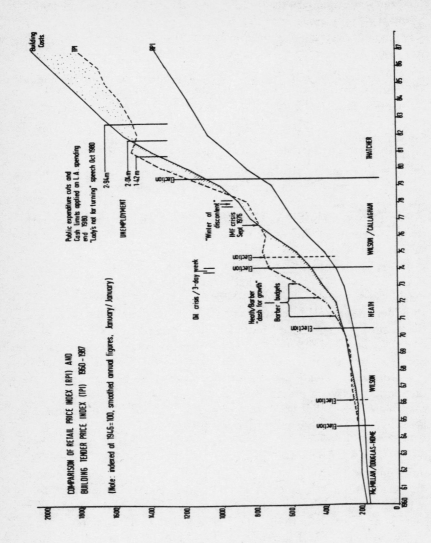

Index of construction costs

Graph showing comparison between building costs (derived from the basic costs of labour and materials), the retail price index and the tender price index (derived from tenders actually received).
The graph indicates dramatically the influences of different factors on construction costs and the speed with which costs react to inflationary influences.

A number of factors affected building costs from the early 1960s onwards causing them dramatically to outstrip the retail price index (RPI), but the absence of a reasonable wage structure and the irresponsible behaviour of the industry, particularly in regard to tendering procedures, turned it into an engine for inflation. The situation was not improved by the Heath government's 'dash for growth', the consequences of which are vividly revealed in the graph. It is a sad fact that even now, in spite of our immense unemployment problem, resources diverted into the construction industry, except on the most carefully regulated and competitive terms, will be more inflationary than reflationary in their effect. As I write this in 1987, the speed with which construction costs react to demand is being dramatically illustrated in the redevelopment of the London dockland. Contractors are being paid as much as £50 per man per day over and above agreed contract rates for such trades as plastering in order to secure completion of urgently required projects.

In 1972 two leading trade unionists – George Smith, general secretary of the Union of Construction and Allied Trades and Technicians, and chairman of the Trades Union Congress (TUC), and Leslie Kemp, national secretary of the Building Construction and Civil Engineering Group of the Transport and General Workers' Union – complained bitterly that a very substantial proportion of the work-load on which their men were engaged was 'cost-plus in disguise'. As a result, they were trying to negotiate an extra shilling an hour for men who were already being paid £50 per week (quite a significant sum in those days). When a cost-plus situation exists on one major site, it cannot be confined within a ring fence and it will spread. It is not taxing the imagination too far to see how the whole of industry has been infected, and remains infected, by the influence of cost-plus in construction. If one accepts that most of the defence industries are cost-plus, that the nationalized industries are cost-plus almost by definition, and if one then adds a cost-plus construction industry, it is not difficult to argue that this makes for a cost-plus economy. There is, of course, no way that a cost-plus economy can survive, and the road back is still going to be a long one.

Power in the industry

If a determined attempt had been made to secure reform in three vital areas – those of definition, discipline and cash flow – there would undoubtedly have been dramatic improvement in the industry's efficiency following publication of the Banwell report. But the fact is that the leaders of the industry were striving for something quite different from what was required by the rank and file, and it is perhaps instructive to examine this dichotomy.

There are two principal organizations that represent contractors' interests – the Building Employers Confederation (BEC; previously the National Federation of Building Trades Employers) and the Federation of Civil Engineering Contractors (FCEC). There are also two other bodies: the National Contractors' Group, whose membership is by invitation and which is organized by the largest contractors active in both building and civil engineering, and who want to protect their particular interests; and also a new group which has grown out of what was previously the Dorchester Group and before that the Third Generation Club, the origins of which are clearly discernible from its title. The Dorchester Group, immensely powerful and influential, was the power behind the scenes that controlled the FCEC. Originally comprised of what one might call master contractors (men who virtually controlled their family companies), members were admitted to the ranks if or when they became so powerful that their presence could no longer be ignored. The pattern started to change in the mid 1970s when, with the passing from the scene of some of the older members and the emergence of big new constructional units such as Trafalgar House, the family element was diluted as there was little alternative but to admit professional managers to the group. From this and other developments has emerged the Group of Eleven, membership of which comprises the chief executives of the eleven former companies which were effectively the Dorchester Group.

Although the BEC is far larger in its membership, the FCEC is more powerful politically and further benefits from the fact that its power is effectively concentrated in a few hands. By contrast, that of the BEC is spread fairly widely throughout its organization and is therefore more susceptible to the wishes and the interests of its general membership. The structure of the FCEC, its control and the location of its power are therefore vital.

The Federation is divided into eight regional sections, one of which is the London and South Eastern Section which has ten members on the council. The remaining seven regional sections are entitled to twenty-two places on the council between them. There is a further General Section into which large contractors who pay the maximum subscription can be admitted on request. This too is entitled to have ten members on the council. One third of the council members retire each year. This means in effect that most of those from the regions other than London, who have on average three elected members each on the council, spend three years on the council and then vanish. In view of the large number of members from the London and South Eastern and the General Sections, their representatives effectively become permanent members. They are reinforced by the past chairmen who automatically become vice-presidents, the president and the vice-presidents remaining permanent *ex officio* members of the council. Admission to this circle is, of course, only possible through the narrow gateway provided by the annual election to the chair. The mode of selection was therefore vital. (I can speak only of the arrangements when I was a member of the council but I know of no material change.)

The chairman and vice-chairman were 'elected' annually by the council from among their own number and at the first meeting of the council after the annual general meeting. In preparation for this a dinner was held at the Savoy Hotel which was attended by the chairmen of all the sections and also by a suitable number of *ex officio* members of the council. At this meeting a name was put forward and approved for nomination for the vice-chairmanship. This effectively secured the succession – not only to the chair but thereafter to vice-presidency. This dinner was a highly portentous affair. Some of the permanent officers were in attendance and after dinner all the members sat around a baize-covered table and were made to feel at home – discussing very weighty matters. In due course a paper was put before them listing the members who were eligible for chairmanship, and after a brief discussion a name was proposed, seconded and approved, whereupon the papers were quickly removed and normal discussion was resumed.

The reality behind this annual charade was a little less democratic, for the Savoy dinner followed an earlier dinner at the Dorchester where the decision had really been made. As this was not an official Federation event, and indeed few among the general membership had any knowledge of it, the basis of invitation was unknown. The Savoy event was nicely stage-managed to secure the endorsement of the Dorchester choice by the regional chairmen and thereby ensure its safe passage through the following day's council meeting.

So it was that the exclusion of any non-conforming voices was assured.

As the chairman and the vice-chairman become *ex officio* members of all the standing committees, and these are chaired by the president

53

or one of the vice-presidents, control is established. There might remain a remote possibility that the intentions of the hierarchy on some matter dear to them could be frustrated at an annual or special general meeting of the membership. This danger however has little reality given the voting procedure at the general meetings.

Decisions at the general meetings can be taken in the first instance by a show of hands, but there is provision for the chairman to direct a poll either before or after the declaration of the result. Furthermore, the chairman can elect to take the poll forthwith or through the post. In this event, each member has one vote for each £1 of his latest annual subscription. Ultimate power is therefore dependent on the amount of subscription paid. In my time, the subscription was levied as a percentage of the wages paid by each contractor. There was, however, a maximum subscription equated roughly with that which would have been paid by a contractor with a turnover of £1 million per annum. Those with a turnover of, say, £50 million per annum were therefore paying at a rate equivalent to only two per cent of the rate applicable to the smaller members. As I recall, the maximum subscription was raised from £450 per annum to £525 per annum when I was on the council. I was very interested to learn from a chance remark that the subscriptions paid by those in this category were always adjusted to a level where they represented over half the total subscription. It must be unique in democratic terms that by the simple procedure of raising the maximum subscription by £75 the members involved had given themselves another seventy-five votes. One can hardly conceive of circumstances in which this ultimate device might be used, but it must be a comfort to those who are determined to control the Federation that it is always there.

If this power had been used in a benign way and for the benefit of the industry and the economy I would not have found it so objectionable. But in my opinion it was not. Of many examples I could quote I will refer to one that is of particular current interest – that of research.

When I was Chairman of the Midland Section, research was high on the agenda. It was proposed to form the Civil Engineering Research Association (CERA) and the question was, how should it be funded? Overwhelmingly the regions were in favour of a levy on turnover – a fixed percentage to be added to every tender. By this means really significant resources were ensured. It became apparent that this was not acceptable at the top. The matter was debated and in the Midland Section a unanimous vote was given in favour of the levy. We had a McAlpine on our committee and I asked him if the fact that the vote was recorded as unanimous would cause him any embarrassment. He said it did not trouble him so far as the Federation was concerned but hoped it wouldn't prejudice his election to the Jockey Club! In spite of the fact that the Midland Section's views were reflected throughout the regions, the decision was taken to make CERA dependent upon voluntary subscription. In this way major contractors, by making apparently generous subscriptions, which nevertheless only represented a fraction of the payment they would make under a levy system, established ascendancy and control over the whole operation which had by then been largely reduced to a public relations exercise. Today, over twenty years later, there are complaints on all sides that research is inadequately funded.

So far as my relationships within the Federation were concerned, those within the Midland Section were as enjoyable as one could wish them to be; the meetings of the section were stimulating and objective and conducted with great goodwill. I made lasting friendships and the members of the section were both individually and collectively very kind to me following the misfortunes of 1973. I was particularly pleased to receive many generous tributes not only testifying to the value of the work that I had done within the section, but also recognizing the attempts that I and my company had made to raise standards within the industry. My relationships with many of the members of the council, including some of the most senior members, were also good, but it was always clear that behind the scenes there was a very powerful caucus which commanded their first loyalties and whose affairs were completely secret. It was clear, too, that the permanent officers were very dependent upon the patronage of its members.

Problems at Blyth 'B'

One area in which Mitchells had specialized knowledge and depth of experience was in the field of power station construction. Our reputation was high and we were usually included on the lists of contractors who were invited to tender for major projects. In the early 1960s the company had in fact carried out over a hundred major contracts for the electricity supply industry, but already attempts were being made to pre-empt this class of work and have it allocated within a small group of contractors on the basis of negotiation. This was a source of very considerable concern to us – as it was to a number of other contractors who were well experienced in this class of work. This concern was reflected in the CEGB itself where, too, there was a division, some being known to favour particular contractors, while others were known to be reluctant to place themselves at the mercy of a small group that already, whether by self-promotion or otherwise, was being widely referred to as the 'super-league' but which was effectively synonymous with the Dorchester Group.

It was against this background that we became involved in the construction of the Blyth 'B' power station in the North-east, and the history of our involvement provides an example, not only of the dilemma facing those within the CEGB who sought to retain traditional practices and relationships, but also of the unfortunate effect a monopoly buyer can have on the ethics of a whole industry.

In 1959 we had been approached by the CEGB with a request that we should tender for the series of contracts that were to be let in connection with a new power station at Blyth. We were informed that the board was concerned because absence of competition in the area led to a virtual monopoly of the work by Sir Robert McAlpine. The consulting engineers for the project were Merz and McLellan, whose general experience was in mechanical and electrical engineering. On major projects they normally used one of the recognized civil consulting engineers, who took responsibility for the civil work. As often as not, they worked with Sir Alexander Gibb and Partners. (Merz and McLellan were to be joint consultants with Sir Alexander Gibb and Partners on the Kariba project.) Though Merz and McLellan did not have the in-house experience of civil work usually encountered on power stations, I understood that this created no problem in their close relationship with McAlpine in the North-east.

Our first problems in tendering at Blyth arose when we found ourselves up against a virtual monopoly of the supply of aggregates for concrete; there was great difficulty in finding any gravel that was free from deleterious material, principally coal. However, we had a very successful quarrying operation within the company and we were able to commission a quarry of our own to provide our requirements at reasonable cost. As a result, we secured a series of contracts at Blyth for the foundations and superstructure of the main and auxiliary buildings and the chimneys.

Merz and McLellan were being allocated additional work in the civil field by the CEGB, partly to compensate them for mechanical and electrical work which had been promised to them, but had not materialized, and while the work at Blyth was progressing we were awarded another contract at West Burton which came under their supervision. We therefore had a very substantial amount of work being carried out under their direction. It was not long before we found ourselves facing difficulties in securing proper valuations and certificates in respect of work done that were quite unprecedented in the company's experience on power station work. By 1961 the cumulative effect on our cash flow resulting from undervaluation had become so serious that for the first, and in fact the only, time in the company's history I enlisted the assistance of Tiny Mitchell, chairman of Mitchell Engineering. We had a meeting with the then engineering member of the CEGB, after which we confidently expected an improvement in valuation and certification. However, the position did not improve and in fact there was a further deterioration.

The form of contract under which we were working was a familiar one that had been agreed between the CEGB and the FCEC. But as the stranglehold on our finances increased, it became a matter of growing concern to us that the contract conditions governing the valuations were being interpreted by the engineers and the client in a manner that was quite inconsistent with previous practice.

Serious underpayment continued, and it was not until January 1963, when I had a meeting with the Board's chief purchasing and contracts officer, that I learned that the Board had formulated and circulated to all its consulting engineers a series of guidance notes in 1959 as to how the contract was to be interpreted. The source of our difficulties was immediately apparent. These guidance notes contained 'definitions', which were quite inconsistent with the terms of the contract, for they provided that payment for part of the work, which should properly have been made as the work proceeded, should be rolled up and dealt with at some future date. The implications of these guidance notes were very serious indeed, for the consultant's duty to act impartially and in a quasi-judicial capacity in interpreting the contract is fundamental, and any interference with that independence is a breach in itself. In other words, it appeared that the CEGB were in breach on every civil engineering contract that had been in progress since the issue of the definitions. It was extraordinary that a nationalized industry should have got itself into this situation and also that the definitions, having been issued, should have remained secret for so long. Inquiry revealed that they were being almost universally observed in the breach on other contracts and by other consultants. Many years later, the Chief Contracts Officer of the CEGB was to tell us that 'some of their consulting engineers' had interpreted the note wrongly and that this had created great problems; but this did not help us at the time, when a harsh interpretation was being rigidly imposed on our contracts.

Representations to the Board and to the consultants proved ineffective and the matter became so serious that it was decided to take the advice of R. D. Stuart Brown, QC, who was head of one of the principal chambers dealing with civil engineering contracts, and was also the legal representative on the Banwell Committee. In a very clear and unequivocally worded opinion, he stated that the definitions were not in accordance with the form of contract. I later drew his attention to a paper delivered at the Institution of Civil Engineers that appeared to endorse these definitions, and he wrote to me, 'I am terrified . . . I think that [this] paper shows vividly at least one of the reasons why contractors don't get properly paid during the course of the work, a point with which the Banwell Committee is very much concerned.'

My first reaction on receiving counsel's very forthright opinion was to take it along to discuss it with the CEGB. I assumed that they would wish to extricate themselves quietly from a situation which could have such far-reaching consequences on all their contracts. It simply had not occurred to me that once responsible people within the CEGB had addressed themselves to the matter they would wish to behave other than properly, and I was therefore very surprised when I could get no response. We could not let the matter rest, because our business was being seriously distorted owing to the heavy work-load we had with this one consultant. My next move was to have a meeting with their senior partner, but I found him chillingly indifferent to both the contractual situation and the fact that we were being so severely embarrassed by underpayment.

The usual form of contract adopted on civil engineering work in the UK is that governed by the conditions agreed between the Institution of Civil Engineers and the FCEC, but the CEGB had wished to make adjustments to the standard form and these had been agreed in 1958 with the Federation. In view of the close liaison that had developed between the CEGB and the legal sector, I referred the matter to the director of the Federation. He immediately recognized the very serious implications for the industry if the definitions gained currency and an attempt was made to apply them generally. I understood that he would support Mitchells and, since the matter raised such important questions of principle, he would discuss it confidentially with other members. He felt it was something that should be dealt with sensitively, with a view to the Federation taking it up officially with the CEGB. Unfortunately a long silence followed and I was unable to get any reply to my further inquiries. After almost another year, during which Mitchells were still expected to finance these contracts, a meeting was arranged at which the president of the Federation would be present. I attended, duly briefed, but the president did not, and the meeting was abortive. I made a number of other attempts to get the Federation to act, two of them through presidents who were clearly sympathetic, but on each occasion promised action was not followed up. The only explanation seemed to be that somebody, somewhere was exercising a veto.

Obviously it is not the Federation's function to pursue individual contractual disputes, although they do intervene from time to time, but it is very much their duty to protect the procedures and agreed form of contract through which the industry functions. I became increasingly concerned at what I regarded as the cynicism with which Mitchells' position was being damaged by the action, or rather the inaction, of the Federation itself. My concern was greatly heightened when I was informed by the CEGB that the Federation agreed with their definitions, that the rest of the membership accepted them, and that, in the circumstances, Mitchells would not be allowed to tender for any other CEGB work unless and until they specifically accepted them as part of the contract. In fact, it did not appear that the definitions were being operated on any contract other than Mitchells' and, although in the last resort we would have had legal redress, we would have had no protection at all if we had accepted different conditions from those on which other contractors were tendering. At this, we again consulted counsel, who strongly advised against entering into any contract incorporating the proposed additional conditions. I had a series of meetings at different levels of the CEGB up to and including the chairman, Sir Christopher Hinton, and subsequently with his successor, Sir Stanley Brown, but the result was always the same – the Federation agreed with the definitions and therefore there was no reason to modify them. However, I could not discover who it was in the Federation who had agreed this matter with the CEGB, or in what form.

The cynicism of the group who were making use of the Federation had become unmistakable. We had, for many years, enjoyed very good relations with the CEGB. They were our largest customer but we were now being squeezed in such a way that, though personal relationships remained cordial, we were forced into conflict with the Board because of our cash starvation. Furthermore, it was clear that the purpose behind the operation was to present Mitchells as 'difficult' and as 'claims merchants' – very damaging labels to attach to a contractor – and that this myth was being carefully and assiduously cultivated.

It was to be several years, during which Mitchells suffered great embarrassment in their relationship with the CEGB, before I learned from one of the legal secretaries who had left the Federation what had happened in relation to the definitions. It emerged that there had been a secret meeting within the Federation – for how else could one describe a meeting which was not disclosed to the council or to the conditions of contract committee (I was a member of both) – where it was decided that the Federation would not intervene, but would leave Mitchells to their embarrassment. It was 'leaked' to the CEGB that Mitchells did not have the Federation's support, thereby provoking a confrontation between the Board and ourselves. The way this was done made it impossible for us to bring it into the open, with the result that our embarrassment was to continue for a number of years. During this period, as will be seen later, the senior members of the Federation used their office to advocate to the CEGB, among others, the concept that all major contracts should be let on a negotiated basis to a handful of major contractors, leaving the rest of the industry to be employed by them as subcontractors. By eliminating Mitchells they would have rid themselves of a principal competitor in the field, and at the same time they would have neutralized the only voice speaking out at that time against negotiation.

The fact that a decision had been taken at a secret meeting of members of the Federation was something I took up directly with the president, who at that time was Robin McAlpine. Although McAlpine maintained that the Federation had no record of any discussion of the definitions with the CEGB he did admit, at a meeting with me, that 'a few of us had had a discussion at which it had been decided not to pursue the question'. At that meeting he also accepted that as we were the firm principally concerned, no such meeting should have taken place without our having had the opportunity to attend. Given the way that communications are conducted, the question of whether or not an official discussion had taken place with the CEGB was academic. The difference being that if there are properly constituted discussions these are recorded and then such influences can be controlled. This was the first irrefutable evidence I had of an inner circle which could conduct Federation affairs and control its directorate without reference to the members. Following these disclosures, and at my insistence, I received the following confirmation from the chairman of the council:

In the view of the Federation the definitions are not consistent with the conditions of contract agreed with the Central Electricity Generating Board.

This letter (24 September 1968) was received over five years after I had first referred the matter to the director. The rules of the Federation provide for support and assistance to be given to members in connection with settlement of claims 'as the Council may deem proper'. I have never known that rule to be invoked for the benefit of the general membership; but, be that as it may, there is certainly no rule which provides for the contrary position – for officers acting in the name of the Federation but with no authority to embarrass an innocent member.

Not only had there been a betrayal of a member, but fundamental principles affecting the whole of the membership had been placed in jeopardy, and indeed great damage had been done. The damage done to Mitchells had been almost irreparable, for as a direct result we had been removed for a period from the CEGB list of tenderers, and this had been used as the basis of a smear campaign. It was put about that CEGB's actions were due to the company being unreasonable over claims. The facts were that Mitchells had one of the lowest claims records in the industry, and indeed the chairman of one large company told me he was astonished by the skill with which this myth had been created. He happened to know that, in the case of the CEGB, the claims of a number of firms, including his own, were not only larger, but a multiple of Mitchells'.

Some time later, at a Federation dinner at the Dorchester Hotel, I suggested to one of the senior CEGB men present, who had been responsible for asking us to tender at Blyth, that we had been very badly let down after we had tendered for those contracts at the CEGB's specific request. He replied that there were two schools in the CEGB: one pro-McAlpine and the other anti. Consequently, when we responded to the request, we automatically made some friends at the CEGB and some enemies. At the same dinner I was told by one of our foremost consulting engineers of the extraordinary influence wielded by the McAlpines. He told me that they had said they would get his company appointed as consulting engineers on a power station and that they had proceeded to do exactly that.

Early in 1963, while we were experiencing these problems with the CEGB, but before they had become insupportable, we were fortunate in securing the contract for the main foundations at Fawley power station. This was followed by contracts for the superstructure and other works. The Fawley foundation contract, which at that time was the largest civil engineering contract that had ever been let by the CEGB, was very important for a number of reasons.

Achievement at Fawley

We do not, of course, accept that the difficulties which have arisen . . . are the result of adverse physical conditions.

Consulting engineer to contractor
April 1964

This was rather special, of course, because the foundations problems there were so appalling once we got the ground opened to build the station: despite an extensive survey before we did this, we were rather taken aback . . . and the remarkable fact is that we managed to build a power station there at all.

Sir Stanley Brown, CBE, chairman of the
Central Electricity Generating Board,
in evidence to a House of Commons Committee
January 1970

I know nothing of what has happened at Kariba apart from what I have seen in the technical press, but I would like you to know that while I have been reading about your troubles there during the last few weeks I have remembered, with satisfaction, the work which you did at Chapelcross and, with gratitude, what you did at Fawley.

Letter from Lord Hinton of Bankside, CBE, FRS
(Lord Hinton, as Sir Christopher Hinton, had been
Sir Stanley Brown's predecessor as chairman of the
Central Electricity Generating Board)
19 February 1973

I have been surprised at the amount of hostility there is in some quarters and my reply has been that David had proved right more than once in disputes and this can be unforgivable. Fawley is a key case and it is important that Lord Hinton wrote to David as he did. Also, the affair after Scunthorpe [Anchor] went to McAlpine probably not only upset them, but also the establishment who can be bad unseen enemies.

Sir Harold Harding, past president of the
Institute of Civil Engineers to Mr E. K. Wright,
president-elect of the Institute of Chartered Accountants
and a member of Mitchells' holding company board
27 April 1973

The award to Mitchells of the contract for the foundations at Fawley in May 1963 had come as a great relief. The contract itself was bound to test any contractor. It was sited on the south-west shore of Southampton Water adjacent to Calshot Spit and on the foreshore saltings. Access had been made possible by the pumping of a raft of gravel some eight feet thick over the site. Excavation for the foundations descended to 75 feet and the basement structure was so large it would have been possible to float two liners the size of the *Queen Mary* side by side within its walls. Because the station was located on the low-lying foreshore, the construction called for extensive coffer dams and similar works: one sheet steel pile envelope alone enclosed an area of nearly 10 acres. In addition to all the normal ancillary works, switching stations, culverts, etc., the station was also provided with its own dock, leading off Southampton Water.

Described by the CEGB as the biggest civil engineering contract they had ever let, within Mitchells it was regarded as a superb and exciting opportunity and one for which we were well prepared. We were able to field a first-class engineering team (Fawley men have gone on to occupy senior positions throughout the industry, as have Fawley trainees) and the proximity of the site to Eastleigh airfield enabled senior head office engineers to fly from our own landing strip in Peterborough at the shortest possible notice.

In spite of the difficulties on the site and the often appalling working conditions, we were able to reap the benefit of our good labour relations. In the three years we were working at Fawley we did not lose a single day through strike action. The response of the men to their own achievements was magnificent and we were, in fact, asked by the CEGB if we would take over the erection of the structural steel work because, apart from ourselves, labour relations on the site were very strained. We had to decline because this would have involved us with another union and good labour relations are not a question of instant gimmicks: they have to be built up in a spirit of mutual confidence over a long period.

Mitchells' performance at Fawley was recognized by the CEGB as outstanding and we went on to win contracts for further works, including the superstructure. By the time the station was completed we had re-established excellent relationships with all for whom we worked at CEGB. But among some members of the 'super-league', who were already making good headway in their efforts to corner all such major work for themselves, our success only caused chagrin. More rumours were generated over the coffee cups, some of them quite vicious, in an effort to neutralize our success. Although this could not detract from our standing with those for whom we had worked, the pressure for allocation of major contracts with a small group of contractors on the basis of 'Buggins' turn', was building up and, notwithstanding our performance, the Fawley contracts were to be the last awarded to us by the CEGB.

Sir Harold Harding's somewhat Delphic comments in his letter to Kenneth Wright showed great perception. Although I had long been aware of the nature of this trouble in which we were involved, I had not at that time realized that it was being so acutely observed by others. Ironically, it was at Fawley that the seeds of our destruction at Kariba were sown. Indeed if it had not been for a chance meeting with Sir Christopher Hinton at a time when the problems confronting the Fawley project were most acute, Mitchells' downfall might have been brought about some eight years earlier.

How it all came about provides interesting parallels with Kariba, as we shall see later.

Before obtaining tenders for the work, the consultant had naturally undertaken site investigations. The contract called for the provision of temporary works necessary to cope with the conditions believed to exist and, of course, the design of the permanent works was based on the same criteria.

Fairly soon after the works were begun, Mitchells became concerned with the ground conditions being exposed, which appeared to be markedly different from those envisaged in the contract documents. These differences were of such a magnitude that they appeared to call for major changes, both in the methods of construction of works and the design of the works themselves. These matters were brought to the attention of the consulting engineers.

Mitchells had not previously worked under the direction of this particular firm of consultants – Rendel, Palmer and Tritton – and whether it was the result of sensitivity over mistakes which might be attributed to them, or prejudice towards Mitchells coming from some outside source, it provided quite impossible to secure an objective appraisal of the problems confronting us. By February 1964 we had commissioned our own soil investigation survey together with engineering tests on the ground, and on 10 February we wrote to the engineers expressing our grave concern and our conviction that a meeting should be held at a very early date to discuss these problems. In reply we received a letter saying that in the engineer's opinion conditions were consistent with what could have been envisaged at the time of tender and there was no need to resort to new methods of construction. Further exchanges between ourselves and the consulting engineers, all along the same lines, continued until June. During the whole of this period, Mitchells, perhaps inadvisedly, continued with the work. We assumed that eventually common sense would prevail and that the efforts we had made in the best interests of the job would be recognized.

By June, however, an entirely new situation had arisen. There had been massive ground movement when a large stockpile of gravel subsided into the ground in one rotational slip. In the meantime, piling around the foundations was found to have moved despite the fact that it was by now tied in with concrete which was to form part of the permanent works. In early June, with the whole construction sliding into the foundation excavation, we advised the consulting engineer that we had become extremely concerned for the safety of our men and our machines in the area, and that we might have to withdraw them if the movement did not stop. At that stage the whole of the concrete slab at ground level had moved $7\frac{3}{4}$ inches towards the excavation, and yet the consulting engineer was still refusing to acknowledge that any movement had taken place. On 26 June, by which time the movement had increased to 10 inches, we wrote to the engineer in response to his pressure regarding programme dates, saying that the only way that they could be achieved would be for us to revert to the original methods with all the attendant risks of collapse involved. We pointed out that necessary plant and equipment were standing on the site and personnel were immediately available, but concluded our letter by saying that 'We have satisfied ourselves that we can take steps to avoid undue risks to the men, and although there will be some risk to the equipment, this can be overcome. The main risk is to the ultimate completion of the project itself, but we accept that the relative importance of this is not a matter for us to decide. Upon receipt of your instructions we will continue to excavate.'

It has to be remembered that this letter was written after many months of dispute and after we had poured over a million pounds of our own money into the project. The engineer's response was to instruct us that we had to continue in accordance with the original methods and programme, and that it was our responsibility to do so without involving the risks to which we had referred. This was manifestly impossible in view of the ground conditions, yet these instructions were given formally, and ominously quoted clause 46/1 of the CEGB conditions of contract, which provides for the removal of the contractor if he fails to comply with the engineer's demands.

Mitchells' situation was grave. We had committed our funds and resources to the project and if our contract was now to be terminated our standing as contractors would be ruined, and indeed the very question of our survival would be in doubt. We felt very strongly that we were not getting a fair hearing and that this could only be because of the climate that had been created following our experiences at Blyth. However, an entirely fortuitous circumstance came to our rescue.

Two months earlier, at the beginning of May, quite by chance, I had met Sir Christopher Hinton at the International Conference on Large Dams which had been held in Edinburgh. He told me he was concerned about the situation at Fawley, and I confirmed that the problems were very serious indeed, suggesting that he should get beneath the surface and find out what was really happening. Sir Christopher was, of course, a most unusual man: from an apprenticeship in a railway workshop he won a scholarship to Cambridge, and later became chief engineer of ICI. After the war, showing quite incredible energy, drive and ability, he virtually created the United Kingdom Atomic Energy Authority, directing construction of the world's first nuclear power stations. (It was under his direction that Mitchells built Chapelcross.) From there he had become chairman of the CEGB.

Following further deterioration of the situation at Fawley – aggravated, it must be said, by our reluctance to continue with work which we were now convinced was unsafe – Sir Christopher arranged for a meeting to be held at the site on 16 July. Quite clearly, the chairman of the CEGB would not become involved in contractual matters at site level except in very unusual circumstances. He was accompanied by the engineering member of the CEGB, the Board's chief contracts officer, its chief engineer and the director and five senior members of the project group. Sir Christopher took the chair. The meeting started in the morning and we soon realized it was not going to be made easy for us and that we were very much on trial. By lunchtime, however, a little daylight had emerged, and we all went our separate ways to eat.

Protracted and difficult discussions in the afternoon failed to provide agreement, whereupon Sir Christopher Hinton took matters firmly into his own hands. He first suggested to me that we were accusing the Board's consulting engineers of being irresponsible. I replied that this was not the case, but that we were in a difficult position. We did have different views and we firmly believed that what we were being asked to do was dangerous and could place the whole scheme in jeopardy. If in those circumstances we disregarded our misgivings, it would be us who were irresponsible. All we were asking was that these matters be properly examined and the matter decided on its merits. I proposed that a panel of three senior engineers be formed – one from the CEGB, one from the consulting engineers and one from Mitchells – to examine these questions and to report back within a fortnight. Sir Christopher Hinton accepted this proposal and all three parties nominated their representatives.

It was agreed that the report of the panel – which became fashionably known at the time as the 'Troika' – should be delivered by 30 July and that the meeting would reassemble on the site on 4 August to consider its findings. One of the Board's members pointed out that 4 August was a public holiday, but Sir Christopher set his seal on the proceedings by saying, 'That's right, ten o'clock in the morning.' The effect of Sir Christopher's involvement was immediately apparent: the Troika got to work the next morning.

One of our most urgent problems was to secure the services of an independent and authoritative expert to act for us in relation to the geology and soil mechanics. This had, after all, by now become a life-and-death matter for the company. Inquiries as to who might be a suitable candidate produced one categorical answer: in view of the parties involved, we could not expect to find a UK consultant who would act for us. I was, however, recommended to approach Dr Golder, one of the founders and earlier chief executive of Soil Mechanics Limited, who pioneered in this country the development of soil mechanics on a combined professional and commercial basis. Dr Golder, who had become an internationally recognized pioneer and expert in the field, had since moved to Canada, where he had set up in practice and was now senior partner in his own firm of Golder Associates in Toronto. I telephoned Dr Golder that night in Toronto, only to find that he was about to leave for an assignment in Vancouver, but he did agree to fly straight from Vancouver to London Airport. Here we met him with our own small plane which flew him to Chichester, where he was joined by a consulting engineer who had agreed to assist him. Together, they were taken by speedboat straight to the site at Fawley.

The report of the panel, signed first by the consultant's partner, then by Mitchells' chief engineer, and finally by the chief engineer of the CEGB, was submitted to Sir Christopher Hinton on 30 July. In brief, it stated that the ground conditions were different from, and worse than, those envisaged at the time of tender. In consequence, the design of the temporary works would have to be modified, and various parts of the permanent works would probably also have to be modified.

At the resumed meeting on 4 August, Sir Christopher thanked the panel for an outstandingly clear report, which he said established that there was substance in Mitchells' contention. He then asked me what proposals Mitchells had for dealing with the situation. I suggested that, having benefited from the example of the Troika, we should form a high-level steering committee from very senior representatives of the three parties, and that this should be responsible for supervising and guiding the project as a whole. I also suggested that there should be a joint engineering team (which appropriately enough came to be known as 'Jet') with responsibility for reaching decisions on the urgent day-to-day engineering matters, which were bound to arise on the site, and that this team should report to the steering committee.

Sir Christopher gave his approval and then asked me if we, as a company, were happy that the job should now go forward on the basis of the existing contract. I replied that we had had serious cause for complaint, but that I was quite sure that the contract could be operated satisfactorily, provided that there was a team of people on the site who could make decisions and deal expeditiously with their financial consequences.

The results of this agreement were quite dramatic. The huge excavations were open and vulnerable to the weather, and speed was therefore vital. Normally any attempt to take a civil engineering job by surprise ends in disaster, but on this occasion weather favoured us. We put in hand a programme which, in addition to excavation, involved the task of placing concrete, much of it in complex work, at the unprecedented rate of over 10,000 cubic yards a week, and we kept up that pace until 236,000 yards had been completed. On 15 August, a Saturday afternoon, at the end of the first week for which this massive placement was planned, I arrived on the site to assess progress. I was astonished to find the site deserted: the programme had been completed, everything was clean and tidy and ready for a fresh start on the Monday morning. Had I been better informed, I would have found all those responsible for this achievement at a well-earned celebration in a hut on the site. As it was I was immensely proud. The magnitude of the achievement was subsequently recognized by a CEGB spokesman at the opening ceremony when he said that work which had been forecast to take one year was achieved in six months.

Fawley had been a daunting experience. At one stage, we had almost been brought to our knees and had encountered that same chill feeling of helplessness in the face of a situation where facts seemed to be of no importance, and compassion or mercy entirely absent, which we were subsequently to experience at Kariba. In the execution of a contract, no contractor seeks to incur the odium of his client or the engineer. Indeed, it goes without saying that it must be in his own best interest to maintain good relations with both. It might be thought, therefore, that at Fawley Mitchells should have taken the easy way out by accepting the engineer's views on the foundation conditions, and letting events run their course until ultimately some engineering disaster engulfed the site, whereupon we would have been handsomely paid to put it right. Indeed, one of the most senior people from the other side did suggest our own interest would have been better served had we adopted this course. Though we never considered this, I am in no doubt that our policy ill-served Mitchells' long-term interests. In spite of the goodwill of the CEGB, the consulting engineers not only refused to include Mitchells' name on future lists of tenderers, but insisted on its removal when it had been placed there by the client. So far as the CEGB were concerned, Mitchells fell victims to the general policy of farming work out to members of the super-league, the policy that had been so long and diligently promoted for securing work on the basis of 'Buggins' turn'.

Fawley was, as I have said, the last major contract which we executed for the Board directly.

There was another consequence. An MP, who had played a very active part in committee work dealing with the nationalized industries, had visited the site during construction and had been most impressed. Later he was invited by Edwin McAlpine to a party in the penthouse suite at the Dorchester. He was taken on one side and told by Sir Edwin that the Fawley problems were the result of a plot by Mitchells who had ruthlessly exploited the situation and made a tremendous profit. For good measure, he was also told that neither Mitchells nor I personally were fit to be allowed to stay in the industry. The MP warned me that McAlpines had a trip-line out for Mitchells wherever we went, and I was able to assure him that I had already been advised of this from many other sources. In fact, Mitchells' profit at Fawley amounted to 7.8 per cent on our costs, which, in view of the enormous difficulties, and the fact that at one stage we were financing the job to the tune of £1 million, was modest enough. The rumours about our exploitation of Fawley and the excessive profits we made were so effectively sown that they resurfaced as fact in newspaper reports at the time of our receivership – four years after the contract was completed.

Progress, but anxieties

While the challenge at Fawley was being met and brought to heel, the company continued to expand. Work was continuing on eight power stations in England and Scotland, in addition to further extensive hydroelectric works. Kinnear Moodie, our soft-ground tunnelling company, emulated Mitchell Construction's many records in the hard-rock tunnelling field by establishing a new soft-ground world record, increasing the previous best performance by fifty per cent, when it drove a mile of tunnel on the Metropolitan Water Board's Wraysbury–Datchet tunnel in eight weeks. On the London Underground's Victoria Line Kinnear Moodie constructed running tunnels and stations, and supplied tunnelling machines and pre-cast concrete tunnel linings for the whole line. They also carried out the complex reconstruction of Oxford Circus, from the new booking hall below street level downwards, an undertaking involving two miles of tunnelling on this location alone. (At the time of our receivership they were carrying out similar works on the Fleet Line, including the new station complex at Trafalgar Square, which drew together the old Trafalgar Square station, the Strand station and the Charing Cross station, with tunnels running east up to Aldwych. Sadly, the benefit of all this had to be passed to others.)

Meanwhile, our very high standing with the Department of the Environment was reflected in the amount of work awarded to us that was of the highest priority. This ran into many millions of pounds and included a succession of contracts for the construction of the new Polaris base at Faslane and the new Telephone Communications Research Centre at Martlesham Heath. Overseas, too, our operations had expanded steadily and profitably, and nowhere more so than in Canada, where on the strength of our reputation we were invited to tender for increasingly prestigious projects.

There was, however, a sinister underlying drift throughout the 1960s which increased as the decade progressed. More and more work was being pre-empted. It frequently appeared that bids were only being used to provide a semblance of respectability and to form a basis for arrangements with an already selected tenderer. Even when contracts were ostensibly open to competition, the usual prompt response to a tender gave way all too often to an atmosphere of secrecy and silence before announcements of questionable awards were made.

This was, of course, the period of Poulson, who was the direct product of this growing fashion for negotiation. While it may have seemed from his trial that all corruption started at Pontefract and was primarily confined to local authority contracts in the provinces, he was in fact a product of the amoral climate of the time, which clearly prevailed in a very wide circle in London. Many will have remained less than convinced that justice had been served by the incarceration in Wakefield Gaol of a provincial architect who did not have the wit, amid all that largesse, to keep himself solvent. When it came to probing the wider implications of the Poulson exposure, there was an extraordinary lack of curiosity.

One avenue closes; but another opens

Among the first casualties of the promotion of special interests had been the nuclear power work. Our construction of Chapelcross nuclear power station had been one of the most successful operations carried out for the nuclear industry, and at Windscale we had built, with equal success, the nuclear chemical separation plant and completed the advanced gas-cooled reactor. It was with immense chagrin that we watched the maoeuvrings whereby all the nuclear power work was removed into the hands of one or two contractors on the apparent basis that these people alone would be able to gain export orders. Some of them had never even entered into really competitive overseas work and the fruits of this policy are yet to be seen.

A two-tier industry with a double price structure and double standards appeared to be spreading throughout the country, with the second-tier contractors becoming victims of a tremendous squeeze. This squeeze was the worse because they were being forced into areas where payment procedures were slow and unsatisfactory.

Thus it was that in the late 1960s Mitchells had to make a general reappraisal following the depredations of the previous ten years. It was against this background that what appeared to be a new opportunity opened up for us: one that started with the construction of a pipemill at Hartlepool for Stewart Lloyds, who were part of the Northern and Tubes Group of the British Steel Corporation (BSC).

The requirement was for a mill to manufacture tubes up to 20 inches in diameter, incorporating a plant for processing the basic tubes into such products as rectangular sections. The site was the Hartlepool works at the South Durham Iron and Steel Company Limited. Tenders were obtained from a number of national contractors and in January 1967 Mitchells were awarded the contract, with access to the site in mid-April. The contract was for the management, design and construction of the new mill, which was to be nearly a quarter of a mile long with piled foundations, 3,000 tons of structural steelwork, fifty production units, 3,600 feet of conveyors, 600 electric motors and generators, 40 miles of cable, 6 miles of piped services, together with railway sidings and associated roads, paving, etc. In addition, there was to be a separate administration block.

The first tube was rolled from the mill only nine months after the handing over of the site – an achievement that brought the greatest satisfaction to everyone associated with the project, both in Mitchells and in the Northern Group of BSC. This, taken in conjunction with work we had previously done within the steel industry, and the fact that our unique performance at Fawley had shown that we had a capacity second to none, led to our being advised that we would be invited to tender for the Anchor project. This was the first major project to be carried out in the massive reorganization programme at that time projected for BSC, and it fell under the aegis of the Midland Group.

Here, at last, a door was opening that might help us make good some of the depredations to the available work-load that had resulted from the concentration of purchasing power in London.

We knew that once a decision was made to go ahead with Anchor it would be an urgent project. It was located near our headquarters in an area where we knew we could be competitive. We therefore started reserving staff and resources at an early stage.

At a preliminary briefing with BSC we were invited to put foward proposals of a general nature indicating how we would handle the civil engineering and building content of the work, and what resources we would make available. Our proposals were presented at a meeting at Scunthorpe on 22 September 1969. After a very detailed examination, they were well received, and it was apparent that we were favourably placed for the award of the contract.

Unfortunately, at this stage it emerged that we had run into one of those periods of reorganization which appear to be an inescapable feature of nationalized industries, with the result that initiatives in the matter of investment were once again transferred to headquarters in London. We were informed that new arrangements were being made and it was anticipated that the work would go out to competitive tendering at the end of October, with the object of securing tenders and starting work before the end of the year. In the event, W. S. Atkins and Partners were appointed consultants and on 7 January 1970 they invited us to tender.

There were a number of features in the tendering procedures which seemed to leave a great deal of licence for discretion after tenders were received, and this caused considerable unease, both to ourselves and others. Tendering for a project of this size is a major operation involving expenditure of the order of £20,000–£30,000, and several contractors sought reassurances on the adjudication process before agreeing to tender. In particular, it was confirmed that all the selected tenderers had been chosen on the basis that their resources were adequate to meet the demands of the project, and that selection would be made according to a purely financial evaluation of the tenders. It was on this understanding that we and others set about the preparation of our tenders.

Tenders were due in by twelve noon on Tuesday 31 March, and our own tender in the sum of just over £28 million was completed and submitted under cover of a letter dated 26 March. Having regard to the urgency and the straightforward procedure which had been outlined to us by BSC, we were disappointed at not getting an early response, but not particularly concerned. However, on 7 April, at a meeting in London, I learned from one of the other tenderers that ours was the lowest tender, information that he seemed to assume was already in my possession. I did not disillusion him, but I was worried. We did not make a practice of exchanging prices with other contractors, and our prices could only have been obtained from BSC or its consultants. One does not have to suffer many experiences of post-tender manoeuvring to develop sensitive antennae for trouble. I knew there was something wrong and was on my guard.

The next day (8 April) I was in London when I received a very worried telephone call from Alan Lightbown, our group director in charge of estimating. The consultants had been on the telephone to say, although they admitted there might be ambiguity, some tenderers had provided for the operation of a bonus incentive scheme in their tenders, and he wanted to know what we would want to add in this respect. Alan Lightbown was quite sure that there was no ambiguity in the documents.

In fact, the tender documents as originally issued did require tenderers to include for the operation of an incentive scheme but thereafter, in a letter of 16 February, the consultants issued a specific instruction that this provision should be deleted. The reason for this was understood to be that BSC wished to avoid embarrassment with their main labour force and to include instead a new clause requiring the successful contractor to participate in consultative machinery set up by BSC to coordinate labour relations and conditions of employment. The intention of the amendment, specifically that no allowances for bonuses were to be made and that any such payments would be reimbursed under an alternative clause in the contract, was verified with the consultants on the telephone and thereafter confirmed in a letter to them of 19 February.

In the circumstances I shared Lightbown's anxiety about the way the matter was being dealt with. For example, although great stress had been placed in the tender inquiries on the propriety of the procedures to be adopted, Lightbown was being asked to give a figure over the telephone that was going to be used in some unspecified way by the consultants in adjudicating on the tenders. Scope was being created, knowingly or otherwise, for the adjustment of tenders after all the other bids were known. However, provided we had priced the job correctly, which we had been at great pains to do, there was no need for us to increase our tender. On the other hand, it appeared that somebody else might be getting an opportunity to reduce his. When this happens, one is helpless, and it has always been my understanding and belief that to give such opportunity was ethically inexcusable. I questioned Lightbown on the telephone, but he was convinced the people with whom he was directly dealing were, as he expressed it, 'down the middle', though he felt that there was something drastically wrong somewhere. He was under pressure to give an immediate reply, but we agreed to call a meeting on the Saturday morning (11 April).

At this meeting we reviewed the contract documents and it was clear to us that, although confusion could be created in an untutored mind, there was no possibility whatsoever of ambiguity, other than contrived ambiguity, in the documents themselves. Contractors develop extremely sensitive antennae in this sort of situation and we were, by this time, reasonably certain that we were indeed the lowest tenderer, and speculated as to who the closest to us might be. Finally, the meeting decided that we should react just enough to warn off anyone who was being 'naughty' without offending the others. And so we wrote a letter to the consulting engineers that morning explaining our misgivings and suggesting a meeting at which any suspected ambiguity could be examined. Our letter contained the following paragraphs:

While, therefore, we would not wish to appear presumptuous, we would infinitely prefer to let our tender stand and to be judged on its merits in accordance with the original enquiry.

In making this proposal we are mindful of the fact that in

estimating the amounts that might be involved the estimate could be so widely divergent as to be virtually useless.

This letter was despatched to the consulting engineers the same day and a copy was delivered by our senior representatives to BSC's chief project engineer at Scunthorpe on the following Monday. The chief project engineer received our people most sympathetically, but said that it was absolutely imperative that our bonus figure should be provided by the following day. In the meantime, we had a telephone call from the consulting engineers who made clear that we could not have a meeting, and that, unless we provided the figures, they would make arbitrary adjustments of their own. While this was going on, a number of suppliers, who are always anxious to know the identity of the successful tenderer at the earliest opportunity, and who have their own well-developed channels of communication, started calling on us at Peterborough. From them we learned that all other contractors, apart from McAlpines, had been eliminated. We also learned from press sources near to BSC that it was felt that there was no reason why the contract should be awarded to the lowest tenderer if there was only about '£200,000 or so' involved. My note made at the time reads, 'If it was not intended that anybody else but McAlpines should have this contract, it is hard to understand why it was considered necessary to occupy our time and that of other contractors in tendering.'

We were in an impossible situation. We could not secure a meeting or an explanation and, if we refused to give a figure, we would be opening the way for arbitrary adjustments to be made, either by way of increasing our tender figure or reducing someone else's. As a way out of our dilemma we decided to stop short of an absolute refusal to comply with the request and offered a more or less arbitrary figure of £75,000. If all parties were operating in good faith, it was thought that they would examine the matter further and perhaps give us the meeting we had been consistently denied.

On Thursday 16 April I attended a Federation dinner at the Dorchester Hotel where I met BSC's project engineer and protested mildly that all our competitors, and even the City of London, seemed to know we were the lowest tenderer. He assured me that the whole thing was being played 'straight down the middle' – by now a familiar phrase – and although I thought he was being sincere I was still suspicious that somewhere along the line there was something very wrong. It was not long before my suspicions were confirmed.

On the evening of Friday 17 April, by which time the whole

industry was rife with rumour, I received a telephone call at my home from someone speaking on behalf of a man who I will refer to as 'X'. 'X' was involved with the Anchor project, and was so concerned he wanted to see me.

I saw him on Saturday morning at my office. He had certain papers with him and had been analysing the contract. He thought something was amiss and wanted to check his reasoning. He felt he had been starved of information and that he would be outnumbered at a meeting where he might be pressed to subscribe to a recommendation without having been able to satisfy himself that it was the correct one. He felt isolated. Having become suspicious, he reckoned we would be the most likely people to explain an alleged ambiguity which he had not been able to understand.

We went through all the documents relating to the treatment of incentives and I told him about the double-talk that seemed to surround us. I advised him of our efforts to get these matters off the telephone and out into the open and in writing. He, in turn, told me that the only information he had been able to get was that Mitchells 'had made a mess of their bonus'. This was patently untrue, and he confirmed that before tenders were invited a policy decision had indeed been made by BSC, who wished to keep control of bonus payments. They had decided not to allow freedom to contractors to make payments which would upset their existing wage structure. It was perfectly clear that Mitchells had not misinterpreted the intention of the tender documents.

My visitor had with him a number of papers, including a summary of the tender results. There was something so obviously wrong that I secured his agreement to my making copies.

It was clear that 'X' had only come to us at this late stage, nearly three weeks after tenders were submitted, because he was determined to risk a great deal to get at the truth. During our discussion, there was no suggestion from either side that any obligation was involved, or being created, and apart from one telephone call from him during the following week no communication of any sort has passed between us since that date: I do not even know whether he is alive or dead. This has been deliberate because I knew there was nothing I could do to save him if his identity became known.

The papers he brought me included copies of a summary of the tenders received and copies of the covering letters submitted by tenderers. The schedule showed that from a straight comparison of prices Mitchells' tender was £1.4 million lower than McAlpines'. It also showed that McAlpines' figure was very close to those of two of the other three tenderers. Examination of the detail, however, showed a vastly different picture, and one which made the McAlpine tender the least attractive of any of the bids. Other considerations apart, the special nature of the contract had led to an undertaking in the documents that the successful contractor would be paid a minimum of his costs plus overheads, unless it could be shown that he had performed incompetently. Tenderers had been required to disclose the percentage they would require in respect of overheads, which would be added to their net costs in order to arrive at the minimum payment. All the tenderers except McAlpines showed a figure of the order of three per cent, whereas McAlpines' figure was a minimum of six per cent. From this it appeared that either McAlpines' overheads were twice as high as everybody else's, or there was a hidden three per cent profit within them. There was, however, one item which was likely to be quite significant before the contract was completed. This was incorporated in the bill in such a way that any percentage addition would not be reflected in the total tender price. In respect of this, McAlpines had increased the on-cost that they would require in respect of overheads to ten per cent.

In the last analysis the McAlpine tender was different from the others in that, unless they performed quite incompetently, which was unthinkable, it provided for a cost-plus job without any risk, while leaving various options open for further enhancing the profit element. According to a report in *Construction News* after the figures were revealed, 'The award of the contract on this basis is a simple licence to print money.' If the summary of the tender figures made it surprising that McAlpines' tender had received further consideration, this surprise was compounded by the contents of their covering letter.

In the first place, the covering letter was addressed to W. S. Atkins and Partners, the consulting engineers, instead of as directed to the Scunthorpe division of BSC. It is customary for contractors to be particularly careful to comply with such directions as failure to do so would normally invite disqualification. The instructions to tenderers further stated, 'Any matter on which advice or a decision is required in the preparation of the tender should be referred in writing to W. S. Atkins & Partners . . . A reply will be sent by W. S. Atkins & Partners in writing and copies sent to all tenderers.' During the tender period Mitchells had been told that this requirement was to be rigidly respected and we were discouraged from raising any queries in writing or otherwise. It was therefore surprising to read in McAlpines' covering letter, 'We would like to thank you most sincerely for all the help we have been given during the tender period.' The fact that McAlpines had been helped and dealt with differently from the other tenderers had caused us concern during the tendering period, when one of McAlpines' own staff had brought it to our attention on more than one occasion, but we hardly expected to see it confirmed in a letter accompanying tender documents for a project which specifically excluded such consultation.

Even more significant than either of these matters, however, was the question of general qualifications to the tender. The instructions to tenderers included the following clause:

> The tender shall be strictly in accordance with the specification, schedule of prices, drawings, conditions of contract and instructions to tenderers and shall not be qualified in any way. Any such qualification is liable to result in a tender, which is otherwise favourable, not being considered. Tenderers should ensure, therefore, that any explanatory or descriptive matter included in their tender does not constitute a qualification to the requirements and terms and conditions as stated in the enquiry document.

Our tender was prepared strictly in accordance with this provision although we, like other tenderers, had to draw attention to certain deficiencies in the bill of quantities. These related particularly to plant items which were inappropriate to the Scunthorpe project. The McAlpine letter contained an unusually large number of explanations and qualifications of varying significance, but amongst them two stood out:

> 1 'All our prices and attendances are based on completion on 30th September, 1972, as indicated in the tender documents.'
> 2 'We have allowed in the quoted rates for operating a bonus incentive scheme.'

The first qualification was, of course, so sweeping that it would have rendered the tender quite valueless in the very likely event of any overrun on time. The second was ambiguous, if not meaningless. In its literal sense it could refer to the administration of some scheme of reward which did not involve actual payments to the men, in which case all other tenderers would have considered it to be included in their overheads. On the other hand, it might be argued that it was intended to cover either arbitrary bonus payments, or payments to be made on the basis of results. If either of these interpretations was intended, then it would be in direct conflict with the instructions to tenderers. At the same time, it was notable that, whereas W. S. Atkins and Partners had stated to us in the first place that 'some of the other contractors had included for bonus', there was no indication of this in any of their submissions.

The importance of the two qualifications taken together, however, was far more serious, for it will be seen that if, by agreement, the contractor was allowed to withdraw his qualifications, he could, in the case of the first qualification, agree to do so on the payment of an additional sum compensating him for the extra risk. In the case of the second qualification, he would be able to agree to deduct a sum in respect of an item which he had not been required to include. In other words, after all the tender results were known, he could, given the agreement of the engineer, enjoy an almost infinite capacity to adjust his tender upwards or downwards to suit circumstances. This does not necessarily imply that he would do so, but it is a cardinal principle of true competitive tendering that such situations are not allowed to arise.

With the knowledge available to us, our anxieties had become very grave. But what were we to do about them? We would have had no compunction at all about bringing the matter into the open had it not been for the risk to our informant. Our earlier policy had been to try to warn off anyone who might be being 'naughty', and it was decided to pursue this policy, only with more emphasis. In the meantime, the copies of the documents were retained in a wall-safe in my office. (It was, in fact, the only time that that wall-safe was ever used, and the covering letters never left it until I cleared my office in 1973.)

Our concern, of course, extended beyond the Anchor scheme. Stimulated by the propaganda in favour of negotiation, tendering procedures had become progressively more lax and all too often one feared that discretion was being allowed to run riot. Civil engineering contracting is a very competitive sphere and much turns on the benefit of a doubt. If one were always to get the benefit of the doubt, it would be a very prosperous business indeed. If, on the other hand, one never got the benefit of the doubt, the opposite would apply. In a severely competitive industry one needs even-handedness. With our experiences on the nuclear power front, and the developments we knew were taking place in other nationalized industries, in particular the CEGB, we had pinned many of our hopes on Anchor. With something approaching despair, we realized that once again we were likely to be deprived of a contract that should rightfully be ours. Although we had been suspicious on numerous previous occasions, this was the first for which we had unequivocal facts and figures.

We decided to press harder. Our resolve was reinforced when we heard on 23 April that McAlpines' general manager in their Leicester office had told an old friend that McAlpines had, in fact, secured the contract. Our attempts to meet the consulting engineers of BSC were unsuccessful, and so we decided to refer the matter to leading counsel in order to get an independent view as to whether there was, in fact, any possibility of an ambiguity which could have escaped us.

In a written opinion, David Gardam QC advised that in his view Mitchells had tendered precisely in accordance with the instructions, and he could see no reason why they should be asked to retender at a higher figure or on a different basis. He could not see how it could be consistent with fair tendering in limited competition to allow tenderers other than Mitchells to reduce their tender. After commenting on other 'disquieting aspects', counsel said that of course BSC could not be compelled to accept any offer but, as Mitchells had plainly tendered in accordance with the instructions, if the contract were awarded to another tenderer, whose tender was higher than Mitchells', Mitchells might have certain courses of action open to them.

Mitchells were interested in contracting and clearly there could be no future in legal action. On the other hand, nor could there be any future in an industry in which we were to be deprived of reasonable opportunities for securing work in competition and on the basis of our skills. Counsel's opinion had removed any element of doubt and strengthened our resolve. We continued to press for meetings at a higher level with the consulting engineers or BSC; but meanwhile, at a meeting at Scunthorpe on 11 May, I was informed by the project engineer that our tender had not been adjusted upwards, though he admitted that other tenders had been adjusted downwards. I suggested to him that this not only made nonsense of competitive tendering, but the method of adjustment after all the figures were known had made the position worse. I gained the impression that the Scunthorpe people had some sympathy with us, and they certainly accepted that it was bad practice to allow tenders to be reduced after they had been submitted. But I also got the impression that the project engineer had no authority or discretion to reopen a decision that had obviously already been made.

In the circumstances I decided to press for a meeting with Dr Finniston, Deputy Chairman of BSC, who assured me on 14 May that no decision had yet been taken, and that it would not be taken until the end of the month. He was about to leave London and would not be back until 19 May, but proposed a meeting on 20 May. Meanwhile, I was not particularly comforted to hear of a luncheon meeting that took place that week attended by representatives of BSC and W. S. Atkins and Partners and Sir Robert McAlpine, at which the McAlpine people indicated they were proposing to take Ray Gunter* on to their board in order to deal with labour relations at Scunthorpe. For good measure, there had apparently been an assertion, quite contrary to the truth, that Mitchells had had very bad labour relations at Fawley.

At our meeting on 20 May, it appeared to me that Dr Finniston and his colleagues had been misinformed regarding the alleged ambiguity in the tender documents. I insisted that there was no ambiguity. I wanted to put those responsible for raising this matter to the embarrassment of supplying in writing an explanation of how and where the ambiguity arose. Dr Finniston and his colleagues suggested that it was a matter that they should take up with W. S. Atkins and Partners, and I adhered to my view that I hoped in due course to get a written explanation from them, at which time the validity of the revisions that had apparently been made to the tenders could be examined.

Notwithstanding the assurances I had had from Dr Finniston that no decision would be made before the end of the month, I returned from my meeting with him to learn that a telex message had that day been received from the consulting engineers advising us that our tender had been unsuccessful. Although there was still no public announcement, reports appeared in the press during the following week to the effect that McAlpines had received a letter of intent regarding the award of the contract.

It was now over two months since tenders were submitted and it was impossible any longer to have confidence in the way that the matter was being handled or in the information that was being passed to us. At this time I had a long conversation with a valued consultant who had been involved in the presentation of our proposals. He had followed the post-tender saga closely, and I disclosed to him the summary of the tender figures which I had in my possession. He was very insistent that they ought to be published, but I could not think of a way of doing it without exposing my visitor of April to very considerable risk. Our consultant was very persuasive, and I remember the occasion well because it was the first time I heard of the Poulson affair. He told me that the question of propriety in dealing with contractual matters and tenders was going to become one of major importance. I knew nothing of Poulson beyond the fact that we had

---

*Minister of Labour in Harold Wilson's Government.

81

once been advised against becoming involved with him. It now appeared that Poulson had got himself into grave financial difficulties. He had kept a regular suite in the Dorchester, where lavish entertainment had taken place, including charity balls organized for local causes, which was going to be the subject of some very searching questions. My friend persuaded me that under the circumstances the best thing to do was to permit publication of the information I had, and I agreed to allow him to arrange this on condition that there would be no possibility of risk to my original informant.

I do not know exactly how the information was passed, but an account appeared in *Construction News* on 11 June 1970. The response was quite dramatic. Apart from McAlpine and ourselves, two other tenders had been received,* each from consortia. Each of them contacted us within the next few days expressing their sympathy and their concern. It emerged that they had both sought reassurances from BSC that tenders would be adjudicated strictly on their merits before becoming involved in the expense of tendering. Furthermore, on receipt of the tender documents, and reviewing all the circumstances surrounding them, they had both gone back and sought a further assurance, which they had received. In the case of one of them, Mowlems, they had already done £4 million of work on the site which was to be incorporated in the main contract when it was concluded. On this McAlpines would get 6.5 per cent – over £¼ million – as Mowlems' chairman, Edgar Beck, said, 'simply for passing the cheque'. This was more than he himself expected to make for doing the work.

In the following weeks the chairmen of the various companies involved made the strongest representation to BSC and to Atkins and, like myself, were informed that there would be a massive programme of work and that the intention was for the existing list of invited tenderers to be preserved until each had had a share.

Meanwhile, there was considerable comment in the press, with speculation as to the possibility of questions being asked in the House of Commons, and – a particularly welcome development – a great deal of emphasis on the desirability of public opening of tenders: a reform for which I had been pressing for a long time. At that stage I was asked by Edgar Beck, on behalf of himself and Sir Godfrey Mitchell, the chairman of Wimpeys, if I would add my voice to a joint protest. Obviously I was prepared to do so.

---

*A fifth tenderer submitted an alternative proposal as a basis for negotiation which did not appear to have been considered.

Although it was an open secret by now that McAlpines had secured the contract, no announcement was made. Representations were made to various members of parliament by most of the people involved in the consortia. I was abroad for a great deal of the month, leading a government-sponsored delegation to Hong Kong to promote British interests in connection with the proposed Hong Kong subway, and then visiting other places in the Far East, including Bangkok, where we were carrying out tunnelling and other work. On my return, I found that public interest had not waned. On 30 July, four months after the submission of tenders on what had been represented as a desperately urgent contract, it was announced at last that the contract had indeed been placed with Sir Robert McAlpine. There was widespread comment in the national press about the unsatisfactory circumstances that surrounded the award, and questions in the House were rumoured once again. *The Economist*, noting that the announcement was originally to have been made earlier and that Parliament was now 'conveniently in recess', went on to say, 'Nevertheless, when it returns members ought to press the new Ministry of Technology for more details. And in due course, one hopes, the Select Committee on Nationalised Industries will shed some more light on the decision.'

Following these public expressions of disquiet, BSC and Atkins took the unusual step of organizing a press conference at the Connaught Rooms on Monday 3 August, at which there was some long and fairly hostile questioning. From this questioning and other comments made by the representatives of BSC, it appeared that justification of the award was being made on three grounds:

1 that after various adjustments and adjudication, McAlpines' price was within six figures, i.e. less than £100,000, of Mitchells' price;
2 that in the circumstances the contract had been let to the firm with the strongest resources;
3 other things had to be taken into account, including strike records.

So far as the first of these items was concerned, it meant that a means must have been found of reducing McAlpines' tender by £1.3 million to bring it within the scope of the criteria leaked three and a half months earlier immediately after tenders were received, namely, that 'if there was only about £200,000 or so involved, there is no reason why the contract should be awarded to the lowest tenderer'. As to the size of the reduction in McAlpines' tender, two points have to be made: first, no matter how big a reduction they made, they were not involved in any risk because, by virtue of the way they had priced the overhead, they were assured of a cost-plus job, which included a substantial profit. Second, although on the face of it McAlpines' original tender was already a full five per cent higher than Mitchells' – a very substantial margin indeed in construction terms – the tender document included some £15 million of prime cost and provisional sums which were at the disposal of the client. If one adds to these £5 million in respect of certain essential materials which had to be common to both tenders, competition was effectively limited to only £8 million of work. If the £1.4 million excess is related to this competitive element of £8 million, then the McAlpine figures were 17.5 per cent higher than Mitchells' when related to the competitive element. These figures are important because construction is basically a service industry, and they show how easy it is to mask a fee which is five or six times the going competitive rate, even in circumstances as exposed as those on the Anchor project. If Anchor did nothing else, it should have illustrated to any potential client of the construction industry the impossibility of making valid judgements in the absence of a competitive process.

As to the ethical issues involved, it is interesting to contrast our experience of tendering for a major contract with the Atomic Energy Authority. There was further work to be done at Windscale, the authority was very well disposed to us, and, as we were already established on the site, they would like to have seen us secure the contract. In the event, our price on a multi-million pound project was second only by a margin of £219 and the authority decided, quite properly, that the contract should be let to the lowest tenderer, and we accepted without question. It may be tempting to think otherwise, but ethically it is indefensible to ask a contractor to tender for a major project knowing that if he tenders the right price the contract is unlikely to be awarded to him, whereas if he makes a massive mistake his tender will be accepted.

As regards the question of resources, Atkins have enjoyed a very long and close relationship with McAlpines and no doubt are well acquainted with their resources. The facts were, however, that Mitchell Construction were the only contractors in the country who had, at Fawley, and on far more complex work, achieved anything like the outputs that were necessary for the Anchor project. The company specialized in heavy civil engineering work of the type that was required at Anchor, which was why we had been invited to tender in the first place. The ownership of hotels, office blocks, freeholds in

84

Park Lane and massive property interests in London are indeed resources, but these in no way implied an ability to outperform Mitchells on a contract which was very near to their location in Peterborough and was ideally suited to their particular resources and experience.

In our original submission to BSC we had included works programmes, method statements, with details of a fully integrated management structure for our own operations, together with proposals for the necessary joint structure to provide full liaison with the client. Our programme was accompanied by named staff, including twenty-four qualified engineers, of whom fifteen were full members of the Institution of Civil Engineers, to fill designated senior management and supervisory functions on the project. As the result of various delays and the retendering following Atkins' appointment, most of this staff, together with plant and other resources, had been held ready for some twelve months so we could comply with the requirement for an immediate start if the contract was awarded to us. We knew that our original proposals had been adopted by BSC as a yardstick to assist them in assessing other submissions, and yet with all this effort we did not have a single meeting or receive a single meaningful inquiry from the consulting engineers. In any fair adjudication of available resources, Mitchells could not have been faulted, but there appeared to be a resolute determination not to allow us to present our credentials.

Finally, it had been particularly galling to me at the time when adjudication was supposed to be taking place to learn of luncheon and dinner parties at the Dorchester, attended at the highest level by representatives of McAlpines, BSC and Atkins. At these meetings the letting of the Anchor project to McAlpines had been taken for granted and the reference to Mitchells' 'strike record' suggested that the information given to me in May was indeed accurate: when making their decision even supposing a valid adjudication had been attempted, there had been a reliance on gossip, rather than proper inquiry.

Disquiet in the industry

Following the announcement of the award, I had messages and representations from a number of major contractors expressing concern, not only about what had happened at Anchor, but about trends within the industry generally. Maurice Laing, chairman of John Laing, had earlier remarked to me that it was absurd to suggest that there was any deficiency in Mitchells' resources, especially since the tender list had been restricted and, in spite of his personal representations, his firm, for one, had not been admitted.

Another of Laing's directors telephoned me asking what we were trying to achieve. Too much adverse publicity, he felt, would affect other statutory authorities, who had 'been got into a negotiating position'. This, of course, went to the heart of the matter, and was the principal reason why we had made a stand on Anchor. The facts were known and it might be an opportunity to turn the tide against the pre-empting of work by a few major contractors.

Among the other messages I had at this time was a telephone call from Mogens Kier, chairman of Kier Ltd, who was facing the same problems and, like us, was extremely concerned that the CEGB were proposing to abandon normal competitive tendering procedures on the contract for the construction of the Isle of Grain power station. He told me that Olaf Kier, chairman of Kier's holding company, had had a meeting with the chief purchasing and contracts officer of the CEGB, who himself had apparently objected to the proposals, but had been overruled. I expressed the hope that with the exposure over Anchor we might have caught in time this movement, which was apparently designed to exclude contractors of our size from projects for a number of nationalized industries. Kier himself hoped that this was true, because he 'could not hope to run his outfit' on the basis of sewage disposal works and road diversions 'involving the usual wrangles with town clerks, etc.' If they could not secure a change the only alternative would be to concentrate abroad – a high risk strategy which demands a strong home base.

Edgar Beck of Mowlems telephoned me on 6 August – he told me that he felt 'livid' and that something ought to be done. However, following upon his suggestion made earlier, on his own and Sir Godfrey Mitchell's behalf, that we should make a joint protest, he had discussed the matter again with Sir Godfrey who felt that this would not necessarily be in the interests of their respective shareholders, although it might be of benefit to Mitchells. Even so he repeated that they were both solidly behind us and I told him that I drew some comfort from this, as I felt rather isolated from time to time. He assured me that this was not the case: 'I am full of admiration for what you are doing and I think you have got guts.' Guts? Why did the situation call for guts? And what was the threat? In fact I had heard so many stories of indiscriminate and defamatory statements about myself and Mitchells, which I had been told emanated from the Dorchester and Sir Edwin, that I had made a conscious decision that nothing could be lost if those hearing them knew that we were not the best of friends with McAlpines.

Sidney Lenssen, editor of *Construction News,* telephoned me to say he had had discussions with a large number of contractors over the previous few weeks, all of whom considered that it was time something was done to clean up the industry. He also told me that a public relations man, employed by one of the parties concerned, had been diligently lobbying journalists, suggesting that 'the more this is looked into the more unfortunate it is going to be as far as Mitchells are concerned', because 'they would get a spotlight focused on their claims record'. There was nothing we would have liked more than to have a spotlight on our claims record, because it would have given us a chance to destroy a carefully nurtured myth.

It was necessary at this juncture to redefine our objectives and to decide what we could achieve or what we should try to achieve. We had been advised by counsel, David Eady QC, that it would be possible to argue strongly that some of the criticism that had been reported had been defamatory, either of the company or of me personally. The advice of David Gardam QC, given before the contract was let, had also allowed the possibility of legal redress. However, although we had sought guidance on these matters, neither of the opinions suggested a course of action which would secure us what we wanted – an opportunity to obtain work for which we were eminently suited in fair and open competition.

There was clearly a limit to what we could now hope to achieve, but any steps which would improve standards and at the same time clear our name must be good. I thought it would be wrong to go to the minister over the head of BSC. The heads of nationalized industries resent government interference and my sympathies are with them. I had not yet had an opportunity to see Lord Melchett, the chairman of BSC, but we would be satisfied if we could obtain the following: (a) an acknowledgement that a serious mistake had been made, (b) an acknowledgement that the corporation had been wrongly advised about our resources, capacity, finance and labour relations, (c) an acceptance that we had suffered as a result of these mistakes and that, accordingly, we should have the opportunity of tendering for further work, with no strings attached, but with a reasonable opportunity of success, and (d) an assurance that suitable steps had been taken to prevent a recurrence of what had happened in the Anchor project.

It was against this background that I wrote to Lord Melchett suggesting that he must be as concerned as I was about the Anchor controversy, and pointing out that there had been considerable press comment, much of it attributed to BSC, reflecting adversely upon my company. I enclosed a memorandum giving a history of our experiences and asking him for an early meeting. I was rather disconcerted when the first reaction to this came from a member of the McAlpine family who congratulated me on what he thought was a very clever case, though he thought he could pick holes in it. Obviously security at BSC was not good at the highest level. Two days later Lord Melchett wrote to acknowledge receipt of the memorandum, but suggested that there was nothing he could add to what had already been said by Monty Finniston. He assured me that the Corporation's decision in no way reflected adversely on the record of my company.

Almost as the letter arrived, I had a telephone call from the editor of *Construction News* telling me that he understood I had received a letter from Lord Melchett which was 'short and to the point'. As I was about to go abroad I could not deal with the matter immediately, but on my return I wrote to Lord Melchett emphasizing that it had been my hope throughout, albeit against a mounting weight of evidence, that some proper and logical explanation of the unhappy events would be disclosed, and that if a mistake had been made it would be recognized and suitable lessons drawn from it for the future. I added that I believed the issues involved were of fundamental importance, both to the industry and to the economy. 'With this in mind, I have at no time been interested in any form of redress which could not be made properly and openly.' I went on to suggest that, while I was quite sure that Lord Melchett would not be personally responsible for any discourtesy, I was extremely concerned that the press should have been informed of his letter to me, and the fact that it was 'short and to the point', before I had an opportunity of seeing it. I concluded by saying that, in view of the Corporation's persistent involvement of the press and the wrong impressions that may well have been created, I felt I had no alternative but to make available to them such information as enabled objective judgements to be made.

In the absence of any reply, I arranged a meeting with a few members of the press on 20 October 1970. At that meeting I released the letters and the memorandum which I had exchanged with Lord Melchett, expressed my concern that the whole competitive system was being brought into disrepute, adding the hope that some healthy attitude of inquiry could be stimulated. While accepting that crusading was an unprofitable pastime, I indicated in response to inquiries that I would be happy to make documents available. I emphasized the fact that Mitchells' tender was beyond any reasonable doubt the lowest, and that certain statements had been made in justification of the award which were quite clearly untrue. I drew attention to the statement in my memorandum to Lord Melchett that the unwarranted adjustment of our own tender for comparison purposes and the apparent disregard of the extremely important percentage additions in McAlpines' tender were but two of the very unsatisfactory features of the adjudication and award. My memorandum had concluded:

I believe that the treatment of our tender and the explanations that had been given raise very serious issues which cannot be ignored in fairness to ourselves or to the British Steel Corporation.

On a wider front, the letting of such an important contract at the present time on the basis that was clearly uncompetitive, and on such terms and in such circumstances that an inflationary thrust on the wage structure was an almost inevitable consequence, cannot be reconciled with the policies that had been put forward by government to combat our economic ills, and must be a matter for public concern.

A proper and if necessary independent examination of this unhappy affair is clearly essential if confidence in our recognised tendering procedures is to be restored and other attendant fears are to be allayed.

Later in the afternoon, my secretary received a telephone call from Lord Melchett's secretary saying that he had been abroad and had only just got back, and proposing that a meeting be arranged. This was fixed for three o'clock on Wednesday 28 October. Immediately afterwards I learned from a message received indirectly from Will Camp, who handled political and public relations for BSC, that they were fearful of a government inquiry, and he thought that 'the ball would be at [my] feet' when I saw Lord Melchett. This information was accompanied by the usual assurances that work would come our way – either the next big contract or the one after. At the same time, it appeared that BSC had at last recognized that I was prepared to be 'a martyr'. In this they were, of course, wrong. Martyrdom was not our objective, but with the information that had come to light it was probably the only chance we would have of striking a blow for securing the only sort of market in which we could hope to prosper.

When I arrived at BSC, Lord Melchett came to the waiting room to conduct me to his office and after a few polite words we turned to Anchor. He opened the discussion by saying that his people had a high regard for me and my company, that he had personally looked into the position regarding the adjudication and that, if he had been in our position, he himself would feel dissatisfied, and even angry. He thought the situation was unsatisfactory, although he could not say he had found any specific thing that had been the subject of improper practice. He was, however, quite prepared to accept that I might have information which I had not disclosed, going beyond this. In any case, nobody quite knew what was going to emerge once QCs, etc., were let loose on an official inquiry. He had simply done his best.

He was satisfied that as 'new boys' to the game they had been less sophisticated than they ought, and that they would make changes in the future. He hoped that we would now allow the dust to settle so that we could all get on with our jobs. I pointed out to him that I could do no better than quote a comment attributed to him the previous day. 'Just fix the rules and let us get on with the play.' As far as Mitchells were concerned, all we had sought was an opportunity to tender in fair competition and to succeed or fail according to our efforts. We could not do this if the rules were going to be changed, as they had been in this case.

My persistence, I told him, had not been directed essentially at BSC or its consultants. It was perhaps unfortunate for them that on this occasion figures had been published which confirmed beyond doubt what we had good reason to believe had happened elsewhere. It could be that the only difference between Anchor and other projects was that this was the time 'that the cat got out of the bag'. He recognized that I was worried by the procedures being adopted by the nationalized industries generally and the influences to which they were being exposed. I made it clear I was not suggesting these influences were necessarily corrupt; they did not involve anything as crude as backhanders, motor-cars, etc., but were more to do with spheres of influence and mutual patronage.

Lord Melchett said he quite understood the wider implications and that they had 'already been taken aboard': BSC had learned a great deal from their experience and would certainly do things differently in the future. He could not say how far this would be extended to other sections of the nationalized industries which he knew we were concerned with, but he thought the whole thing had been pretty widely discussed, and as for what I was trying to do in the industry generally, I could count upon his support as a 'personal ally'. He accepted that much damage had been done both to BSC and Mitchells, but that we had suffered the most. He assured me that in future he and his senior colleagues would all be personally involved in contractual arrangements to ensure that they were satisfactory. He did not think we had to continue our battle further because it would seem to serve no purpose. Certainly, we would have the opportunity of tendering for future work, for they had many projects coming up which were even bigger than Scunthorpe. He suggested that the matter should be dealt with at our level, taking the widest view.

I replied that it was not our wish to collect scalps or initiate a witch-hunt: we were solely concerned to have proper procedures and a healthy competitive climate in which we could work and survive. If normal work in the nationalized industries was going to be pre-empted, then certainly we should have to look around for another calling than civil engineering, and we might as well do it in 1971 as be forced into it in 1975. In this particular case, the matter had gone so far that it was just not possible to let it drop: some explanation would have to be put forward, otherwise people would make assumptions. Lord Melchett agreed that it would be unfair to us to expect the incident to be left without an explanation. He proposed that we should issue a joint statement, saying that BSC had looked into the matter, that they were satisfied that we had had grounds for complaint and that they were going to alter their method in future, having learned lessons from what had happened. He would submit a draft to me in suitable form which I could 'chop about'.

Granted that the Anchor project had now gone beyond recall, Lord Melchett's proposal encompassed everything I could hope to gain. I was impressed by Lord Melchett, by the fact that he had obviously gone to some trouble to acquaint himself with the background of this matter, and by his sincerity. In the circumstances, it would have been churlish, if not foolhardy, not to have agreed. He suggested that the involvement of the press had been unfortunate, and he thought that BSC had handled the whole matter very badly, particularly in having had a press conference. He suggested that if we made a joint statement, we should not elaborate on it to the press. With this I agreed, if only because I had already learned that my company had neither the time nor the resources to match the press relations machinery of the Corporation.

As it happened, there was a meeting of our holding company board on the following day, at which I was able to report very fully on my discussions with Lord Melchett, and they welcomed the fact that an acceptable solution had been found. I also wrote to a number of other people who had become involved, including Sir John Eden, who was at that time Secretary of State of the Department of Trade and Industry, telling them of this outcome.

Anchor had been a very disrupting influence, and if I acted precipitately in accepting that the matter would now be closed, it was because I was under very considerable pressure before going overseas. It was therefore with great disappointment that I received from Lord Melchett an inadequate draft statement, which he proposed I should issue personally. We had a further meeting at which we considered the wording. It was not nearly as strong as I would have wished, but Lord Melchett argued that a sophisticated observer would not miss its significance. He was very sensitive because he had a lot of people in BSC to consider. In agreeing with the statement, I emphasized that for me the choice had been between precipitating a tremendous row or settling for having a powerful ally in my attempts to secure reform in the tendering procedures generally, and particularly in the public sector. The understanding reached between us had been a personal one: we both knew the intentions and I was quite satisfied that we would both observe them.

In the circumstances, it seemed to me that the most sensible course would be to bring the matter to an end. I did, however, emphasize again that Anchor was part of a much larger story, and I would not want any misunderstanding to arise regarding our future course of action: while I quite agreed that no further comment should be made to the press, I was equally sure I could not sacrifice my freedom of action to bring Anchor into the open in any future discussion. I did undertake not to say or do anything which would embarrass him personally and we agreed the arrangements for releasing the statement the following day (12 November).

Unfortunately, I had suffered a family bereavement, involving a funeral from my home that day, and I was very fully occupied until the evening. I also had an early start from London airport the following morning to fulfil my long-standing overseas commitment. It was therefore with considerable chagrin that I learned that BSC had distributed the statement by hand, on unheaded paper, and that they had managed to imply that the best thing to do with it was to dump it in the wastepaper basket.

Perhaps because of the pressure I was under at the time, I acted naïvely, but I had formed a very high regard for Lord Melchett. Even though BSC's handling of the statement did not accord with the spirit of my discussions with him, I did not think he was responsible, nor did I believe it would in any way undermine the commitments he had made.

During the period when we were quite certain that the contract for Anchor had been vouchsafed to McAlpines, despite the absence of any announcement, it so happened that we received an invitation to tender for a project at Kariba, and in view of the unused capacity we now had on our hands, we had submitted a tender for the project in early October. When I returned from overseas I found that the campaign during the Anchor saga that had caused us to seek counsel's advice was still being pursued. This time it was sinister. Our tender was being considered favourably and as big international contracts require performance bonds, normally underwritten by a bank or major financial institution, we had entered into negotiations to arrange the bond in London. I soon learned that one broker, with whom we had never had any association, was generating rumours as to our financial stability. As the story was linked to an alleged disastrous experience in the West Indies, and as our maximum exposure on the contract in question was £25,000, it was not difficult to show that this was not the sort of stuff disasters were made of. On the other hand, it was clear that a further and very active campaign to damage the company was under way.

Perhaps I had been naïve, too, in not appreciating the dangers to which Lord Melchett's assurances exposed the company. Certainly I had no idea then that we were not to be allowed to survive to enjoy the possible benefit from the commitments which he had entered into. In the months and years that lay ahead, through our experiences at Kariba and the whole process of receivership and liquidation, I was to learn a great deal more of how the establishment conducts its communications, of the power of rumour and of gossip, and of the obstruction and suppression that renders useless and inaccessible all the remedies whose apparent existence brings us comfort in times of approaching adversity.

There was a further ironic sequel to Anchor: Ray Gunter's appointment notwithstanding, the contract had within weeks joined a number of other McAlpine jobs, including the National Theatre and the Barbican, as a major centre of industrial unrest. Nor could the men be bought off. Within months the rates of pay for labour on the Anchor site were double the local rate, with still no sign of long-term peace. Anchor therefore became another classic case of the syndrome which caused us so much concern: a cost-plus environment with escalating and ill-controlled labour rates, which destroyed the wages structure for an area of 30–50 miles around the site and exerted inflationary pressures throughout the industry, and indeed on all those other occupations serving major construction.

There were other respects in which Anchor provided a classic example of the malaise of the day, which will take a long time to eliminate, and for which we will be paying dearly for many years to come. In a nationalized industry decisions to spend £3 billion had been made by people who had nothing at risk, and who were spending money as if it had gone out of fashion. There was, of course, the accompanying assumption that government money was by definition almost inexhaustible. Employers, contractors and unions all had their feet in the trough. Who was making the value judgements? Who was deciding that, for the sake of this one project, the wages structure of a whole area should be destroyed? One only has to look at Anchor to see a microcosm of a pattern which would inevitably bring any economy to its knees. Did we learn any lessons? I would suggest one lesson above all emerges. When an employer has too much money and a contractor is on a cost-plus job, it is idle to blame the unions if some of the men decide that what is good for others is good enough for them.

Notwithstanding the hope expressed in *The Economist,* the Select Committee on Nationalized Industries never did shed light on the Anchor decision. A senior engineer from the Anchor site did tell one of our managers that the escalation on the contract had been 'enormous and would make your eyes pop', and I have been informed that the final cost exceeded £60 million, but this has never been confirmed. When the McAlpine prospectus was published in September 1972 it contained only an enigmatic statement which gave no clue regarding the true cost of the project to BSC.

The 'super-league'

Although the establishment rapidly closed ranks, persuaded as they had been by the promises given to them by BSC that this was the best course to follow in the interests of their shareholders, the rest of the industry enjoyed no such reassurance. It was by now an open secret that tremendously heavy lobbying was going on in government circles and within the nationalized industries for a move to a policy whereby a super-league of contractors would employ the rest of the industry as subcontractors. In this way, and by some mysterious process, efficiency within the industry was going to be improved, but how this was going to be brought about merely by the creation of another tier, while the contractor who was actually doing the work was being reduced to a second-class status, was obscure. For clients, the concept was intended to conjure up visions of a cosy life, in which what they didn't see they wouldn't have to grieve about. For the major contractors it was just another variant of the many devices which had been promoted to enable them to insulate themselves from competition.

I shall refer later to some of the disastrous consequences of this form of contracting, but within the industry it was undoubtedly seen as a threat to the competitive market, and the fact that contracts – such as the Isle of Grain power station for the CEGB – were seen to be going the same way as Anchor was causing widespread concern. Not surprisingly, a number of contractors, who did not consider themselves one whit less efficient than some of the so-called 'super-league', did not regard kindly the prospect of being relegated to subcontractor status in a wasteful and confused management structure, which could only blunt efficiency, confuse communications and, in so doing, undermine the first requirement of good labour relations. Since that time, most major contractors, in self-defence or otherwise, have jumped upon the creaky bandwagon and offered their services as so-called management contractors, and have vied with one another in a proliferation of seductive material prepared for the gullible.

Part of the bait being used by the small circle of contractors who stood to benefit by these proposals was the elimination of 'claims'. Those within the industry know full well that it is the major contractors who have the most awe-inspiring machinery for formulating and making claims. Indeed, one of the foremost proponents of the concept had been struck off the CEGB tendering list for a while because of his intolerable claims record, and had only been reinstated after very influential intervention. No doubt the principle of poacher turned gamekeeper appealed to some public sector clients, but, if so, it was totally misconceived.

Immediately after the Anchor debacle, I was approached by a number of contractors with a view to making a joint representation in parliamentary and other circles in an endeavour to counter the aggressive promotion of these concepts. A meeting was arranged with the chairmen of six major construction companies, Tarmac Construction, Kier, Gleesons, Monks, W. C. French and ourselves, to talk the matter over. It emerged that a number of them had been taking independent action, and we agreed that some sort of joint action would now be desirable. For obvious reasons the Federation no longer provided a satisfactory forum, although it was hoped that with the forthcoming election of E. C. Beck (now Sir Edgar Beck) as president, better channels of communication might be established and reforms made possible. In the existing circumstances, however, we decided that rather than trying to form a splinter group, our first objective should be to secure reforms within the Federation so that it truly represented its members. With this in mind, each of the six members who attended the initial meeting agreed to make themselves responsible for recruiting two more, making eighteen in all, and that these should be geographically spread right across the United Kingdom in order to secure representation through the various section committees.

Beck had undoubtedly been shocked at what had happened in the Anchor adjudication, and I had found him very genuine and forthcoming. As he was president-elect he did offer the best entrée, but it was considered inappropriate to embarrass him or ask him to be directly involved with our group. However, it was arranged that I would have a talk with him, and I met him for lunch (25 May 1971) two weeks after his election as president. He was very open and told me that his company, Mowlems, was at that time suffering seriously as a result of delayed payments, coupled with a particularly adverse experience on one major contract. It did indeed look as if we might have an ally. I was therefore greatly disappointed when, in early August, he visited my office in Bedford Square for a working lunch, and suggested that, after all, there was merit in the proposal that work should be shared out among the larger contractors, and that Mitchells should be included in the group. In this way we could all be ensured a steady work-load at satisfactory prices. I had to tell him that this was not the way I saw the competitive system operating, or even surviving, and I could not compromise that belief.

Our own liaison group – now eighteen – had had its first meeting at the Savoy Hotel on 13 July, at which we had explored the question of the 'super-league'. It was noticeable that there was a certain nervousness expressed, particularly by the two Scottish members, about the reaction from the establishment, because 'some of them are very powerful', but the group accepted that a choice had to be made – either we insisted on our right to an independent existence, or we submitted to the patronage of our bigger brethren.

I reported the outcome of my meeting with Beck to the group on 14 September, when it was decided that three of our members, myself and the chairmen of W. C. French and J. L. Kier, would have lunch with Beck in his role as president at the Connaught Hotel. We expressed our total opposition to the concept of the super-league and the way that the Federation's resources were being devoted to promoting it. Beck, as usual, was very open, but we were astonished when he responded that it would be difficult for the Federation to change course in view of its commitment to the policy of management contracting and the representations that had been made over a long period, and at the highest levels, in support of it. We protested very vigorously at this. The Federation had regular meetings at permanent secretary and ministerial level, and were represented by the president, the chairman and some vice-presidents of the Federation, but we pointed out that at no time had we, as members of the council, ever been consulted about matters to be discussed at these meetings, nor had we received reports of what went on. Above all, none of us had ever given a mandate to our representatives to promote concepts which were the commercial concern of particular companies, but diametrically opposed to the wishes of a large number of the members. Beck's response was devastating in its simplicity: 'I was born with a golden spoon in my mouth and I intend to keep it there.' I have always liked Beck, but the naïvety of that response I found quite staggering: although he had taken shelter, he was never really intended for the role of predator!

After Beck's candid disclosures, it was clear that we had a federation within a federation, and furthermore one over which the general membership had no control. Moreover, this could only be possible if the officers and permanent staff of the Federation were in fact the creatures of the establishment rather than committed representatives of the general membership. Our group met once or twice to discuss it. There was no doubt that the Anchor business had produced strains in the higher echelon, and it was decided that our concern should be brought out into the open in the interests of the industry at large. We sent a letter to the president of the Federation expressing a desire for a change in the conduct of the Federation's business.

As a result, a meeting took place between representatives of our group and the president, vice-presidents and chairman of the Federation some two months later, at which it was agreed that these matters would be further explored. But, although some progress was made, the fundamental power structure has remained. Of the five signatories to the letter, only one would still be in his position five years later. I know nothing of the circumstances of the others, but my own fate and that of Mitchells have provided a salutary lesson for anyone with the temerity to think it is possible to reform the construction industry against the will of its establishment.

The National Economic Development Office

By the late 1960s I had long since become reconciled to the fact that there was to be no role for me within the Federation, and it had even ceased to be a source of frustration. I had been informed that a veto had been imposed at the highest levels on our companies being represented on important committees, on the grounds that we were 'politically unacceptable'. To one who had always regarded himself as being rather to the right in politics, it was intriguing to find myself in the role of a radical! However, the implication obviously owed more to an entrenched resistance to reform than to my own political inclinations. At the same time, I was becoming accustomed to sustained attacks behind the scenes on me personally and on the company, but at the beginning of 1969 an event occurred which suggested that my opponents were beginning to suffer from overconfidence, and a chink was opening up.

In May 1969, under the auspices of NEDO, a conference was organized by the Civil Engineering Economic Development Committee on 'Civil Engineering since Banwell', to be held at Solihull. One of the papers to be presented was on the subject of Pre-planning and Claims. I had never had anything to do with the Economic Development Committee (EDC) or anybody associated with it. Obviously inquiries had been made as to the most appropriate people to give papers and, maybe the temptation proved altogether too strong, I was nominated to give the paper. I must confess that my first reaction was one of chagrin, but I decided that if it was the only thing I was to be allowed to talk about, so be it. Claims are the greatest indictment of the industry and of its clients; almost by definition they are the manifestation of incompetence and inefficiency. They are not the monopoly of wicked contractors, nor of small contractors: quite the reverse; it is not small contractors who build nuclear power stations. In the absence of claims, how could the cost of Dungeness 'B', for example, escalate from an original estimate of £88.5 million to £537 million, or its companion stations at Heysham and Hartlepool from £322 million to £1.5 billion? Although the first word in the title of my proposed paper, 'Pre-planning', was anathema to me, having been coined by public relations people to whom the concept of planning in construction was so novel that it had to be given a meaningless prefix, I accepted the invitation. What better opportunity could there be to demonstrate where our problems really lay, and expose some of the hypocritical and emotive nonsense that was being generated to promote a commercial purpose and mask a very real evil.

The conference, which was held under the chairmanship of Sir Frederick Catherwood, at that time director-general of NEDO, was attended by some 300 senior representatives from the professions, municipal authorities and the industry. It was a considerable success and my own paper, which was well received, was subsequently reported in full in *Construction News*.

The ploy, if such it was, appeared to have backfired, and a door had been opened which gave an opportunity for wider expression of my views and also brought me within the ambit of NEDO and the Civil Engineering EDC. Nevertheless, it came as a surprise when at a Federation dinner at the Dorchester Hotel in May 1970 I was introduced to Gerard Bonham Carter, head of the construction group of the National Economic Development Office, who asked me whether, if an invitation to join the Civil Engineering EDC were extended to me, I would accept.

My surprise at his proposal must have been equalled by his surprise at my response: 'You must be joking!' I asked him if he had permission? What did I mean? I nodded towards the president on the top table and said, 'Have you asked him?' Bonham Carter was obviously puzzled, but I had made my point, and I simply laughed and told him that nothing would please me more. In fact, it was to be some months before I received my invitation and joined the committee. In the meantime, the inevitable luncheon had taken place between Desmond Misselbrook, the EDC chairman, and Sir Robin McAlpine, as president of the Federation, at which Misselbrook was apparently told that my appointment would be out of the question and that the industry would not have it at any price. But for once the matter was not allowed to rest there; at a subsequent industry meeting a number of people were canvassed and their reaction was generally favourable. Short of putting his personal veto on the appointment, Robin McAlpine had little alternative but to go along with it.

Ironically, no sonner had the door opened than it seemed to be closing again, for whether or not the Federation resented an unwarranted intrusion into its power, it was not long before the Civil Engineering EDC had to face a determined attempt by the Federation's establishment to have it abolished. However, with the benefit of my experience at the Federation, and the impression that I had rapidly gained following my involvement with the EDC, I was able to submit a paper which Sir Frank Figgures, Sir Frederick Catherwood's successor as director-general of NEDO, assured me played a decisive part in gaining general appreciation of the EDC's value, and the role it could play, and thereby in securing its reprieve.

I enjoyed my period of service with the Civil Engineering EDC. I approached it with a strong belief in the potential of British industry and, above all, thanks to my experience both in this country and overseas, with respect for its skilled, intelligent and politically sophisticated work-force. I was convinced that there was no limit to what could be achieved if we could act together. At this time, too, I was encouraged by other developments: an invitation to join the council of the CBI, and then a further invitation 'in recognition of my services to management' to become one of the two per cent of the Fellows, now Companions, of the British Institute of Management.

But on another front there was continuing cause for concern as delayed payments in the public sector continued to shackle our ability to develop as we would have liked. However, there appeared to be some sign of increasing public interest when I had an approach from Andrew McElroy who was introduced to me as an established journalist and whose credentials had been cleared by people I trusted. He told me he had been commissioned to write an article, or a series of articles, for the *Sunday Times* dealing with aspects of the construction industry known to be near my heart and in particular relating to the negotiation of contracts and also slow payment in the public sector. Mitchells were one of a number of contractors he would be consulting.

Over the ensuing months we had a series of meetings and he carried out certain researches within the company. He asked for and was given a great deal of information, much of it confidential and sensitive. It included details of public sector clients for whom we were working, and the sums of money outstanding on individual contracts, which I would not have liked to fall into the hands of a hostile competitor. However, I was very busy and accepted his assurance that its significance would emerge when it had been added to similar details collected from others and it had been processed 'in the *Sunday Times* computer'. He promised me that confidentiality would always be respected and that his notes would be destroyed once the article was compiled. I was a little surprised when, on a later visit, he asked me to let him see some particularly confidential documents. I did not feel at liberty to pass them on to him, but he said I need not be involved: I had only to leave them on my desk and he would have copies by the morning.

It seemed to me that we were moving into a world I had only read about. I became increasingly uneasy as the articles remained unpublished, despite repeated assurances that they were about to appear. Finally McElroy told me that the entire series had been locked away in the *Sunday Times* safe and that he could not tell me the contents because he had not kept copies. When I asked other contractors who I had been told would be included in the survey I was informed that they knew nothing of it.

I have made a number of attempts to contact McElroy to seek further explanation of this extraordinary incident, but without success. I have since learned that Gordon Brunton, chief executive of the Thomson Organization, which at that time owned the *Sunday Times,* had a great interest and involvement in the construction industry. So it is indeed possible that the article was commissioned as a result of *Sunday Times* interest, but why it should not have been published and yet merited lodgement in the *Sunday Times* safe remains a mystery.

But whatever else emerged from this experience there was certainly no improvement in public sector practices – indeed matters seemed to get worse as in the ensuing months we repeatedly found that, while relationships on a number of large DOE contracts continued to be good, our experience with payment actually deteriorated and all too often it seemed that payments agreed at one level would be blocked at another. It was worrying because although there was no doubt in anyone's mind that we were owed a lot of money, we could not secure its release.

Meanwhile two other developments had taken place: I had been appointed chairman of an EDC working party which was to look into the question of public sector purchasing and from which I had high hopes of reform; and second, having been awarded the contract for the Kariba project, we were finding that matters here, too, were anything but as straightforward as they appeared on the surface.

II
Kariba

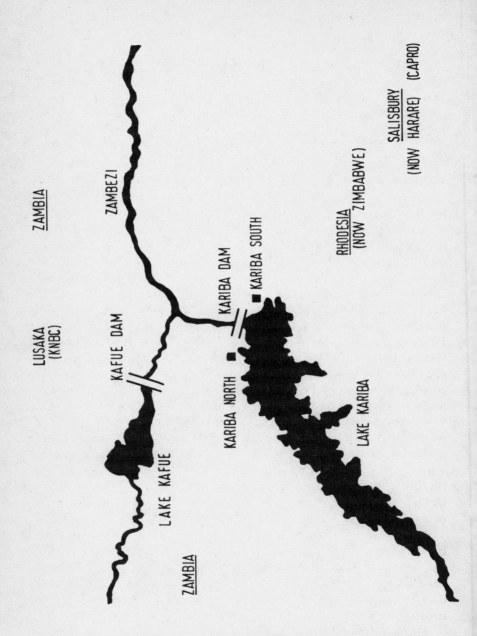

Map showing the location of the Kariba and Kafue Hydroelectric Stations.

The contract

In the late 1960s, the developing republic of Zambia desperately needed more electricity. Copper, on which the new country was heavily dependent, was booming and there was great concern that the demand for electricity at the mines would soon outstrip supply. It was therefore proposed to double the capacity of the Kariba hydroelectric scheme on the Zambezi by building an underground power station on the Zambian side of the river, the north bank, similar to the one which already existed on the Rhodesian side, the south bank. The Kariba North Bank Company (KNBC) was set up, an entity that was wholly owned by the Zambian Government, and Sir Alexander Gibb and Partners were retained as the consulting engineers. Surprisingly, the Salisbury-based Central African Power Corporation (CAPCO) was appointed as the agent for construction. We were told that this was considered necessary because CAPCO had been responsible for the original Kariba project and the running of the two power stations would necessarily involve some cooperation. Furthermore, CAPCO was familiar with the problems associated with an undertaking of such magnitude, whereas the Zambians had no similar expertise. Eyebrows were raised at this very close involvement of Rhodesia at a time when the bitter struggle over the Unilateral Declaration of Independence (UDI) was at its height, but there was no reason to question the explanation.

It was to be many years, and long after the company's receivership, before it was discovered that these statements concealed more than they revealed. If the concealment of vital information, which would have led contractors reasonably to refuse to tender, is deceit, then deceit there was, and the events that followed were rooted in this original deception.

Speed of construction to allow the earliest possible commissioning of the station was the keynote of the contract, which was awarded to

Mitchell Construction to the sum of K21.4 million, in April 1971. The work included the building of an underground power station contained in a huge main cavern, some 132 metres long by 25 metres wide and 48 metres deep, together with all the necessary tunnels, shafts, intake and outfall works associated with the scheme.

In construction of this kind the quality of the rock is all-important, because it determines the design and the speed of construction. At KNC2, the project number allocated by the client, both were predicated on conditions assumed to be ideal. Thus, a wide flat arch design was adopted, a design that makes the maximum demands on the compressive strength and homogeneity of the rock. This, in turn, allows for rapid and continuous excavation without the necessity of providing concrete lining or other support as the work proceeds. It cannot be emphasized too strongly that this choice of design was critical, for it was unsuitable for anything other than first-class rock.

But on this score we had no doubts. As tenderers, we had been given a detailed geological report, which advised that conditions in the working area were ideal. This report had been carried out under the direction of Gibbs in 1961, and was accompanied by detailed logs of core samples taken over the area of the projected works. Furthermore, these logs were *warranted to be accurate*, a unique feature in the experience of the many experts who have since become involved. Our contract specifically provided that if they were found to be inaccurate, any resulting change in our conditions of working would be treated as unforeseeable and we would be paid for any additional costs incurred. Alas, this report was fatally inaccurate, and its errors were not marginal, but fundamental and inexplicable.

Mitchells' special interest

Mitchells' particular interest in Kariba derived from a number of different factors. The company had long since recognized the growth potential in underground works and had specialized in tunnelling and associated techniques. In doing so it had been responsible for many innovations which in turn had contributed to economy and therefore growth in the field. We had not tendered for the first Kariba project because of its size and remoteness. Nevertheless I had paid two visits to the site when the project was under construction and had agreed with Gibbs' resident engineer – for Gibbs were consulting engineers on Stage I too – that UK contractors could do at least as well as the Italians. Indeed I noticed methods being adopted there which were acknowledged to be derived from reports that appeared in the technical press on techniques we had developed in Scotland. My tours of Africa had been part of a general plan because the construction programme of the North of Scotland Hydro Electric Board was coming to an end and we had to look overseas if we were to find outlets for what had become a very large pool of tunnelling expertise and resources. At the same time the failure of the British contracting industry to compete effectively for both Kariba Stage I and other overseas hydroelectric work had been a great source of disappointment to the British Government. Mitchells had reacted by establishing overseas companies to act as sounding-boards and bridgeheads for major works, particularly for hydroelectric and tunnelling works that might arise in the future. One such company had been established in Northern Rhodesia, and our Kariba involvement was therefore the result both of particular circumstances and long-term planning.

As it happened, we were in a unique position to tackle the Kariba scheme, because of the large engineering force we had earmarked for the Anchor project which would not now be required. The result was that we were able to submit a competitive tender, albeit one that was qualified to take into account and limit the risks of local conditions, of which we were aware. We were also able very quickly to assemble a team whose experience in hydroelectric and underground work must have been unrivalled anywhere in the world. In addition to the off-site supervision, the team included a resident staff of no less than seven men who had experience as agents and subagents on major projects, six of whom were chartered civil engineers. And, equally important, we had seven general and trades foremen with long experience in every aspect of tunnelling and hydroelectric works.

Such was the camaraderie of the Mitchells staff and the enthusiasm for the project that two further men, both with excellent records, rejoined the company in order to assist in training Zambian labour. One of these had retired, but had formerly been the agent on the company's Glenmoriston hydroelectric contract, where we had received the highest praise from the North of Scotland Hydro Electric Board for our performance. He had also been the agent on the Chapelcross nuclear power station and the Windscale nuclear chemical separation plant both of which had won the approval of the Atomic Energy Authority. The other man had been Mitchells' works manager on tunnels when the National Coal Board had sent a working party to study Mitchells' methods and who, with the company's agreement, had subsequently gone to the National Coal Board as chief tunnelling

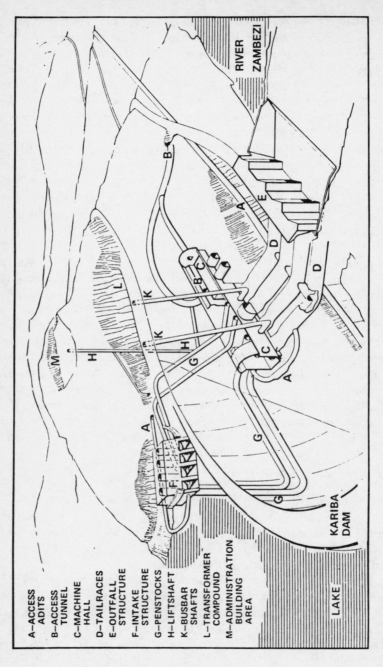

A—ACCESS ADITS
B—ACCESS TUNNEL
C—MACHINE HALL
D—TAILRACES
E—OUTFALL STRUCTURE
F—INTAKE STRUCTURE
G—PENSTOCKS
H—LIFTSHAFT
K—BUSBAR SHAFTS
L—TRANSFORMER COMPOUND
M—ADMINISTRATION BUILDING AREA

Schematic drawing of North Bank Power Station.

engineer. The senior Mitchells staff – twenty in number – attending the first site progress meeting had between them over 200 years' experience with the company, and I do not believe that any international contractor could have marshalled a team to equal it.

Apart from the sheer size of the machine hall, the project itself was not a particularly large one, and in contrast with contracts we had carried out in Scotland, which sometimes spread over as much as a hundred square miles, it was conveniently concentrated in a small working area. We were encouraged to field such a strong team, not only because of the demands of the programme, but because there were big bonuses to be earned by early completion. Many of the men who went to Kariba had already been associated with outstanding achievements on hydroelectric works during the course of which six-figure bonuses had been earned. With this powerful team, our plan was to ensure that a vitally important momentum was established from the start. Unfortunately, we were frustrated by obstacles beyond our control.

What then went wrong? To establish this we must review the history of our contract on the site. It is a disturbing story, whose implications and importance extend even beyond the wilful destruction of the company.

What went wrong?

It is very important in major projects of this nature, particularly if they are in remote areas, that an advance party prepares the ground by arranging the necessary services and accommodation before the main work-force arrives at the site. In our company it was normal practice, when we were responsible for the whole of the works, to treat this preliminary work as a separate contract, giving it to a different agent whose responsibility was to hand over the completed services to the main project agent on a given date. Experience had shown that embarking upon the main civil engineering works without having the essential services and facilities already in place inevitably proved counterproductive in the long run.

In the case of Kariba, these preliminary items were the subject of a separate contract let by KNBC before the main project went out to tender, and time ought to have been saved. It was therefore a great disappointment to find that very little of this work had been completed when the advance party arrived in Central Africa. Access roads necessary for the heavy and continuous traffic, including the transport

109

of constructional equipment, had not been prepared and a 40-mile dirt access road was still the only means of reaching the site. The client had completely failed to provide the facilities we needed – family and bachelors' quarters, social amenities, a school, roads and services. Indeed, many of these were still not available twelve months after our arrival. It was too late to stop the flow of essential expatriate staff going forward, many of whom were accompanied by their wives and children. Even without the heat, work on a project such as Kariba is hard and demanding, particularly in the early stages before a rhythm is established. The absence of essential services was an enormous additional burden and it was a great tribute to the enthusiasm, determination and resourcefulness of the men, and to their supervision, that these setbacks were solved without a disintegration of morale.

Thanks to this spirit and the recruitment of additional, and in some cases very senior, men from the UK, it was possible to handle many very difficult problems, but not, of course, without a setback to the programme. Mitchells' performance at this stage may best be judged by quoting from a letter sent by the chairman of CAPCO to the chairman of KNBC on 8 December 1971 – eight months after Mitchells had started work on the site – with a similar letter to the Zambian Minister of Mines: 'It is clear that the contractor himself has the necessary organisation, capacity and enthusiasm to meet his obligations under the contract. There are several areas, however, in which he is being prevented from applying his capacity and resources to the proper execution of the work.' This letter was written at a time when we were still suffering from the failure of the Zambians to provide amenities and services – but notably it made no reference to the much more serious disruption which by this time was being caused by rock conditions. Everyone on the site was made aware of the serious consequences to the Zambian economy that could arise from delay and for this reason there was constant consultation with Gibbs in an effort to find means of making up lost time. It was as a result of these discussions that a fundamental and potentially disastrous change in the method of excavation of the machine hall was agreed upon. In view of its implications, it is important to examine how that agreement came about.

The machine hall excavation

The original method statement and programme, agreed with the engineer, was based on what might be regarded as the 'normal' method for carrying out an excavation of this sort. The key to the operation is the driving of a tunnel along the crown of the vault; the whole roof is then exposed by progressively opening it out on either side. In this way the stresses are gradually transferred to the haunches as excavation continues. Obviously, the limiting factor is the availability of working faces, and to overcome this it was decided to open up headings on either side of the crown, thereby giving two working faces rather than one. (See Sketch pp. 112–13.) This change of method had one very considerable drawback, in that when the central pillar was finally removed a shock load would be transmitted throughout the crown, instead of having the stress transferred by degrees. The new method would, therefore, be quite unsuitable for any excavation other than in the exceptionally high quality rock upon which the original design was predicated.

However, with the knowledge then available to us there were no fears on this account. The 1961 report repeatedly emphasized the very high quality of the rock, classifying it as homogeneous sound gneiss which Gibbs' partner who had been in charge of the original Kariba project specifically equated with granite. The introduction of the word 'granitized' and the use of the conventional symbol for granite on the core logs clearly indicated that the works would be carried out in this type of rock – the underground man's favourite and most reliable material. It is not clear where this fiction of a homogeneous mass of sound gneiss originated but had we known that Gibbs were at that time suppressing two geological reports that made it clear that the rock we would encounter was likely to be anything but the expected 'granite', not only would the revised method not have been adopted but the entire history of the contract would have been changed.

One of these reports, submitted by Dr Dubertret, their retained geologist, in March 1971 – before Mitchells had even started work on the site – included the following reference to the findings of the 1961 report:

> Sound rock means here rock . . . where physical properties had not been altered by weathering . . . Sound rock is commonly bluish in colour while weathered rock becomes yellowish. In the Kariba gneiss there are bands exclusively of biotite which, if sound, is black but soft.

The 1961 report itself had been prepared by a young and inexperienced geologist under the overall direction of Dr Dubertret, who was held by Gibbs to be the supreme expert on Kariba geology. The most

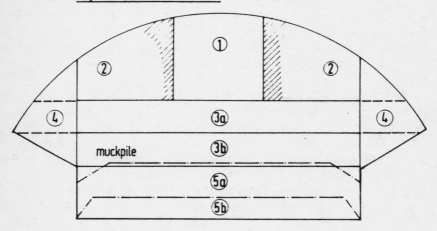

SEQUENCE AS TENDER PLAN

① Crown Cut full length.

② Side Cuts staggered to follow ①

③a ③b Benches down to haunch base

④ Corners linear drilled staggered behind ② and ③

⑤a fire to clear haunch concrete, trim muckpile for haunch and roof construction

⑤b Clear muckpile trim down to loading bay

Sketch showing alteration in method of excavation in order to provide two working faces instead of one, thereby accelerating progress.

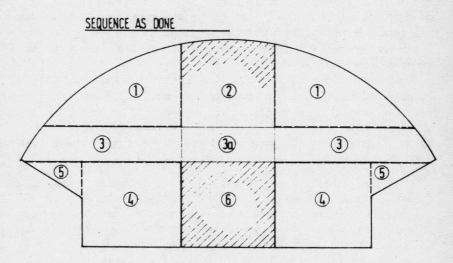

SEQUENCE AS DONE

① Side cuts to vault roof
② Remove vault dumpling / prop.
③ 3 metre cuts to full width springing 393·00
④ "9 metre" cuts to loading bay level 385·00
⑤ 30° slope cuts to form haunches
⑥ Remove vault access dumpling

generous explanation of the extraordinary sequence whereby Dr Dubertret's black soft material was eventually equated with granite is that it may have been due to a language difficulty. In any case, it is shocking that neither Dr Dubertret nor CAPCO nor Gibbs considered the matter worthy of further inquiry, because, as it emerged, a very considerable amount of published material on the geology at Kariba was available to them, quite apart from the information they must have acquired during their experience of the south bank scheme. All of this was totally inconsistent with the 1961 report. It is also shocking that Dr Dubertret's March 1971 report, with all its implications for the contract, was not passed on to us.

The matter does not end there. At the specific request of the general manager of KNBC who, under Zambian law, had direct and very onerous personal responsibilities for the safety of the work-force, the Zambian Department of Geological Survey commissioned a report from Dr G. D. Matheson, the government's senior petrologist. Dated June 1971, his conclusions differed from those of the 1961 report. He wrote:

> The entire north bank project is located in the complexly folded and highly metamorphosed rocks of the basin system . . . In underground workings biotite schist bands are common and vary in size from a few centimetres to several metres in width . . . These rocks are potentially the most dangerous in the project area . . . The pattern indicates that such rock types [biotite schist] can be expected in all the workings.

According to information we subsequently received, the report was suppressed at the insistence of CAPCO. The reason for this will become apparent, but it should be said at this stage that, had these facts emerged, then it would have been seen that the whole financial plan upon which the project was based had collapsed with possibly disastrous consequences for CAPCO.

Be that as it may, the suppression of this vital information, combined with the endorsement of the revised method of working, was an invitation to, if not a guarantee of, disaster. It was reckless and inexcusable, and all those who had a part in it are exposed to very serious indictment. Indeed, in the light of this information, any modification to the original plan should have been directed towards further precautions rather than courting additional risk or, as in this case, inevitable danger. Gibbs were of course acting entirely in accordance with instructions emanating from CAPCO, based as it was in Salisbury and staffed entirely by Rhodesians. The country was sanctions-bound and on a war footing and, as will be seen, the Kariba North Bank scheme was vital to its economy. It is apparent from the records that considerations of safety came a very poor second when the choice was between safety and progress.

The harvest

It was not long before the problems associated with the bad rock began to manifest themselves in a series of dangerous falls. During this period, Dr Back – Gibbs' London partner with responsibility for the project – and Dr Dubertret repeatedly insisted that the rock was still excellent and as described, while maintaining that what was happening was only the result of local difficulty requiring temporary support.

However, by November the gravity of the situation had become inescapable. The financial burden of carrying heavy overheads unsupported by full production was also becoming acute. On 6 December 1971, the company served the required formal notice under the contract invoking the procedures for dealing with unforeseen physical conditions and for recovering the costs necessarily incurred. Gibbs' site organization referred the matter to their head office, a procedure familiar to us. We were disappointed to receive, on 21 December, a formal rejection of our submission. However, most contractors will recognize this as a Pavlovian reaction, which was indeed how we treated it at first.

Our concern would have been very much greater had we known that Gibbs' site resident engineer had dispatched a telex to Dr Back in London on 3 December in which he advised that there had been a series of rock falls in the machine hall. He had gone on to say that during the early hours of 2 December a further rock fall of about 20 cubic metres had pulled out six rock bolts, each of them 3 metres long forming part of a 2-metre grid which had been installed in an effort to stabilize the rock. He had added that he couldn't understand why the bolts had not held the rock and that the present appearance of the roof made it obvious that more falls were going to occur. In his opinion, the only safe solution was to install the vault concrete before any further excavation of the vault was undertaken. This, he had said, would clearly mean some major rethinking and replanning of the whole works in the machine hall, and that Dr Back should visit the site as soon as possible so he could assess the situation at first hand and advise.

These 3-metre rock bolts were designed to act like *rawl bolts* in the roof and the people on the site were naturally at a loss to understand

115

how they could be pulled out in the massive falls of rock. Dr Back, however, ought to have understood because the bolts were, of course, passing through the fractured rock on the surface and into one of the layers of soft black material about which he had been fully informed, both in Dr Dubertret's March report and in the subsequent report from the Department of Geological Survey. But his reaction was to send his resident engineer an astonishing reply in which, after asking for further information regarding the availability of rock bolts, he wrote, 'For your information, consider present rock falls may be due to longitudinal sagging of the vault and may therefore stabilise fairly quickly.'

There were probably 100 men working under that rock who, although accustomed to danger, were mortal like the rest of us – their lives dependent upon the competence, judgement and integrity of those who were able, or should have been able, to assess and limit risks to an acceptable level. And yet the response of these same experts to the massive falls of rock was simply to say that they would probably stop. Had any of the men working in the machine hall known of the message and of the reply, they might well have felt entitled to ask, 'When?'

Thus, another opportunity to put the project on a sound footing was lost. The beginning of 1972 saw the people on site grappling with problems whose true nature and magnitude were hidden from them, while it was being insisted, against all the evidence now available, that they were still working in a homogeneous mass of sound gneiss. It was to be a traumatic year, during which the consequences of these deceits began to take terrible effect.

The experts are called in

The early weeks of 1972 showed none of the hoped-for improvement we had been led to expect by the consulting engineers and Dr Dubertret. The rock falls continued, resulting in a great deal of damage to plant and equipment, but, miraculously, in no loss of life. Progress was necessarily slow as attempts were made to secure the rock under which the men had to work, but with the continuing failure of Gibbs' engineer to endorse the changes in methods and programme necessary to limit the dangers, the Zambian Department of Mines moved in and insisted that work be suspended. At the same time, the Zambian Department of Geological Survey instigated a further investigation and report, this time under the direction of three geologists: Drs Matheson, Kepje and Vrana.

This report (18 May 1972) not only confirmed the presence of a set of strongly developed, steeply dipping joints which had caused rock falls, but also recorded the presence of numerous biotite schist bands and drew attention to the great danger of further rock falls where these were located in or above the roof. The report also revealed that detailed underground mappings had been made by the Geological Survey Department in August 1971 and March and April 1972, and brought into the open the earlier report made by Dr Matheson in June 1971. No amount of geological semantics could any longer disguise the weak and hazardous state of the rock, and the senior mines inspector summed it up when he said, 'I don't mind what you call it – it's soft and it's crumbly and it's dangerous.' But despite this new report, Dr Back seemed unwilling or unable to accept the seriousness of the situation and even pressed for continued blasting.

Mitchells' position was becoming very grave. Income from measured work had virtually stopped, massive overheads continued, losses amounting to over £1 million had been incurred and were accumulating at a rate of some £200,000 per month. It was in these circumstances that I became personally involved. I had the first of a series of financial meetings with Gibbs' senior partner, Angus Paton, in April, which led to an understanding that he would recommend to CAPCO an immediate payment of K1 million* – a sum which, we agreed, would afford temporary relief, but nothing more. He also agreed to put forward a proposal that the contract be revised at this stage to take into account the conditions that had been encountered.

As I have already pointed out, the terms of the contract required the engineer to certify for reimbursement any additional costs incurred by the contractor in overcoming adverse physical conditions which he could not reasonably have foreseen. He is supposed to perform this function with strict independence in a quasi-judicial capacity. However, as a matter of courtesy, and in order to avoid embarrassment, it is not unusual for him to seek to carry the client with him. What is unacceptable, and would certainly have been unacceptable to us had we known of it at the time, was that the engineer's terms of engagement provided that he had no right of certification of any additional costs in excess of K2,000 (approximately £1,200) without the client's prior approval. This condition was completely incompatible with one of his most important duties under the contract, and in

---

*Zambian currency. At that time £1 = 1.71429 kwacha; US$1 = 0.71429 kwacha (£1 = $2.4).

fact made him the creature of his client. In the circumstances at Kariba this effectively meant that we could only receive payment as the result of a consensus decision shared by Gibbs, CAPCO and KNBC and, as was to emerge very much later, the conflicts between them made consensus unlikely, if not impossible.

The anticipated early relief did not materialize and after a number of requests, I received notification on 31 May that CAPCO considered there were no grounds for certifying additional payment or making revisions to the contract.

Another month had been wasted

This continuing refusal to acknowledge the lethal working conditions was now assuming a sinister, rather than merely perverse, aspect. We could either withdraw, but that was unthinkable and anyway would have meant dispersing a superb team that could never have been reassembled, or we could go on trying to use persuasion and logic. In any case, it was clearly vital that we should arm ourselves with our own independent geological report. To that end we decided to approach Professor Anderson of Cardiff University, who had exceptional experience of underground work, and Professor Shackleton of Leeds, who was recognized as probably the leading expert in African geology.

We were fortunate: they both agreed. They acted separately and in due course we received reports from each of them, which were both clear and conclusive in their condemnation of the 1961 report. I met Professor Anderson on the site and he personally assured me that the matters at issue were not questions of opinion, but of fact, and that no geologist who valued his reputation would assert otherwise. Professor Shackleton was equally forthright: he stated that the 1961 report was 'tendentious by repetition, misleading by omission, and in places incorrect'; that 'the errors and omissions are not random, but consistently implied rock conditions better than those actually found', adding, quite simply, 'that the information given in the borehole logs was inaccurate'.

Trapped

From the end of March major excavation in the machine hall could only proceed on a piecemeal basis as the situation became steadily more desperate. We were trapped under a huge area of unstable and unsupported roof where any small vibration was likely to cause, and

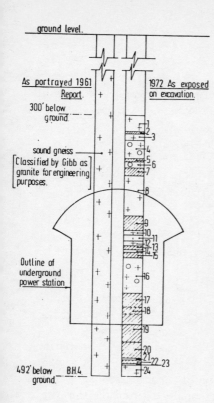

1 Massive grey quartz-biotite-felspar gneiss.
2 Coarse biotite-felspar schist.
3 Light felspar-rich biotite gneiss,a few vertical joints.
4 Massive pinkish biotite gneiss with abundant pink felspar porphyroblasts.
5 Coarse biotite-felspar schist
6 Massive pinkish biotite gneiss with abundant pink felspar porphyroblasts.
7 Coarse biotite-felspar schist with some migmatitic injections and a few inclined joints.
8 Massive light-grey biotite-felspar gneiss, a few steep F.e. joints.
9 Coarse biotite-felspar schist with a few migmatitic injections.
10 Light grey massive biotite-felspar gneiss.
11 Light grey biotite-felspar gneiss with steep joints.
12 Light grey massive biotite-felspar gneiss.
13 Biotite-felspar schist
14 Grey gneiss with minor folds and some pyrites.
15 Biotite-felspar schist.
16 Massive light pinkish gneiss with abundant pinkish felspar.(Augen)
17 Fairly massive migmatised biotite-felspar schist.
18 Biotite-felspar schist
19 Coarse migmatised biotite-felspar schist.
20 Biotite-felspar schist with a few migmatitic injections.
21 Massive light grey biotite-felspar gneiss
22 Coarse migmatised biotite-felspar schist
23 Massive grey biotite-felspar gneiss.
24 Broken grey gneiss with thin biotite schist band.

"Borehole N⁰4"- through centre of machine hall

Borehole No. 4 (Through centre of machine hall)

Core logs are derived from a physical examination of the rock actually recovered from the borings when the site investigation is made. In the present case, they were stored in Rhodesia. The column on the left – sound gneiss (granite) – was the information given in the contract documents and warranted to be accurate. That on the right shows the results of re-examination (by Professor J.G.C. Anderson of Cardiff University) of the same cores – with their dangerous bands of biotite schist – after the problems in the machine hall had been encountered. Although Borehole 4 is featured because it passes through the centre of the power station, it is nevertheless typical of the misinformation given in respect of all the other boreholes in the area.

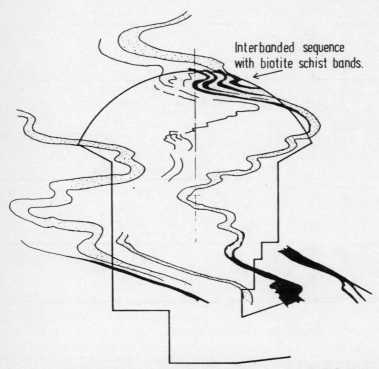

Interbanded sequence with biotite schist bands.

Rock profile within the machine hall as drawn by the Zambian Geological Survey. This shows how the black bands of biotite schist fold round other rocks leaving dangerous noses.

The sketch illustrates two of the problems encountered in the machine hall: a) a typical; 'foldnose' can be seen just above the springing of the arch on the right-hand side. There is no continuity or adhesion between the different types of rock; b) the rock at the crown was heavily fissured and it was necessary to bolt it in order to secure it until concentrating took place. Unfortunately, the bolts were, in many cases, located in the soft rock (shown dotted) with the result that they simply pulled out.

120

did cause, further falls of rock. Many experienced men considered the conditions so dangerous that they refused to go underground, and those who were working below, and particularly those in charge, were showing considerable strain. All blasting had to be stopped while concreting to the roof was edged forward in extremely dangerous conditions in an attempt to introduce stability. On 3 May there was a series of rock falls into the newly erected shutter while concreting to the roof was proceeding. Some 20–30 tons of rock was removed from the shutter, again in desperately dangerous conditions, while the rest had to be concreted in and can be seen in the roof to this day. Huge blocks of rock had become detached and were hanging by bolts which were themselves pulling out, since they were only anchored in the soft layer of rock above the roof. A few days later a large slab of rock fell within inches of John Hudspeth, Mitchells' section engineer in charge of the power station. Water was lying around and he was drenched by the splash just as he was leaving to go above ground for a progress meeting. The meeting had scarcely begun when he received an urgent message to return below. A series of falls was taking place and all the men had been cleared from the station. He went below where he was joined by Tommy McPherson, one of our key foremen. They sheltered on one side while rock continued to fall.

Gibbs' attitude to all this was quite extraordinary: they pressed for more blasting and accused us of sacrificing speed to safety. According to their resident engineer, the Zambian Chief Inspector of Mines was 'just going through the regulations and looking for items which he considers he can bring up to further frustrate the works'.

Although they were notified regularly of rock falls, Gibbs refused to acknowledge their seriousness or discuss their cause. Their attitude was that unless there was something with which they violently disagreed they did not bother to acknowledge notification of rock falls. Sometimes they did disagree. Concerning one rock fall, for example, they wrote that they had witnessed it and their estimate of the quantity of fallen rock was of the order of 1 ton rather than the notified 4 tons. This was hardly a constructive approach, and, irrespective of which estimate was nearer the truth, would have been small comfort to anyone standing beneath. In addition, it became clear that the word 'schist' was proscribed in the Gibbs organization; instead, all sorts of euphemisms – 'biotite-rich', 'black biotite', 'dark rock' – became commonplace. At that time we did not know that there had been a major arbitration following completion of the south bank contract which hinged upon the presence of biotite schist; it had gone against

CAPCO, and by inference against Gibbs. But it had already become clear that the defence of the 1961 report was more important to Gibbs than anything else on the site.

However, by 24 May even Gibbs had become concerned and, unknown to us, they had issued drawings and instructions for the installation of anchors to stabilize the rock. Unfortunately, their resident engineer had by now got the bit between his teeth. Instead of issuing the appropriate instructions, he telexed his head office saying that, whereas Mitchells had blamed their difficulties on bad rock, he had always countered with criticisms of their blasting techniques. He went on to say that instructing the addition of more anchor bolts would undermine Gibbs' arguments. He was particularly worried about issuing instructions to install these anchors so soon after the Zambian Government report because it would greatly strengthen the Mitchell case. He added that so far he had implied to Mitchells that if they chose to put in extra anchors it would be their responsibility. He apologized for querying instructions from his head office, but said he preferred to have further information before advising Mitchells.

The astonishing reply to this telex, which he received the same day, thanked him for his comments and acknowledged that notification of the change would be 'contractually awkward' and followed with instructions that 'the revised drawings of the anchor bars should therefore be withheld for the time being'.

The following day (25 May) Tommy McPherson was supervising men as they erected shuttering for the concreting of the next section of the machine hall roof, but as one of his men drilled a hole for a fixing bolt, the vibration caused a single block of rock weighing approximately 8–10 tons to fall from the wall. Two men were injured, but McPherson took the full impact. No Africans would go near and his colleagues and the senior site personnel had to do what was necessary.

Tommy, who had been with the company since he was eighteen (he was thirty-eight when he was killed) was one of those men who inspired that special brand of affection which the industry reserved for the first-class tradesmen who are the backbone of its achievements. He left behind a wife and three children, who had accompanied him to Kariba and I saw them at London airport a few days later when they returned to face a future without him.

I had been pressing Angus Paton to mobilize our combined skill in order to achieve the maximum progress compatible with safety, and had met with no response at all. In fact, his reaction following Tommy McPherson's death was to say, 'We expect men to be killed on hydroelectric work.' Nothing in my contracting experience has ever upset me more. Mitchells probably had more tunnelling experience than any other contractor in the world, but we have never 'expected' men to be killed. In all our underground work, including over 100 miles of hard-rock tunnelling and the construction of several underground power stations and associated chambers, we had never before lost a man in a rock fall.

An independent inquiry

My April meeting with Paton to discuss financial matters had been preceded by an abortive visit in March when I had been shocked to find that, far from accepting that the rock conditions were bad, he was blaming Mitchells for the lack of progress. It was obviously pointless to discuss, in London, conditions in Kariba, and so it was agreed that Dr Paul Back and Mitchells' chief engineer, David Harries, would visit the site and, if possible, draw up a joint report on the geology. During this visit they encountered the Zambian Government geologists and Dr Kepje conducted them through the underground workings. David Harries then prepared a written report which he agreed with the resident engineer, and although Dr Back declined to sign it, on the rather curious grounds that his partners never signed such documents, there was no reason to suppose that it would be the subject of dispute.

It was only after Dr Back returned to London and repudiated these findings that I became really worried. A disturbing situation was now beginning to look positively sinister. Site morale, which is all-important on a project of this nature, had been badly damaged by months of unrewarding effort. A large number of men was refusing to go underground, something unique in our experience, and although the supervisory staff continued to put in a tremendous effort they were also showing signs of strain. The two men who had returned to the company full of enthusiasm for training Africans had decided to leave.

Apart from under-certification, there was another cause for concern. On World Bank contracts it is customary for the bank to pay for all the plant and equipment purchased abroad, and for the contractor to reimburse the cost by deduction from the certificates once production is in full swing and a positive cash flow is being generated.

At the suggestion of the consultants a moratorium on these payments had been initiated until such time as it was possible to generate earnings on the site. Similarly, Gibbs were certifying generously in respect of the provision of the overall management and operation of the site. These payments constituted a forward liability for Mitchells because although they temporarily eased cash flow the company would still have to provide the plant, the management and the other services at a later stage and at that time there would be no payment. There was an even greater danger attached to these items: as they were merely a substitute for paying us money to which we were properly entitled and could at any time be suspended or withdrawn, they constituted a noose around our necks: a noose which was to be drawn tight when it suited their purpose.

In view of the gravity of the situation at Kariba and the massive monthly demands being made on the group's liquidity, it was obvious that I had to make myself very familiar with the whole problem. I therefore went to the site on 15 June 1972, in order to inspect the works and prepare for a meeting in Salisbury with CAPCO.

Arriving on the morning of 16 June, I toured the works, interviewed all the senior staff and during the weekend prepared a detailed report. Armed with this and samples of the rock taken from the excavation, I went on to Salisbury and for the first time met James Ward, chairman of CAPCO, and E. M. Shepherd, his general manager. Having described the problems we were encountering, the steps we were taking to overcome them, and the need for a cooperative joint effort, I showed Ward the various samples of rock which I had brought with me from the excavations. I took one piece of the 'granite' in my fist and squeezed it, whereupon it burst into a shower of small grit which sprayed his desk. I had not expected quite such a dramatic demonstration and, not without embarrassment, the three of us brushed it up.

Or rather, *I* was embarrassed, for I was disconcerted to see that neither Ward nor Shepherd showed any sign of surprise. But then for the last fifteen months they had been in possession of Dr Dubertret's undisclosed report, in which he had stated that part of the sound gneiss consisted of black biotite which was 'sound but soft'. The one satisfactory outcome of this meeting was that Ward proposed that Angus Paton should come out for a joint meeting in Salisbury on the following Friday.

I returned to the site where I was very fortunate in making the acquaintance of Professor Anderson who was making his inspection. His personal account of the geology made a great impression upon me, and I was completely convinced by his assurances that we were dealing with matters of fact and not of opinion. Incidentally, he told me that things looked so bad he had been reluctant to stand for long in certain parts of the cavern.

I returned to Salisbury on 23 June for meetings with Ward, Shepherd and Paton, which were bewildering as well as unsatisfactory, largely because of Paton's attitude. Briefly, his opinion was that the problems were of Mitchells' own making. He also maintained that 'biotite schist' and 'sound gneiss' were the same thing from an engineering point of view. Coming from the senior partner of an experienced firm with an international reputation, this submission was astonishing, but nothing I could say would move Paton from it.

Following these meetings Paton and I went by chartered plane to Kariba, accompanied by Paul Back and David Harries. Our first call was at the compound on the Rhodesian side to examine the rock cores which were stored there in steel boxes, some of which had been opened in readiness for our visit. Paton walked along the boxes jabbing the rock with his penknife and without pausing in his stride pronounced all of it 'sound rock'. It was clear that further examination was not going to be fruitful, and so we proceeded to the site itself. After we made a joint inspection of the whole works, Paton accepted that conditions in a number of sections could not have been anticipated and agreed that new rates should be considered. But he refused to acknowledge that the same conditions obtained in the machine hall.

Even his partial acknowledgement would afford us temporary relief from our appalling financial drain, and since tentative proposals had been made for an inquiry into the machine hall we thought there was at least some possibility of the position being stabilized. We were not to know that an agreement to keep daywork records, on the basis of which new rates were to be agreed, would be reneged on as soon as we left the site. Although we did get some payment on account, the net effect of all this was to add yet another month to our cumulative embarrassment.

As a result of the loss of confidence we had suffered following the first abortive visit of Paul Back and David Harries to agree geological conditions on the site, we had consulted with Keith Goodfellow QC, and on my return to London I had a further conference with him at which I reported fully on my visit to Central Africa. Goodfellow expressed himself in exceptionally strong terms on the implication of Paton's insistence that sound gneiss and biotite schist were the same from an engineering point of view. He was aware of the arbitration that had followed the construction of the south bank station, which had turned precisely on this point, and he found it indefensible that Gibbs should be deploying the same arguments again.

125

The panel is appointed

At the meeting in Salisbury, Paton had suggested that an outside opinion should be obtained about the rock. I had by now learned to be cautious and, while anxious that this proposal should be adopted, I was also concerned that it should be truly independent. Equally I wanted it to have proper terms of reference and defined procedures. In short, I felt that we were perhaps being led into a trap and that if we had a three man panel, the evidence would be so overwhelming that no expert would dare refute it in front of his peers. Our proposals, after initial resistance, were finally adopted. Apparently, however, my suspicions had not been entirely unjustified: CAPCO wrote to KNBC suggesting that Mitchells' insistence on a three man panel of separately nominated experts had delayed progress and had largely defeated the consultants' intentions to obtain expert advice which could act as a guide and would be acceptable to those who 'genuinely wished to progress the works'. We were to learn later that Gibbs had on other occasions proposed 'independent' experts whose independence was at least questionable.

After much negotiation the constitution of the panel and the procedures to be adopted were agreed. Brigadier Charles Edney CBE, FICE, FIEE, a barrister, was nominated by CAPCO as chairman. Gibbs nominated Dr (now Professor) John Knill, one of their regular geological consultants. Although Dr Knill could hardly have been regarded as independent, we were quite happy to accept him, given Professor Anderson's unqualified assurance that there could be only one outcome of the geological argument and no geologist who valued his reputation could find otherwise. This also influenced our own nomination. If we had one geologist on the panel, why nominate another? We also had good reason to fear that if the panel was comprised primarily of geologists Gibbs might, after the presentation of its findings, accept them from a geological point of view but deny the engineering implications. We had already had a hint of this danger in the reaction to the earlier geologist's report, when 'sound gneiss and biotic schist' were declared to be 'the same from an engineering point of view'. As a result, we nominated Dr Charles Jaeger, probably the world's leading expert on rock mechanics.

The panel was asked to express its views on the conditions in the machine hall, the factual accuracy of the borehole records, and the question of whether conditions in the hall could reasonably have been foreseen by an experienced contractor.

After a meeting between Brigadier Edney and representatives of Gibbs and Mitchells, at which procedures were agreed, the panel began its deliberations. It received from Gibbs and Mitchells their various written submissions, its members visited the site, and in due course it reconvened in London to examine witnesses and consider its findings which were due to be published on 26 August.

Before recording the panel's findings, I would like to mention two significant matters which occurred during the period of their appointment.

First, we had long suspected that the published information attributed to Dr Dubertret was selective and that there could be other reports, or edited parts of reports, which had not been disclosed to us. In the teeth of considerable resistance from Dr Back we sought and obtained from the chairman a direction that these, if they existed, should be disclosed. In response Dr Back did produce further reports but, despite his assurance given to Brigadier Edney that all Dr Dubertret's reports had now been made available, he had still not produced the damning report of March 1971 in which Dr Dubertret had stated that the 'sound gneiss' was interbanded with layers of soft material.

The second matter concerns an incident on the site after the various members of the panel had completed their inspection and had returned to London. The date was Sunday 20 August, and the July valuation was still being discussed between Gibbs' and Mitchells' staff. I went down into the Kariba Gorge very early in the morning and returned in the afternoon to find George Cummings, one of our directors, looking tired and ill. Cummings was an indomitable character, who had proved his resilience in over twenty years of command on major projects. Though no stranger to responsibility, he had borne the major burden of keeping the site together during this very difficult period and the experience was clearly taking its toll. He told me that out of a total of K5 million of disputed items relating to rock and to other contingencies, Gibbs had certified only K25,000 (approximately £14,600).

He was shocked and I was outraged. Paton was on the site and I drove immediately to his office and demanded an explanation. I suggested that there was something going on that had nothing to do with civil engineering, hydroelectric work, or the normal administration of contracts. Site staff, reinforced by head office staff from both sides, had been labouring for a week to produce this result. The sheer absurdity of the situation was quite beyond belief.

127

Paton replied that Gibbs were unable to certify until publication of the panel's findings, since the whole matter was *sub judice*. I refused to accept this and pointed out that as the engineer he had a responsibility to issue a certificate to the contractor for work completed. Finally, I threatened to suspend operations. Paton was immediately most conciliatory. He promised that instructions regarding specific work in the machine hall would be issued immediately. Even more significantly, he revealed that he already knew the outcome of the panel's findings.

Neither CAPCO nor Gibbs had observed the arrangements laid down for the visits of the panel members to Kariba, which were designed with a view to their comfort and convenience while ensuring their impartiality. On his arrival at Lusaka, Brigadier Edney had been met with a private charter plane and conducted to CAPCO's guest house on the Rhodesian side of the border, where he had been entertained throughout his visit by senior representatives of the other side, including Paton. It speaks highly of his attitude that Brigadier Edney's main concern was that this arrangement was inconvenient, since the curfew and formalities at the border imposed irksome restrictions on his working day. However, these breaches of propriety had apparently yielded no dividend because Paton was able to inform me that the report was not going to be 'grey', as he had anticipated, but 'black-and-white'. He added that it was going to be 'black' on the engineer's side and 'white' on Mitchells'. Although this was not a surprise, it was a great relief, as was Paton's next comment. He had obviously had plenty of time to consider the matter, for he said it was clear to him that the only possible method of dealing with the contract was one based on costs with an addition for overheads and management. It was a matter we could consider and agree between us on our return to England and if we encountered difficulties we should no doubt enlist the good offices of somebody like Sir Harold Harding (see Introduction), for whom we both had a very high regard, to arrive at a fair solution.

Paton was still unwilling to reopen the July valuation, but I was sufficiently relieved to accept the position. At least the way ahead was now clear, subject only to the publication of the panel's findings. I returned to our own site office and gave orders that there should be no relaxation of our efforts in the machine hall, because Paton had promised me personally that appropriate instructions would be issued.

It was ironical that during my visit I had been remonstrating with our senior staff about the initiatives they were taking without any formal instructions or commitment to payment from Gibbs. On previous occasions when Paton had given me assurances they had been broken. By this time I should have learned my lesson. The instructions were never received. Another month had been lost.

The panel report

The panel's report was published to all the parties simultaneously on 26 August. Its findings were as follows:

> The panel, having visited the site, having put questions to representatives of the parties and others, and having considered all the allegations and evidence of the contractor and the employer, by his agents, respectively regarding the disagreement which has arisen DOES HEREBY MAKE and PUBLISH ITS UNANIMOUS FINDINGS as follows:
> As to the factual accuracy of the borehole records referred to in clause 12(3)(b)(i), the panel finds that they were NOT factually accurate
> As to whether the conditions encountered in the machine hall could or could not reasonably have been foreseen by an experienced contractor at the time of tender, the panel finds that the said conditions could NOT reasonably have been so foreseen

It concluded with a tribute to the enthusiasm and good sense displayed by the site staff in the face of their difficulties and expressed the hope that its recommendations would contribute to a successful and harmonious conclusion of this 'complex and demanding project'.

In view of the role played by Dr Dubertret it was unfortunate that it had proved impossible to secure his attendance before the panel as his evidence would obviously have been of the greatest interest. However, the panel did have an opportunity to examine K. S. Jones, the member of Gibbs' staff who carried out the original logging of the cores and who had prepared the 1961 report. In a paragraph which I subsequently learned was agreed verbatim with him before its insertion, the panel recorded, 'He [Jones] explained to the panel how he physically carried out his task and that the logging was the result of his direct observations as the cores become available. He agreed that, in the light of the express wording of clause 12(3)(b)(i) of the Conditions of Contract, taken in their ordinary and precise meaning, his logs are not factually correct.'

This was an admission that was to set the phones buzzing between Angus Paton in London, James Ward of CAPCO in Salisbury and their long-time close associate, Charles White, at the World Bank in Washington. But not between them and KNBC.

'Agreement' is reached

Following publication of the panel's report a series of meetings took place between Gibbs and ourselves to agree the revised contract arrangements based on a cost/target form along the lines proposed to me by Paton on the site at Kariba on 20 August. In the event it did not prove necessary to refer to Sir Harold Harding as a referee, and on 29 September a telex was sent by Gibbs to CAPCO confirming that details of the altered form had been agreed jointly with Mitchells, setting out the details, and asking for CAPCO's agreement or their comments on the recommendations in order that the matter could proceed without delay.

On 11 October Gibbs sent a further telex to CAPCO recommending that a press release be made in view of the widespread interest in the national and technical press, and they enclosed a proposed draft which had been agreed with us. This draft recognized the good progress that had been made in spite of the fact that Mitchells had been hampered by the failure to provide facilities. It then referred to the complex nature of the rock and to the steps that were being taken to agree upon additional works and revised methods. At last it seemed that the most traumatic and prolonged crisis in the company's history was resolved. For many months it had been a source of major disruption to the whole of our business, forcing itself as an overwhelming priority on all our most senior executives, including myself. I had in fact by this time shouldered the main burden of the Kariba negotiations in order to reduce the disruption to the rest of the company. It was therefore with considerable relief that I felt able to inform senior staff that I intended to withdraw from executive participation in Kariba. I emphasized that we should now lose no time in restoring the pattern of our business to normal. This done, I left for ten days' much-needed holiday in Greece, from where I flew on to make a final visit to Kariba.

My anticipation that normality had been restored was perhaps the triumph of hope over experience. For while the revised form of contract was being agreed between Gibbs and ourselves in London, there was a development which could only cause misgiving. When Paton had proposed an independent inquiry, I was deeply suspicious – which was why I had insisted on arrangements which would ensure true independence and clear terms of reference. Presumably anticipating what a truly independent report would say, Gibbs had, while the panel was making its inquiry, insinuated on to the site two 'experts', ostensibly to give them independent advice. They were employees of an American firm of contractors whose major achievement in underground work seemed to have been that one of them had once been involved in the driving of a 9-foot diameter tunnel. Soon after the official panel report was circulated we learned that another report, described as being from a consultant and not from a contractor, had been circulated in confidence to KNBC and the World Bank. CAPCO of course knew all about it, having been a party to its commissioning. The report was scurrilous and Gibbs were outraged that we had been allowed to learn of it. I wrote to the American contractor concerned and received a reply from their chairman saying that they had gone to the site in response to a request from Gibbs 'who are old friends of ours'. And so my conviction that Paton had not intended a truly independent report was vindicated, and any hopes that we might in future encounter some good faith from the other side were dashed. In due course CAPCO vetoed the press release recommended by Gibbs and refused to issue it. Having followed the long trail of deceit, broken promises and unfulfilled assurances, perhaps I half-expected it. After all, it was a long time since logic had played any part in the client's administration of the contract, and there had still been no rational explanation of their behaviour. That explanation was to be long delayed. Had it not been for the operation of the Official Secrets Act the outcome of Kariba would have been very different.

Betrayal

I arrived in Lusaka early on Wednesday 25 October, intending to make a brief courtesy call on the chairman of KNBC and then go straight to the site. Instead I was met by the project manager, Taffy Farthing, and by the group's chief engineer, David Harries, who had flown out from the UK. During my absence a series of meetings had been hurriedly convened to start in Lusaka on the following day, which were to be attended by no less than twenty-three officials from the Zambian Government, headed by two permanent secretaries, and from the World Bank, CAPCO, KNBC and the consultants.

There was an inauspicious start: when I arrived at the Ridgeway Hotel I found that Gibbs, CAPCO and the World Bank officials were all transferring to the Intercontinental, something in itself which must have taken a bit of organizing in Lusaka, where accommodation was desperately short. It set the scene for what was to come. There were to be no courtesies, no opportunities for informal discussion, only an atmosphere of secrecy and confrontation. We were conscious of a continual round of official and unofficial meetings taking place at ministries and in hotels where Gibbs and CAPCO were supported by men from the World Bank who were obviously old friends and with whom they appeared to be hunting as a pack. Meanwhile, we were back in a role with which we had become familiar, that of the victim in a game of blind man's buff.

We had no idea what was going on – or why. We didn't even have the contract papers with us, and in what appeared to be a sustained show of discourtesy, my role and that of my colleagues was limited to being summoned to and dismissed from their meetings. These meetings seemed to be in almost continuous session; when we were called in, we were confronted with a bewildering set of changing situations. Otherwise we were waiting around in hotels and anterooms. One thread, however, became increasingly clear: the defence of the 1961 report had become a central issue and an attempt was being made by Gibbs and CAPCO to place all the responsibility for delays and additional costs at the door of either Mitchells or the Zambians. In our case, it was suggested that we had performed incompetently, and in the Zambians' that they had failed to provide facilities in accordance with the contract and had hampered progress through the interference of their Mines Department and Department of Geological Survey. These allegations were made in spite of the fact that by now no less than eleven experts, none of whom had any previous association with Mitchells, had rejected the 1961 report, stressing, sometimes in the most uncompromising terms, the treacherous nature of the rock. Of these eleven, two were respected professors of British universities, three were members of the independent panel, one was Gibbs' own geologist responsible for the report, and no less than six were public servants of the Zambian Government. Against this overwhelming array there appeared only to stand the elusive Dr Dubertret, who had failed to appear before the panel. His undisclosed reports were fully consistent with the findings of all the other experts involved and quite inconsistent with the description of the rock as it had been prepared at the time of tender.

As the meetings progressed it became increasingly clear that a rift had developed on the other side and that Gibbs and CAPCO were seeking to divide the Zambian politicians from their technical advisers and the KNBC. On top of this, I received further disquieting evidence of intrigue. Our representatives in London, who were finalizing details of the contract with their opposite numbers in Gibbs, sent me a telex dated 25 October advising me that the Gibbs representatives had become 'unimaginative and uncompromising', and that our people had gained the distinct impression that they had been told to mark time – 'They act like men conscious of something quite dramatic about to happen and about which they wish to remain silent.'

Eventually we were called into yet another meeting at four o'clock on the afternoon of 26 October. The meeting was chaired by Mr Siwo, the permanent secretary of the Ministry of Power, Transport and Works, who was assisted by Mr Chibwe, who was permanent secretary of the Ministry of Finance. Mr Siwo opened by saying that the proposals being advanced were not acceptable to the World Bank and that work would have to proceed on the basis of the existing contract, with variations as necessary. Whatever had been said to the Zambians, this simply was not true. The World Bank had already given their approval in principle to a revised contract based on cost – this was confirmed by correspondence that came to light later and also at my meetings in Washington. What *had* happened was that after receiving the panel's report and after the terms of the revised contract had been agreed, KNBC had gone on to the attack. Though accepting the recommendations, KNBC was questioning the competence and responsibility of both Gibbs and CAPCO. As a result, Gibbs, CAPCO and their friends from the World Bank had closed ranks and gone back to denying there was anything wrong with the rock. We felt that the Zambians were being led into a trap, but we could do nothing to persuade the World Bank people to listen to us or even give us the opportunity of a discussion. The only solution now acceptable to Gibbs and CAPCO was one that did not take rock conditions into account, but placed all responsibility for any delays and additional expense on to the Zambians, by attributing the failure to provide facilities to them and to the activities of their Mines Department. This was totally unrealistic: the vehicle simply wasn't big enough to carry the burden and, furthermore, the position resulting from the Zambian failures was by now largely relieved.

Mr Siwo informed us that there was no time for detailed discussion, but that in the next two days a broad framework had to be outlined on which the parties would agree. We asked for a short-term solution while the longer-term one was being worked out, whereupon Shepherd of CAPCO asked for an adjournment of the meeting. We were sent outside in the usual way and recalled 15 minutes later to be told that both solutions must be found at once. It was the beginning of a process whereby Mitchells were throttled, for we could only obtain short-term relief by accepting commitments which were quite unrealistic in terms of the ultimate cost. Siwo then informed us that the matter had been fully discussed with the consultants and that we now had to sit down with them and agree the revised proposals.

We were given an office for our use, and secretarial services, and after some hours of discussion with Paton and Back final proposals were agreed. The record of the meeting, duly signed by Paton and myself, noted that due to the many disrupting influences that we had suffered we should be reimbursed our costs together with an addition for overheads and management charges to date. It was also agreed that various matters which had added to our difficulties – problems in getting work permits, import licences and facilities and amenities generally, should be discussed with the client with a view to effecting improvement. Copies of this agreement, which had been signed in the early afternoon of 27 October were immediately tabled at the main meeting, but without us being present. This meeting continued behind closed doors until 3.30 p.m. on the afternoon of 28 October. We were then called in to be told that once again agreed proposals, endorsed with the engineer's signature, were being withdrawn. This time we were given a verbal ultimatum: we would be paid on a basis of cost up to a certain date and thereafter all the terms, rates and conditions of the contract would continue in full force and effect. Cost was loosely defined: after the figures had been audited, Gibbs were to be allowed to decide on an admissible sum. In view of the inadequacy of the existing rates, the fact that Gibbs were firmly committed to a completely unrealistic figure that took no account of the conditions, and also that Gibbs were to be granted the right to make arbitrary deductions from our actual costs in order to arrive at the 'correct' cost, it was obvious that this new proposal was quite unacceptable.

Confronted with this set-back we were only concerned to find a formula for survival. We offered to continue, or to withdraw, on the basis of net cost only. As an alternative, we offered to submit to any other independent panel or tribunal. All to no avail. We were simply pawns in the game.

We were told that if we did not agree immediately our non-acceptance would be regarded as a refusal. Even our attempts to have the proposals put into writing were refused on Gibbs' recommendation – they said it would be dangerous! After a further unsuccessful attempt to establish a dialogue, we finally had to accept that there was no purpose in our staying any longer in Lusaka. It was apparent that relationships between the other parties had been very strained, but there was much else we did not know.

Appeal to the World Bank

Although we did not know it at the time, Gibbs had formally sacrificed their independence. Nor did we know that our only chance of salvation lay in a consensus between Gibbs, CAPCO and KNBC – which was most unlikely, given that their own interests were so conflicting. As it was, our anxieties were sharpened by the reappearance of the bad faith we had suffered throughout the year.

Mitchells still had the organization, capacity and enthusiasm to which CAPCO's chairman had referred nearly a year before, but our resources had been drained over these twelve months, and the question was now whether we were justified in persisting. In fact, we had already stayed too long. The problems had been so self-evident that it had been inconceivable, as they escalated, that they would not be acknowledged and dealt with. But after the Lusaka meetings the main issue was survival.

Although discussions between Gibbs and Mitchells were resumed in London, there was no evidence that they were being conducted with any more sincerity, and so we had urgently to find new means of achieving a solution.

It was now obvious that the World Bank should be involved at the highest level. In August, for the first time, a visiting World Bank engineer had taken the trouble to find out the true position. During a visit to the site, Eric Arnold had been both surprised and dismayed by what he learned. Clearly, the World Bank had not previously been properly informed, but following his inquiries Mitchells had his support. This was important as revisions to the contract would obviously have to have World Bank approval. Arnold had not been present at the October meetings in Lusaka and the representation of the World Bank had been anything but impressive. In the circumstances I approached the Foreign Office and the Department of Trade and Industry in London and through them arranged to go to Washington for meetings in early December.

These meetings, presided over by Bernard Bell, a vice-president of the World Bank, were reassuring because the Bank made it clear that they were encouraging the Zambians to enter into revised contract arrangements. I was told that the Bank had given its approval to any form of contract – including one based on cost – acceptable to the other parties. At that time the British Government's representative on the World Bank was Derek (now Sir Derek) Mitchell, and he told me during my visit that he had discussed the whole Kariba problem with

Robert McNamara, the Bank's president at that time, who was very well informed but, 'like all of them', found himself in a very difficult position *vis-à-vis* 'the complex legal situation'. McNamara was, however, putting his full authority behind Bell and giving him every encouragement to bring pressure to bear on the Zambians to find a solution.

There was, of course, one major difficulty. Because Gibbs and CAPCO were still refusing to admit that the rock was bad, the responsibility for additional costs would be placed in its entirety at the Zambians' door. Apart from commercial reasons, there were many political reasons for their baulking at such injustice. Nor was it surprising that they mistrusted the advice they were receiving.

When I left Washington it was with an assurance from Bell that he was impressing on the Zambians the tremendous costs that would be entailed if no agreement was reached, adding that I should get in touch with him at any time and that he would appreciate being kept informed.

Meanwhile, ever since the October meetings, Gibbs had kept us under intense pressure to produce full details of our costs. We had been very reluctant to do this in the absence of an agreement defining their use, and also because we had learnt, to our surprise, that on another major hydroelectric contract carried out by an international consortium under Gibbs' direction similar conditions had arisen. This consortium had been paid money on account, too, and, like us, had then been subjected to a financial squeeze until they produced their costs. Once the costs were audited, massive sums had been deducted on the strength of alleged incompetence and 'correct' costs had been declared, which involved the consortium in losses which we were informed amounted to seven million rand.

We did, however, eventually produce all our costs, which were fully examined on site and in London and subjected to a formal audit. Gibbs notified CAPCO that they were reasonable 'on first examination', but our worst fears were realized in the last round of abortive negotiations when we found that our costs had been cut by massive and completely unjustified amounts.

Brigadier Edney and Sir Harold Harding re-enter the scene

In the meantime, there were developments elsewhere. It emerged that following the publication of the panel's report two of Gibbs' partners had sought a meeting with Dr Jaeger in Switzerland on the pretext of obtaining his advice in dealing with certain rock conditions. Thereafter they had secretly circulated what purported to be an account of that meeting which was obviously intended to undermine the panel's report. When Dr Jaeger learnt of this account he was extremely annoyed and communicated with Brigadier Edney, who visited him in Switzerland to discuss the matter. Brigadier Edney was so disturbed that, in spite of considering himself *functus officio*, he felt compelled to come back on the scene. The first thing he did was to contact Sir Harold Harding, who had originally nominated him, and inform him of what he regarded as improper behaviour by Gibbs. Then he wrote to Paton inviting him to meet him in Sir Harold's presence. In his letter, he explained that during the panel's investigation he had discovered extremely disquieting information, and he thought it was in the best interests of all concerned, including Gibbs, that he and Paton should discuss the matter.

Harding, too, wrote to Paton, reinforcing Edney's request for a meeting. A lifelong friend of Paton's, he too was very concerned, and he concluded his letter with Cromwell's words to the Kirk: 'I beseech you, in the bowels of Christ, think it possible you may be mistaken.'

But he did not know what Paton knew.

Edney, who was in his seventies, had been so distressed that his doctor had ordered him to rest, and so the meeting took place at his home in Surrey. After some discussion, during which Paton looked very uncomfortable, Edney handed him a prepared statement:

Statement by Brigadier Edney to Mr T. A. L. Paton, senior partner to Sir Alexander Gibb & Partners
Following the correspondence regarding the panel and its findings which has been carried on between the various parties since the publication of the panel's report, and following my visit to Dr Jaeger in Lausanne, I felt it my duty to visit Mitchell Construction Company and obtain copies of correspondence to which Dr Jaeger had drawn my attention. Also, at my request, I attended a conference with Mitchells' legal advisers to inform them of my annoyance as chairman of the panel, with the way Dr Jaeger had been treated and of my intention, unless it would embarrass Mitchells, of writing to you, as I subsequently did, on 8th November. I also told them in general terms of the evidence obtained by the panel as to the preparation of tender information by your firm.

I have endeavoured throughout to preserve my professional independence in these matters.

From my own appreciation of the situation, as at the present time,

137

it appears that Mitchells is being grievously and unfairly wounded and under such circumstances it is to be expected that, if they are to fall, they will avail themselves of every recourse legally open to them to ensure that those whom they consider responsible for their plight shall fall with them.

I find it most distressing to contemplate the evil effects which these events are having, and are likely to have to a far greater degree, on the reputation and efforts of the British construction industry overseas.

In the meantime, the task concerning all concerned still remains that of bringing to a satisfactory conclusion, within a reasonable time, at a reasonable cost, having regard to the changed conditions, the construction of the Kariba North Bank power station.

Neither I, nor the other members of the panel, have any intention of being drawn into further technical argument. All the evidence which was placed before us, and such further evidence as we were able to obtain by visual inspection and by oral examination, was carefully considered in the drafting of our report. If evidence was withheld from us, that surely was the fault of the party concerned. The moment we published our report we became *functus officio*. What has occurred since publication of the report appears to me to be nothing less than a studied attempt to belittle the work of the panel and to cloud and besmirch its findings. If the contractor is to be able to continue, it is clear certain things will have to be done to make it possible. This can only be effected by careful, patient, speedy and just negotiation between the parties, in which given words are bonds, adhered to in the letter and the spirit.

Let there be no doubt whatever, as I know from my own very personal experience, that, if the contractor is driven from the site, the extra expense to the employer is likely to be very heavy indeed and the time to completion very much delayed. In my opinion, the acts and the omissions of the employer and/or his agents have cost the contractor much extra expense for which he is entitled to reim-bursement, which, if not justly dealt with now, will undoubtedly be recovered by him eventually through the arbitrator's award or through the courts, again at greatly increased cost to the employer.

On the evidence obtained by the panel, it is clear to me that the tender documents and other tender information issued by your firm contained serious misrepresentations as to conditions on the north bank. These misrepresentations were caused at the best by gross carelessness by members of your firm and, indeed, in some instances it would seem that statements which were known to be wrong were made. In the report of the panel these matters were not directly mentioned as they were not within the panel's terms of reference. It is my opinion that your firm has lain itself open to an action for damages by Mitchells for negligent or fraudulent mis-statement. Mitchells could sue you in England and I think that if they are forced off the job, they may well do so. The effect of such a step, whatever the final result, on the reputation of your firm and of British consultants generally would be most damaging.

I must make it clear that I do not know what Mitchells intend to do, and they probably do not at present have all the information which the panel obtained. I do, however, think that you should seriously consider what may be the consequences for your firm if a solution is not found which will enable the contractor to be fairly reimbursed, and to proceed with the work.

Finally, my sincere hope is that a satisfactory solution to the present problems may speedily be found, but it will not be found without genuine goodwill on all sides which depends on individuals.

The meeting, which lasted for three hours, took place on 29 November.

At this time we came under massive pressure from Gibbs to make us accept the conditions laid down at the October meetings. The plant moratorium was suspended and K167,000 was deducted from the certificate issued in November. A similar deduction was due to be made from the December certificate, and so I contacted Sir Harold, who invited Paton to a meeting with us both at my office in Bedford Square. This took place on 8 December. Sir Harold emphasized to Paton that in his view there was more than sufficient information available to enable him to certify very substantial sums, and he added that in the matter of certification Paton had to act with complete professionalism as a consulting engineer and not be concerned to protect himself and his partners. Paton said he would consider the matter and make a recommendation to the client, but on being pressed he agreed he would issue a certificate: 'I am going to think of a form of words for doing it within 24 hours', he told us. This phrase struck me as very odd and I queried it with him, pointing out that all that we wanted was the engineer's certificate in accordance with the terms of the contract. But then I did not know that he was not empowered to issue a certificate without the consent of CAPCO, and he did not enlighten me.

On the Monday morning (11 December) I learned that nothing had been received from Gibbs. Paton had in fact left for Pakistan without issuing a certificate or leaving any instructions. After several unsatisfactory attempts by our senior men to obtain information from Gibbs, I telephoned their partner, Anthony Norris, who, I understood, was familiar with the Kariba contract. When I expressed my shock that Paton had gone away without fulfilling his undertaking, Norris replied that any of the other partners could issue a certificate if he so chose. I pressed him, but he would only say, 'We know you are entitled to additional payment; as to how long it takes us to decide how much, I would not like to forecast.' This was such an extraordinary statement that I wrote it down, read it back to him, and subsequently confirmed it in writing.

The crunch

In the middle of December, acting under pressure from the World Bank, the Zambians convened a series of meetings in London. They were led by Mr Siwo, in his capacity as permanent secretary of the Ministry of Power and as the newly appointed chairman of KNBC. At the first meeting (19 December) no representatives of Gibbs or CAPCO were present, but there were three representatives of the World Bank. Mitchells were accompanied by Ian Andrew and George Gilbertson of accountants Coopers and Lybrand – in a role quite different from the one they were to assume later – and by Keith Goodfellow QC. On this occasion, Mr Chandri of the World Bank confirmed that the Bank would support any proposals that could be justified; the principle of reimbursement on the basis of costs plus overheads as well as management charges had already been accepted by the Bank. After the second meeting, Ian Andrew of Coopers was able to report to our holding company's board that discussions had gone well, that he was impressed by the Zambians, and that he was confident there would be an early payment of between £1 million and £2 million, though he thought £1.8 million might be the limit in practice.

But, on that very day, 20 December, when relations with the Zambians seemed to be at their most fruitful, Gibbs sent an urgent message to Salisbury requesting the presence of Shepherd, general manager of CAPCO. Despite the fact that he was on a Rhodesian passport, which we understood meant he could not enter the UK, he was in London early the next morning. He returned to Salisbury on Friday 22 December, and it was not long before my worst fears were confirmed. The meetings restarted after Christmas on 27 December, but the tone had changed disastrously. We were told that we would be paid K750,000, far less than we had been led to expect a few days before, and we were also told that, since the alleged difficulties in the machine hall were behind us, all the rates and conditions of the original contract would come into effect once more. Finally, we were told there was now no reason why the final cost of the project should not be determined.

These terms were quite unacceptable, and the fact that the Zambians could propose them showed that once again they were being misinformed. The meeting was adjourned until two o'clock that afternoon, but not even the experience of the previous twelve months could prepare us for what was to come.

The two o'clock meeting was repeatedly postponed until four o'clock. What was taking up so much time? It turned out that Gibbs had been closeted with their lawyers processing a course of action that had apparently been agreed with Shepherd before Christmas. As soon as we were reassembled, Siwo handed us two documents, which we all read with mounting disbelief. The first was a draft supplementary agreement to be entered into between Mitchells and KNBC which provided that Mitchells would be paid K1 million over and above the K10.4 million which they had already received, in full and final settlement of all sums due to them to date. This hardly compared with our cost of K15,992,000, which was not comprehensive and contained no provision for the unforeseen financing which the company was having to provide. The draft agreement went on to stipulate that the remainder of the works would be constructed and completed in accordance with the rates contained in the original bill of quantities. A sub-clause was attached to the effect that in pricing the original bill Mitchells would be deemed to have had knowledge of all nine reports which the panel of inquiry had considered and even of the panel's report itself. In this way Mitchells' rates were understood to include provisions for conditions which had been specifically excluded in the original contract. Thus, they were to be deprived not only of the remedy to which they were entitled by the warranty, but of the fundamental protection provided by the standard conditions of contract themselves.

On Mitchells' initiative, many weeks had been spent with Gibbs' representatives agreeing a detailed programme and method statement taking into account the geological hazards so far as it was now possible to predict them, and analysing the additional plant and resources which would be required. This programme had been agreed at the most senior level by Gibbs. The draft supplementary agreement now provided that it should be incorporated in the contract with a programme of heavy penalties which took no account of further hazards and placed Mitchells in an impossible situation. To accommodate all the extra costs, including the essential extensions of time, a further lump sum of K1 million would be added to the contract, which included an estimated K750,000 in respect of additional plant and equipment necessary to make up lost time.

We were now confronted formally with a package which was directed solely towards securing completion for a fixed sum, irrespective of the merits of our case and incorporating no recognition of the changed geological conditions.

At a stroke Mitchells' conviction that Gibbs and CAPCO had never intended their costs to be reimbursed had been rudely confirmed.

In discussions with our bankers, the Midland, I had already been asked what would be the financial outcome if we were compelled to complete without any acknowledgement of the conditions, and I had advised them that my estimate of the potential loss would be between £5 and £10 million. Indeed, I had been over the ground so many times that I knew at a glance that these proposals fell squarely within that bracket.

This astonishing document showed that Gibbs' lawyer had done his job well. It made no concessions to reality, but in accordance with instructions he had no doubt received, it ensured that the works would be completed for approximately K25.5 million, assuming that Mitchells would be able to survive the massive losses that this would entail.

Grossly inequitable as it was, this draft supplementary agreement would, however, have left Mitchells with one avenue of redress, which the lawyer had recognized and closed – for another document had been tabled. This was an extraordinary 'deed of release' to be entered into not only between KNBC and Mitchells, but including CAPCO and Gibbs, and including their agents and servants. It was an astonishing and even brazen document, and it provided that in consideration of CAPCO and Gibbs agreeing to recommend the supplementary agreement to KNBC, Mitchells would release them

> from all actions proceedings accounts claims and demands whatsoever arising out of any matter or thing occurring before 1st January 1971 in connection with or in any way related to the works and whether arising under the contract or otherwise and will indemnify and keep indemnifying the employer the agent and the engineer against all such actions proceedings accounts claims and demands which may be brought against them or any of them by or through any

of its associated or group companies of the contractor or any sub-contractor servant or agent of the contractor or any of its associated or group companies.

Keith Goodfellow was the first to react to these extraordinary documents and he said it all. He could not relate the draft supplementary agreement to any of our discussions over the past nine days; in fact, it bore no relation to them. He also wanted to know what was the purpose of the deed of release and why it was considered necessary.

We spent the next two days trying to keep discussions going in an effort to find any formula which would offer us a prospect of survival, but to no avail. Either the Zambians had been persuaded that the final cost should be no more than K25.5 million or they intended to call Gibbs' bluff by not entering into a firm contract that exceeded that figure. The position was all too clear. Through a succession of assurances and promises Mitchells had been encouraged to stay on the site far too long. This had been in the best tradition of the company, and indeed of the industry, but now the noose was tightening. So far as the Zambians were concerned, the impression was being given that now that Mitchells had completed the vault the principal hazards belonged to the past. With these physical problems behind them, they would benefit to the tune of some K10 million immediately if Mitchells could be forced from the site, i.e. some K5–6 million due to Mitchells which they would not be able to collect once they had become insolvent, and a further K4.1 million which would be payable to the Zambians under the terms of the contract performance bond.

There could be no doubt in that final conference what was at stake. Ian Andrew of Coopers spelt it out with the utmost clarity. He informed the Zambians that Coopers would almost certainly advise that no further Mitchell money be put in Kariba, and that Mitchells could not go on 'pumping money into a job like this. It would be suicidal.' Gibbs sat silent. The Zambians, who had already indicated they were leaving that night, were confused and frustrated; abruptly they collected their papers and left.

Paton and his partners, faced with what they had just brought about, and Mitchells, who now faced disaster, watched them go in silence. Both were equally nonplussed.

Goodfellow then reminded Paton of his duty to certify and of the numerous assurances he had given.

'I was doing this when the Zambians arrived – I hoped thereafter for a package deal, Mr Goodfellow.'

'In that case within what period will you certify?'

'I will study the figures and let you know by Tuesday.'

On Tuesday he sent this message: 'We are unable to agree at the present time, based on information available to us, and which you have provided, that further certification of any substantial sums is justified.'

What else could be done? The situation was so absurd, so illogical, so immensely harmful not only to Mitchells, but to the Zambians. In terms of total cost it would be a disaster. What was it all about?

Implacable

I decided on another approach to the Foreign Office in London. They had always seemed to have some underlying sympathy and through them a meeting was arranged at the Department of Trade and Industry (DTI) on 2 January. P. M. Foster, who was head of the Central and South African department, came from the Foreign Office, B. E. Bellamy, undersecretary in charge of commercial relations, represented the DTI, and the Department of the Environment was also represented.* Paton had been asked to attend and he was at his most implacable; Mitchells, he said, were not entitled to a single kwacha. Foster was clearly sympathetic, but I got no similar vibrations from Bellamy. According to him there was no basis upon which they could intervene in what was essentially a dispute between two British firms.

There are occasions when non-intervention takes on a positive function. Had I known what Paton, Bellamy and Foster then knew, I would have realized that this was such an occasion. Behind their apparently neutral façade, Bellamy and Foster knew far more about the contract than they indicated to me, not least because Paton and Bellamy had kept each other informed throughout. The meeting petered out. No dialogue could be sustained, and no progress could be made in the face of Paton's intransigence. But as we left, Foster opened up one small chink: why did I not seek a meeting with Phiri, the Zambian High Commissioner in London? He was a very pleasant and reasonable man, and some good might come of it.

---

*The presence of the DOE man was never explained. The department had nothing to do with the project. On the other hand it was a major debtor to the company and its presence could have been either beneficial or sinister. Suffice it to say that huge sums of money continued to be denied to us that were subsequently paid to our successors after the receivership.

Immediately on my return to my office I tried to contact Phiri, but it was 8.30 p.m. before I eventually spoke to him. He had just arrived home and could see me at ten o'clock. He was both helpful and curious. There was obviously a general belief among the Zambians that they were the victims of a plot in which all the Europeans were involved. I sympathized, because I thought they were right to suspect their European colleagues. But not of course Mitchells, who were also victims. He found this difficult to understand. In such a situation, Zambians would certainly stick together. However, I easily persuaded him not only that we were not involved in anything other than a contractual relationship, but also that the consequences for Zambia if we were forced off the site would be disastrous.

By the time I left him in the early hours of the morning of 3 January we were on excellent terms. He was satisfied as to our good faith, and suggested a further meeting the following morning with him and his trade commissioner, Mr Mwambasi.

I quickly formed a very high regard for Mr Mwambasi: and when Phiri suggested making arrangements for me to go to Lusaka, I readily agreed and asked that Mwambasi might accompany me. We left London on the same flight on Sunday 7 January, arriving in Lusaka at breakfast time the next morning.

Fate was not on our side, for on 9 January came the closing of the Rhodesian/Zambian border and chaos reigned in Lusaka. With ministers and senior officials attending a seemingly endless series of meetings, it was not until 12 January that I was able to see the Minister of Transport, Power and Works, Mr Mulikita.

The meeting was a brief one and his message perfunctory. He had been assured that it was now possible for us to give a fixed and final price for completion of the works. This was the figure of K25.5 million which Gibbs had insisted was adequate. K2 million was available and could be paid to us immediately, but no payment would be made unless and until we entered into the revised agreement. He would not accept that the matter was being oversimplified or discuss a more flexible approach. As we had only been paid little more than K10 million, I paid particular attention to his assertion that funds were available and his choice of words raised new doubts in my mind. It is important to note that World Bank funds are only available for the purchase of plant and equipment from abroad, i.e. which requires foreign currency. All local costs, which include the major part of the civil engineering work, have to be met from local funds. Had I but known it, K2 million represented the *only* funds available at that time to complete the whole of the work. Against this, Mitchells were already owed K5.6 million. For six months CAPCO and KNBC, the British Government and the World Bank had been arguing among themselves as to how the work was to be paid for. But this fact had been safely hidden from Mitchells while Gibbs were fighting for their lives.

During my five days in Lusaka, I was in constant touch with the High Commission. I had been warned that my room was probably bugged and my telephone was tapped, but I had nothing to hide. The beds in my room were deep in paper as our project manager, Taffy Farthing, our chief surveyor, Terry Wheeler and myself explored in endless detail the practical and financial aspects of what had been done and what remained to be done. The results were always the same. Without some revisions to the contract, we faced a certain loss of at least £5–10 million. I had no alternative but to ring England and advise my colleagues that the situation was as grave as it could be, and that the plant, equipment and personnel lined up for the site must not go forward.

Before leaving I considered an approach to President Kaunda: we had always got on extremely well and he had never denied me a visit. I broached the matter with our acting High Commissioner, Christopher Diggines but he was opposed to it. He had always been very helpful and I accepted his advice. Had I known more of the nature and extent of the British Government's involvement and the restraints under which Diggines was working I would have acted differently.

My own feelings can be imagined, but it was also a sad Mwambasi who flew back on the same flight to London. We did not sit together, though we had long talks at Lusaka and at Frankfurt. He was convinced that what had happened had been very bad for Zambia, but explained that the Zambian dilemma was inescapable. Gibbs were absolutely insistent that the final cost should not exceed K25.5 million. He himself was convinced this figure was unrealistic, and he was certain that if the consultants admitted the job was going to cost K30–35 million it would be acceptable. But in the meantime, Zambia could not take the risk of overruling their consultants' advice.

To the World Bank again

Discussions had continued meanwhile with Gibbs in London and my fellow board members had been persuaded that it might still be possible to accept a modified agreement in order to survive. I briefed my deputy, J. A. Sneden, and he returned to Zambia, where I had left

The author in 1970 (photo: Tom Hustler).

Chapelcross Nuclear Power Station, near Annan, Dumfriesshire
(photo: British Nuclear Fuels plc).

"Of course you can play, but you can't bat or bowl!"

Comment on the Anchor project (*Construction News,* 21 May 1970).

Kenneth McAlpine, the author, Sandy Shand, Bobby McAlpine at a dinner of the
Midland Section of the Federation of Civil Engineering Contractors
(photo: *Birmingham Post*).

Fawley Power Station: dock, screen, forebay and intake area
(photo: Central Electricity Generating Board).

Windscale (now Sellafield): Mitchells were responsible for the construction of the nuclear chemical separation plant and for the completion of the gas-cooled reactor (photo: British Nuclear Fuels plc).

The author with President Kenneth Kaunda at the new terminal of Lusaka Airport built by Mitchells (photo: Zambia Information Services).

Kariba site staff at their regular Tuesday meeting – with over 200 years of experience with the company between them.

Vault of the machine hall at Kariba, after concreting and before main excavation.

SECTION VIII - THE FINDINGS OF THE PANEL

The Panel, having visited the site, having put questions to representatives of the Parties and others, and having considered all the allegations and evidence of the Contractor and the Employer, by his Agents, respectively regarding the disagreement which has arisen

DOES HEREBY MAKE and PUBLISH ITS UNANIMOUS FINDINGS as follows:-

(a)   as to the conditions encountered in the Machine Hall, the Panel found them to be as set out in Section IV hereof

(b)   as to the factual accuracy of the borehole records referred to in Clause 12(3)(b)(i), the Panel finds that they were NOT factually accurate

(c)   as to whether the conditions encountered in the Machine Hall could or could not reasonably have been foreseen by an experienced Contractor at the time of tender, the Panel finds that the said conditions could NOT reasonably have been so foreseen

The Panel has made certain recommendations which are recorded in Section VII hereof.

Member   Member

                              Chairman

26 August 1972

Findings of the Independent Panel of Inquiry: last page of the 35-page report.

MITCHELL RUINED BY DELAYED PAYMENTS

The Construction News team trace the factors which led to Mitchell Construction's shock announcement of the appointment of a Receiver. The report begins on this page and continues on pages 9, 10 and 11.

MITCHELL CONSTRUCTION

MITCHELL COLLAPSE SHAKES INDUSTRY

A company killed by cash starvation

This week's disclosures about the true state of Mitchell Construction's affairs will enable the industry to form a better assessment of the real reasons for the company's failure. It is now abundantly plain that the British Government's stranglehold on finance was a major contributory factor.

Difficulties with the Kariba power station contract are a matter of public record. But these difficulties have to be set against the battle Mitchell was having to extract money from its Government and public authority clients.

Mitchell Construction — debtors named

THERE WERE 12 contracts awarded to Mitchell from the Property Services Agency of the Department of the Environment and other public sector authorities which ceased trouble.

THE FIRST contract was awarded in 1969 for Martlesham Heath Post Office Research Establishment at a total value of £7,600,000. At the

Since the receiver was called in to Mitchell Construction in January, Construction News has followed the events closely. Fresh information, unearthed by the news team, reveals that the company was owed a massive £11 million from public monies at the time of collapse.

Details of the contracts are listed here together with the reasons they went sour.

the original road was virtually rebuilt when bad ground was found. Earthworks quantities were more than ten times those tendered. It is thought that the Northumberland CC was seeking extra grant from the DoE.

THERE ARE other projects which are not directly for Government Departments but public finance ultimately sanc-

Industry reels over shock of Mitchell's sudden collapse

THE SUDDENNESS of the Mitchell Construction collapse took the industry by surprise, and to many it has come as a real

submitted a marginally lower bid.
The decision to give McAlpine the work was strenuously defended at the time by the British

One of the prizes would be Kinnear Moodie, with its good contracts and high reputation in

experienced elsewhere in the group, has produced an unbearable strain on the group's resources.

The failure is a heavy blow, both personally and financially, to the chairman, David Morrell. A well-known figure in the civil engineering industry, he rose from the position of chief sur-

SHARE MOVEMENTS

Shock from Mitchell but Market steadier

A happier week for share prices generally was featured by shock news for Ordinary shareholders in Mitchell Construction who

 Tarmac **MITCHELL CONSTRUCTION**

Francis moves in to sort out Mitchell

A MAJOR part of Mitchell Construction has been taken over by Tarmac.

group staff engaged on construction, tunnelling and plant activities in Britain and Northern Ire

The Financial Times Saturday April 28 1973

The Financial Times Thursday April 26 1973

Tarmac takes over £14m. Mitchell contracts

BY NICHOLAS LESLIE

Mitchell liquidation likely to take years

BY NICHOLAS LESLIE

IT NOW LOOKS as if completion of the liquidation of Mitchell Construction Holdings and its subsidiaries will not be completed until 1976 at the earliest. Since the beginning of February, the company has been in the hands of a Receiver, Mr. Paul Sizwell, appointed by the company's debenture holders, Prudential Assurance and Midland Bank.

The possible length of the liquidation emerged at yesterday's meeting of creditors of Mitchell Construction, Kinnear Moodie Group, the co-ordinating subsidiary, where unanimous approval was given to the appointment of Mr. Michael Jordan as liquidator. The move to appoint Mr. Jordan, a partner in City accountants W. H. Cork Gully, was made to give us

vary widely according to how successfully each of the subsidiaries is liquidated

Kariba power station hustle

That Mitchell thunderbolt

IF THE Kariba power station contract was the cause of Mitchell's collapse, then it should have been dealt with by placing the construction company into liquidation.

This is the main finding of the report by Greene and Company, the City broking firm and construction industry specialists, being issued next week.

CONTRACTORS are showing great interest in taking over the jobs outstanding work in Zambia's north bank

Charcon take over part of Mitchell empire

UNCERTAINTY OVER the future of Kinnear Moodie (Concrete) following the collapse of Mitchell Construction Holdings has now been removed with Charcon agreeing in principle with the receiver to acquire the assets concerned.

The purchase price has yet to be settled and a further statement is expected in due course. Kinnear Moodie (Concrete), of Ashford, Middlesex, and Kirby-in-Ashfield, Nottinghamshire, employs more than 400 people.

Also included in the agreement are certain assets of Mitchell Camus of Newmains, Lanarkshire, where precast tunnel

Relocating viable parts of Mitchell

"EVERY EFFORT to relocate those parts of the group that are economically viable" will be made by Paul Shewell, the accountant appointed as receiver of Mitchell Construction.

This was the view given to Construction News by John Gillum, a director of Samuel Montague, the merchant bank advisers to the group.

Mr. Shewell will also be very

Tarmac to take over the MCKM assets, would not be available

CONTRACTS with outstanding work worth around £14m. have

cent. of the group's outstanding workload in the U.K. before the £25m. respectively, while the total of work taken on by Tarmac was originally valued at £35m.

Mr. Bill Francis, managing director of Tarmac Construction, said yesterday that continuation of the contracts should help maximise the likely return to Mitchell creditors, but he gave no indication of what such a figure might be. Unsecured creditors of Mitchell are estimated to be owed some £10m.

value of £7.6m., £12.2m. and

Retained

Another outcome of the transfer of work is that Tarmac has been able to retain around two-thirds of the staff and operatives previously employed by Mitchell Kinnear Moodie group.

The next major step in the Mitchell situation, which arose after the company ran into major problems on its Kariba North Dam site in Zambia, will be a meeting of unsecured creditors to-morrow.

It is expected that Mr. Michael Jordan, a partner in City accountants W. H. Cork Gully, will then be appointed as liquidator of Mitchell Kinnear Moodie.

Press reaction to Mitchells' crash.

Comment on the Kariba settlement (*New Civil Engineer*, 5 June 1980).

the door open, in a last-ditch attempt to find a settlement. While these discussions were proceeding in Lusaka, I also telephoned and wrote twice to Bernard Bell of the World Bank, arranging for the letters to be delivered by hand in Washington. My first letter concluded with these words: 'Since the panel report Mitchells have been subject to an intolerable financial squeeze until it has become a fight for survival. I cannot believe that this is the way in which the World Bank consider it proper to bring about the adjustments to such a contract.' The second, and longer, letter concluded, 'Sooner or later the facts will have to be acknowledged and the costs will have to be met and, in the last resort, the breaking of a contractor will not obscure the real issues in terms of time and cost.'

On 25 January Mitchells received further evidence of the massive squeeze designed to subjugate them when the consultant issued a nil certificate in respect of work done in December. He even maintained that Mitchells had already been overpaid. Notwithstanding the previously agreed plant moratorium K0.5 million had been deducted from certificates since October, and now we received notification from the Zambian authorities that exchange control facilities were being withdrawn. The K0.5 million overdraft facility which we had with Barclays Bank in Lusaka would have to be paid by 31 January. To put this into perspective, it should be noted that it had been agreed at the time of tender that we would have a facility of K1.5 million at Barclays, but it had been reduced to K0.5 million as a result of exchange control restrictions. This was a time when the Yugoslavs, who were working on the nearby Kafue project, had been extended a facility of K13½ million.

Sneden returned to England on 29 January, having made no progress, and at a board meeting on the evening of 30 January, which was attended by our financial advisers, the decision to ask for the appointment of a receiver was confirmed.

Even then our course was not run because on the morning of 31 January I received a telephone call from Hugh Peppiat. Peppiat was a partner of Freshfields, solicitors to the World Bank in London, and later became president of the Law Society. He informed me that he knew of the impending receivership and had had urgent instructions from the World Bank in Washington to intervene and stop it. This at any rate was one leak I would have condoned, and I rapidly put him in the picture. He asked me the name of the consulting engineers and, when I told him that it was Gibbs, he exclaimed

'What, again?'

'Yes, again!' I answered. I wasn't alone in knowing of their problems elsewhere.

He asked me to contact Samuel Montagu and clear his authority with them, whereupon he would take over. I immediately telephoned John Gillum at Samuel Montagu only to be told that it was 'too late'.

This was an incredible response considering the source of the request and the strength of the underwriting that would ensue, but I could do no more than leave it to Peppiat to pursue the situation as best he could. He made contact with John Gillum and in what has been described as an unencouraging encounter he was persuaded that the company's position was so bad that there was no point in going on with the matter.

In trying to find some explanation for John Gillum's conduct one has to take account of the fact that it was now over nine months since I had described to David Montagu the problems we had confronted at Kariba, which at that time he had fully understood. Meanwhile, all concerned had been fully informed. Not only was the company rich in assets in land, buildings and plant, whose book value was nowhere near their real value, but Gillum had been present at the board meeting (20 December) when Ian Andrew had reported that the Zambians accepted that Mitchells were entitled to substantial payment and that he expected an early certificate for £1.8 million. Gillum was also present at a meeting of our advisers on 19 January to which I refer in detail later, when Keith Goodfellow confirmed that in his view very substantial payments would have to be made to Mitchells for Kariba and, furthermore, the least he anticipated from an arbitration in progress concerning work done by the company at Peterborough Hospital was a payment of £1 million. In response to an appeal for help, John Gillum had himself been in touch with Lord Bridges at the Cabinet Office in an attempt to unlock the government coffers. One result of this was that on 26 January he telephoned John Cuckney (now Sir John Cuckney), at that time chief executive of the Property Services Administration at the Department of the Environment, who accepted that the PSA owed the company a lot of money. It was just a question of time. One wonders what would have persuaded John Gillum and David Montagu to rally to the company's support.

The appointment of a receiver was brought about by the company as a response to circumstances which made it appear the only responsible course. In the light of experience, I would now say that acquiescence to the appointment of a receiver by anyone concerned for their moral obligations to all their creditors, and not just their secured creditors, is a reckless act as long as the faintest hope of survival remains.

There is now, of course, a new Insolvency Act, but this is directed primarily at controlling the 'cowboys'. Given the behaviour of the 'professionals' at Kariba, and apart from the possibility that a liquidator might have intervened to exert control over the receiver from the start, I cannot see that we would now be in any better position to protect ourselves.

In Mitchells' case, there can seldom have been such a deliberate and calculated act of destruction. In a few short brutal weeks the heart of the company was torn out.

In the June birthday honours list, Angus Paton received his knighthood.

Catch-22

How to explain the inexplicable? A contractor forced into receivership and ultimately into liquidation, a first-class organization broken up and a client forced to take measures that were bound to delay completion and lead to an eventual cost which was a multiple of what Mitchells were asking and many times what Gibbs were prepared to recommend. Why?

Throughout 1972 there was deep and growing tension between KNBC on the one hand and Gibbs and CAPCO on the other. Any attempt by KNBC to protect what they believed to be Zambian interests evoked deep resentment and hostility from Gibbs and CAPCO.

What was at the root of the Zambians' mistrust and of Gibbs' and CAPCO's reactions? Did the geological report, with all its optimism, owe more to politics than to geology? Was this in some way the underlying significance of the warranty? Unique in our experience, this had at first been heralded by us as an enlightened advance by a responsible and forward-looking client and engineer. It now looked as if it might have been introduced to frustrate opposition. Certainly by this time this seemed to me to be the most probable explanation, but if we had known more of Kariba's history the mystery would not have been so great. There was indeed plenty of reason for mistrust and, had we but known it, Zambia was going through an experience which it had previously suffered when, as Northern Rhodesia, it had been part of the Federation ruled from Salisbury.

At the beginning of the 1950s, with the growth of demand for power in the copperbelt, Northern Rhodesia sought to promote a hydroelec-

tric scheme on the Kafue River in Zambia. In this they had the
support of the mining companies and, in particular, the Anglo-
American Corporation. Salisbury preferred Kariba which, being on
the River Zambezi, would be on the border and within their control.
In his book *Damit* Dr Olivier (Gibbs' partner in charge of Kariba
Stage I) describes the 'Machiavellian' manoeuvres with which Sir
Godfrey Huggins (later Lord Malvern), the Prime Minister, outwitted
the North and secured the preference of Kariba over Kafue. Many
disagreed with the decision at the time and, as World Bank money was
to be involved, a panel of inquiry was set up. The panel admitted that
Kafue might initially be cheaper, but considered that in the long run
Kariba would be the more economic. As the battle raged, Sir Godfrey
Huggins, 'spinning his web in Salisbury', announced that Kafue could
not be financed because international sources would only lend to the
Federation and not to the individual states. At the same time he let it
be known that 'totally independent' French engineers had been asked
to make a final appraisal between the two schemes. He had asked the
engineer André Coyne to assist in examining the French reports and in
due course he found in favour of Kariba. It was not an auspicious start
and to quote Olivier, 'now the cat was truly among the pigeons. Up
north there was talk of secession and there were protest meetings and
resignations from the power board. The very existence of the infant
Federation was threatened!'

In a sequel Dr Olivier describes how he was called to a meeting at
the Prime Minister's office: 'When the door was closed behind me I
realised I was alone with him.' After dismissing the possibility of
examining other sites, as had been recommended, Sir Godfrey Huggins told him, 'André Coyne has been immensely helpful to me in
getting out of the political mess arising from the Kafue and Kariba
controversy and I want him to have a share of the project. You will, of
course, find he has hangers-on . . .' Dr Dubertret was introduced to
the scheme by André Coyne and was one such hanger-on. The deep
resentment in Northern Rhodesia can hardly have been assuaged by
André Coyne's reward for his part in assuring the ascendancy of the
Kariba project. Such an appointment, following an 'independent'
expert recommendation, is surely undesirable, but it seems to happen
very often in international contracts. After the scheme had been
adopted, the still 'resentful north' raised a further query about the
geology on the north bank, suggesting it was porous.

It was perhaps significant that once the Kariba contract had been
confirmed, CAPCO's chairman decided to appoint a geologist other

than Dr Dubertret to investigate this particular aspect, on the grounds that the report should not only be 'neutral', but be seen to be so. There was, therefore, a deeply-laid foundation of mistrust in Zambia. Now, Kariba was once again being given priority over Kafue on the basis of financial and technical reports emanating from Salisbury. As for doubts about Dr Dubertret's objectivity, they clearly predated his association with Kariba Stage 2. Nor has history exactly endorsed the claim made by Gibbs on his behalf that he was the supreme expert on the area's geology.

As either Dr Dubertret's neutrality or his skill must have been under suspicion as a result of his failure to forecast the geology on the south bank, it was surprising that he was proposed by Gibbs to undertake the same job on the north bank. The decision to appoint him was rooted in a confidential letter to Sir Duncan Anderson on 11 January 1961 in which Paton drew attention to the possible effects of the geology which would be encountered, both as regards design and cost. Sir Duncan Anderson, who was then chairman of CAPCO, replied suggesting that he would like to discuss this personally with Paton before bringing it to the attention of the CAPCO board. The CAPCO board, of course, included Northern Rhodesian members with whom there had been a long history of suspicion and disagreement. The meeting between Duncan Anderson and Paton appears to have been the first step towards the now notorious 1961 report.

Once again, as on the south bank, Salisbury was to obtain a geological report which suited their purpose and with which they must have been well pleased. Nor was there any shortage of specious explanation for the dramatic change which appeared to have taken place in the geology from one side of the river to the other. Looking back one might well be shocked that a report so singularly inconsistent with all the other information that was then available to Gibbs could have been produced in their firm and issued under their imprimatur without apparently causing them to have a very serious look at it. It is also curious that the logs, which like the report were prepared by Gibbs' very young geologist, K. S. Jones, under the guidance of Dr Dubertret, also came to be accepted – apparently without question.

There were, as we have seen, grave and early doubts on the Zambian side. Their economy is dependent upon mining for its very existence, and as a result they have an extremely efficient, dedicated and well-equipped geological department. It is no coincidence that their geological forecasts, reports and maps have remained unchallenged as the fullest, most detailed and accurate information regarding the

151

geology at Kariba. These records will stand forever as an indictment of the 1961 geological report and its warranty. No less shameful is the fact that the persistent and clear warnings issued by the Zambian Department of Geological Survey, and taken up by KNBC, were stifled.

Mitchells, of course, had some knowledge of all the political trials, tribulations, and indeed confrontations, in the earlier south bank dispute, which had, after all, received fairly wide coverage in the technical press and had featured in the correspondence columns of *The Times*. However, we had no idea that they were continuing, much less that the seeds of a far greater dispute had been sown. We learned too late that the relationship between KNBC and CAPCO was nothing like the one we had been led to believe in – a benign, multinational guiding Zambia to fulfil its dreams of possessing a great power station on the Zambezi which would remove its dependence on Rhodesia, as well as its 'fears of a power cut-off instigated by Rhodesia as a retaliatory measure for any Zambian sins or omission in the confrontation' (*Financial Times*, 2 November 1972). The one obvious interpretation of the growing tension between CAPCO and KNBC was that the Zambians were deeply resentful because they felt they had been lured into the project by a report which, innocently or otherwise, had misrepresented the nature of the task. Perhaps we were unduly naïve, but there was a far more fundamental and, indeed, sinister constituent of which we remained ignorant for many years.

A question of scale

Dr Goebbels was a great advocate of scale in practising the art of deceit. The bigger the deception the less likely it was to be challenged. Thus it was with Kariba Stage 2 for, stripped of its camouflage, it was quite simply the product of sanctions-breaking on a massive scale. The incredible fact was that the Kariba north bank power station was being built for Rhodesia with international aid provided through the World Bank. The Kariba North Bank Company, though wholly owned by the Zambian Government, was simply a façade. It provided a medium through which World Bank funds could be channelled in order to purchase all the imported constructional equipment and permanent installations without the Bank itself suffering direct contamination from Salisbury. At the same time the Zambian Government provided exchange control facilities to enable the Rhodesians to meet local costs. On completion of the project CAPCO was to get – and did get – a 35-year lease and control of all the power in exchange for a rental equal to the amortization of KNBC's loan with interest at seven per cent. At the end of the lease the power station would revert unencumbered to KNBC: in other words that would be their first pay-off.

At best, all this must have been very distasteful to the Zambians, as well as being politically dangerous. One does not know how badly their arm was twisted to make them accept. To say they were forced might be an exaggeration but they were told by a British member of the World Bank team that if the project went off smoothly 'there would be no reason to suppose that IBRD [the World Bank] would not assist with Kafue Stage 2 [Kaunda's favoured solution to Zambia's power problem] in due course'. But, together with the World Bank, the British Government and indeed all those who were parties to the arrangements, the Zambians had at a stroke made themselves hostages to a clandestine pact in which they all had more to lose than Rhodesia. Furthermore, buried in the documentation, was a Catch-22, a clause which was going to influence, if not dominate, the relationships between all the parties. This was the guarantee required of the sponsoring government in respect of all World Bank loans making the guarantor responsible for raising any additional funds should this prove necessary to complete the project. Zambia was destined to be more than a mere conduit for funds: she was to be forced to provide the majority of those funds herself before the work could be completed. And this would be at a time when she was in very straitened circumstances due to the collapse of the price of copper.

The potential for political embarrassment can hardly be exaggerated. Here was a power station located in Zambia, largely paid for out of Zambian funds, leased and operated by what was, stripped of its disguise, a Rhodesian entity, exporting all its power to Rhodesia. One can imagine the Zambian reaction when they realized the true nature of the deal in which they had become ensnared. The ensuing row was not to surface publicly until December 1979 when, with the return of British rule to Rhodesia, the Zambians took up the cudgels and the matter was referred to the World Bank for arbitration. At that time it was reported (*Sunday Times*, 3 February 1980) that the Kariba arrangement had cost Zambia hundreds of millions of pounds and given Rhodesia some of the cheapest electricity in the world: that Zambia had in fact supplied Rhodesia with two-thirds of her power, without receiving any payment. Rhodesia 'had in effect been stealing Zambian power in vast amounts'. The article commented that, for different reasons, neither side wanted to publicize the dispute, and in a subsequent article (*Sunday Times*, 10 February 1980) it was reported,

'Zambian and Rhodesian officials have acted swiftly to defuse the secret row over Rhodesia's reluctance to pay for electricity supplies drawn from Zambia'.

I wonder how many of Mitchells' creditors and shareholders realized when reading this who were the real victims of this dispute? Certainly, the whole scheme was a wonderful gift to Rhodesia's siege economy: 600 megawatts of power, equivalent to 750,000 gallons of fuel oil per day, at a time when the world was hearing outraged reports about a few tankers crossing the Beit bridge. No wonder there was such a cavalier attitude towards safety and that CAPCO was demanding progress at almost any risk to human life. And no wonder they were able to outwit or blackmail the other parties into footing the bill.

Of all the parties involved only Mitchells were in the dark. While they floundered more and more, and hostility between Zambia and Rhodesia grew more acute, the British Government continued to insist that the true nature of CAPCO's involvement should be kept secret. I have said before that we felt we were the permanent victims of a game of blind man's buff, but now I feel rather foolish, and angry, thinking back to all those meetings with Gibbs, CAPCO, the British Government and the World Bank, in which Mitchells alone were unaware of what was going on. Would any other government encourage its industrialists to go overseas to fight for export orders and then treat them in this way?

As the problems with the rock conditions emerged, dissension had grown. Gibbs and CAPCO reacted by suppressing information and trying to bluff it out, while the Zambians seemed to want the situation to be acknowledged and put right. Failure to grasp the nettle resulted in unnecessary delay and expense, but at the heart of the matter was the question of who was to supply the necessary additional finance. The Zambians had, of course, given the guarantee, which made them responsible in the last resort, but CAPCO, supported by Gibbs, sought to deepen the Zambians' obligation by blaming them alone for the delays and additional expense. Mitchells did not know that the project was still not properly funded, but found itself caught unwittingly in the middle of an ever-worsening crisis as the Zambians were relentlessly forced into commitments they had not expected and could hardly afford to meet.

When Mitchells' tender was received in October 1970 it was some K7 million higher than Gibbs' estimate, made in April, on which the financial agreements between CAPCO, KNBC, the British Government and the World Bank had been formulated. Following receipt of

Mitchells' tender, the various parties had agreed that CAPCO would enter into a supplementary loan agreement whereby they would provide the additional sum. Unfortunately, although all the other agreements were dealt with most meticulously, the supplementary loan agreement was not signed before the contract with Mitchells was entered into. By mid 1972 KNBC was in a very unhappy position indeed. Work had almost stopped in many areas because of the geological conditions, and at this point CAPCO reneged upon the signing of the supplementary loan agreement until *Zambia* could show how the project was going to be financed to completion. At the same time *CAPCO warned that the original K13 million which they were to provide to cover local costs was approaching the limit* and that in any case from then onwards they would want permission to borrow short-term loans in Zambia in order to furnish the K7 million they had previously promised. This development confirmed the Zambians' fears that Rhodesia would not be able to finance her part of the project and that Zambia would have to fill the gap.

It was against this background that the panel's report had been received.

Scapegoat

It was perhaps a pity that the panel's report had to be 'black-and-white' rather than 'grey' as Gibbs had hoped, but given the circumstances this was inevitable. Although written in conciliatory terms, it was bound to imply criticism of the design and the administration of the contract by the consulting engineer. The panel had identified the reason for the rock falls, and the steps that should be taken to provide support; but in doing so, they endorsed as necessary the recommendations put forward by the Zambian Inspector of Mines. This must have been unpalatable to Gibbs and CAPCO.

After publication of the report, the Zambians had finally given vent to their frustration and anxiety. Before entering into new contractual arrangements some explanation was due to them as to how errors of such magnitude had occurred, particularly, as they pointed out, having regard to the time that had been available for the preparation of the documents and the technical expertise that had been deployed. Against the background of such explanations they wanted to examine the performance of Gibbs as consultants and CAPCO as agents for construction to determine whether or not questions of negligence and/or professional incompetence arose, and whether there should be some deliberation as to the position of the consulting engineer in respect of the remainder of the works. Finally, in view of the extra costs which would arise, KNBC had to consider at board level whether they would have to reserve their position in respect of such costs.

There is no need to look further for the reasons behind the volte-face at the October meeting. Gibbs and CAPCO could no longer afford to admit responsibility. Some four months earlier, Angus Paton had commented to me that the Zambians 'were determined to have one of us', and this remark must by then have acquired a personal relevance for him. Nor had we helped ourselves by completing, without help or instruction, the stabilization of the machine hall roof. In a report dated 25 October, Dr Dubertret informed Gibbs, 'With concreting, the vault to chainage 77, the most dangerous section, where large slabs appeared already loose, is stabilised. This is an appreciable success. The revetment will contribute to support the end section of the arch. The danger of rock falls in the central section dragging large slabs in the end section is overcome.'

Mitchells had signed their own death warrant. Difficulties and dangers remained in the rest of the works, but these would not be apparent to the layman, whose attention had been focused on the machine hall, and it was now possible to suggest that the problems belonged to the past. As a result, a new strategy was possible: if Mitchells could be driven from the job, the money payable to them and the penalty due under the performance bond, which together amounted to K10 million, would become available to close the yawning financial gap. The temptation was too great, and the opportunity was seized. No wonder Arnold of the World Bank, having acquainted himself with the true position in August, had twice suggested to me that the best thing for Mitchells to do was to walk away. But then he presumably knew both sides of the story, whereas we knew only one.

It was very unfortunate that the team fielded at the October meetings did not include Arnold because he was the only World Bank representative that I met either in London or in Zambia who took the trouble to inform himself. When he had arrived at our site office in August, fully inculcated with prejudice, I was in a state of despair. He did, however, respond to my request that he spare me a little time and go into the facts of the situation and it did not take long for him to appreciate the true situation on the site, the problems with which we were confronted, and the extent to which he had been misinformed. He no doubt suggested that we should walk away because of the problems which he must have known lay ahead and to which he could see no solutions.

As regards the other people that we met from the World Bank, I have yet to understand the value of having a whole team of World Bank officials travelling around in one another's pockets, constantly on the phone to one another in London, Washington, Lusaka, Salisbury, Iran and Pakistan, living in the same hotel and seemingly utterly incapable of making an independent judgement. Of those present at the October meetings in Lusaka I literally pleaded with them to sit down and examine the facts because I was convinced that the Zambians were being led into a trap. I was wasting my time. Either they didn't want to be embarrassed by the facts or they were incapable of assimilating them. Not only did they throw all their weight against any compromise which would have allowed Mitchells to survive, but they failed to intervene when, to the undisguised joy of CAPCO, KNBC's political masters were isolated from their own technical advisers. Thus in one clean sweep Mitchells' fate was settled beyond redemption. At the same time (27 November 1972) the Zambian Government passed Statutory Instrument No. 243 whereby the Kariba North Bank Project (Safety and Health of Workers) Act 1971 – the intention of which had been to reinforce the Zambian Government's determination that her hydroelectric projects would not 'be built on Zambian bones' – was terminated with effect from 28 November 1972. The Kariba north bank project had been thrust into the same twilight conditions which had prevailed when the south bank station had been built and where over one hundred men were killed – many of them in the most gruesome circumstances and as a result of appalling negligence. (These deaths had been accepted by Dr Olivier in his book, and by other writers who presumably got their information from Gibbs, to be *within actuarial limits* – whatever that might mean!) Nor was that all. The chairman of KNBC was forced to resign and KNBC's general manager, who had fought valiantly against overwhelming odds to protect Zambian interests, was dismissed. The field was cleared. KNBC and the Zambians no longer had anyone on their side who was technically competent to advise or defend them. And Mitchells, of course, stood alone.

In view of the ruthlessness of this operation, it is interesting to note that the senior geologists and the senior mines inspector from the Zambian Government have gone on to hold very senior appointments in other parts of the world. This was not so, however, for Alastair Davidson, general manager of KNBC. Davidson had left the North of Scotland Hydro Electric Board in 1967 to take up the post of deputy general manager for the Copper Belt Power Company in Zambia. In

1968 he was appointed director of electrical engineering and chief adviser to the Ministry of Power, Transport and Works on all electrical developments in Zambia, where his duties embraced the forward planning of power supplies in Zambia and the development and construction of power stations and transmission lines. In this connection he was concerned with Kafue Stage I which was under construction and Kafue Stage II which was wanted by Zambia and was a rival to the Kariba north bank scheme.

· With the formation of KNBC, Davidson became acting general manager and thereafter, from March 1971, general manager. There is no doubt that the Kariba/Kafue dispute had run deep and that for a number of reasons, including the fact that CAPCO had aspirations to build additional plants down the Zambezi, the involvement of Davidson with his commitment to Zambian interests and his knowledge of the electricity supply industry met with suspicion and even hostility. He was, in fact, the only person on the Zambian side who could form technical judgements of what was proposed. Even before the north bank contract went out to tender, the hostility intensified as he became concerned about the geological conditions and noticed that the intakes to the power station on the Zambian side were some nine feet higher than those on the Rhodesian side. This obviously put the north bank station at a disadvantage at times of low water level in the lake, in so far that the north bank station would have to cease generating long before the south bank would need to do so. Davidson's insistence that an adjustment in these levels be made resulted in a further deterioration of his relationships with Gibbs and CAPCO which was further aggravated when he introduced Dr Matheson to the site. We now know that Davidson saw clearly, and argued clearly throughout, that it was crucial to recognize the realities of the geological situation and deal with them at the earliest opportunity. In this he was undoubtedly right, but it caused yet greater friction with CAPCO and Gibbs. At one time Paton lost his temper with Davidson: 'don't you think of ever going back to the UK, because I will see you never get a job there' – no idle threat. Davidson and his wife were completely shattered by their experience in Lusaka.

A false dawn, and the noose is tightened

By the time of the December meetings, and following the involvement of the World Bank at the highest level, I had no doubt that the Zambian representatives had come to London with every intention of arriving at an equitable solution. As recorded, the December meetings opened well, and good progress was made until Shepherd, CAPCO's general manager, was summoned from Salisbury. By the time he returned, Gibbs had devised their new recommendations, which were so devastating in their implications. They would either force Mitchells to accept a 'take-it-or-leave-it' offer of K25.5 million (£15 million) to complete the works, or 'expel them on the grounds of non-performance or insolvency' – a state which, by starving the company of liquidity, they would themselves create.

No wonder that their counsel, in drawing up the draft supplemental agreement, advised that a deed of release was needed. When we rejected these proposals, as we were bound to do if we were to preserve any rights in the disaster that was to follow, Gibbs effectively cut us off from every avenue of intercession or appeal. They insisted not only to KNBC and the World Bank, but also to the British Government, that their proposals had been reasonable and that only our intransigence had prevented our accepting them. For good measure they added that we had been overpaid and were using funds from Kariba to finance the rest of our business, which, given that they had had access to, and had both checked and approved, all our costs, was unforgivable.

In the event the works were completed by Energoprojekt, a Yugoslav contractor, who were given a contract which provided that they would be reimbursed all their costs together with additions for overheads and profit. (There was provision for these to be converted to measured work at unit rates – a subterfuge from which they were hardly likely to suffer.) Under these arrangements the final cost of the works included in the original Mitchells contract was, according to Barlow, Lyde and Gilbert (Gibbs' lawyers), £35 million. And of course this figure did not include the sum that had been saved by breaking Mitchells. The figures obtained from the World Bank, but not confirmed, indicate a slightly lower figure, but even allowing for the huge additional costs occasioned by the change of contractor, they show that acceptance of the only offer to us would have involved *additional* losses substantially in excess of the £10 million which had been the upper limit of the assessment we had given to our bankers. Were Gibbs' figures really the best assessment they could make at the time? Had they really 'bent over backwards' to assist us? Whatever the truth, the figures must now stand as an indictment either of their integrity or their professional competence.

Subsequently, Gibbs circulated among the press a most damaging story to the effect that Mitchells' difficulties, and ultimate fall, were

159

not attributable to their experience at Kariba, but to problems elsewhere. Table 1 shows the amount of Mitchells' operating overdraft with the Midland Bank during the last ten months of their trading as reported by the liquidator, Michael Jordan, FCA, at a meeting of the creditors held on 27 April 1973. Alongside are the amounts which would have been due to Mitchells if the form of contract agreed with Gibbs following the panel's report had been honoured.

Table 1

Date	Bank overdraft	Kariba under-certification
April to July 1972	Approx. £1 million	£2,400,000
Sept. 1972	£1,954,000	£2,475,000
Oct. 1972	£1,638,000	£2,750,000
Nov. 1972	£1,509,000	£3,038,000
Dec. 1972	£1,413,000	£3,520,000
31 Jan. 1973	£1,824,000	£4,100,000

The increase in bank overdraft in September was caused by an interruption to cash flow as a result of strike action during July and August which was targeted on high priority government contracts – several of which we were working. But there was no way in which Mitchells could staunch the massive haemorrhaging which was going on at Kariba – this could only be brought about if certificates were issued and thereafter honoured. But there were at least two factors which must have militated against the issue of proper certificates by Gibbs – who as the months went by became more entrenched. First, they feared KNBC's reaction to an admission that the engineering properties of the rock were different from those warranted – after all the delay that had been caused by their refusal to acknowledge and deal with the facts when they emerged: the Zambians had reserved their right of action against Gibbs for the damage they had suffered. Second, as CAPCO had warned in July that funds were running out and no further funds had been received, what would have happened if they had issued a certificate that CAPCO could not honour and how would they obtain CAPCO's agreement to the issue of such a certificate? By January 1973, Mitchells' dilemma was inescapable.

Our bankers, who had been monitoring Kariba for many months and were underwriting part of the performance bond, were completely opposed to sending further funds to Zambia in the absence of some evidence of good faith. There was no such evidence. Of course, we could have entered into the draft supplemental agreement and signed the deed of release. The choice was ours and had we accepted the proposal the bank would undoubtedly have been satisfied for there was no other aspect of our business that could have involved contemplation of receivership. But this satisfaction would have lasted only until the temporary relief, bought at such great cost, was exhausted and then, saddled with the revised agreements and having signed the deed of release, our position would have been beyond any redress. There was no way that we could fathom at that stage, let alone demonstrate to others, the depths of deception to which we were being exposed. On the other hand, to have entered into such agreements knowing their implications would have been an act of utter recklessness and irresponsibility.

I had already discussed the matter fully with the Prudential and Excess Insurance Companies, at a meeting which I will describe later, and they had been very insistent that we should refuse to continue at Kariba unless promises we had received in the past gave way to immediate and substantial payment. And, as will be seen, they gave me an important assurance of what would be their attitude, and that of the Midland Bank, if as a result of what was happening we were forced into receivership.

This assurance was, of course, tremendously important, for if we were forced into receivership we would not have the freedom to fight on our own behalf. It was therefore a source of considerable comfort to know that in the last resort we had behind us resources which could be equal to any demands made upon them. I cannot emphasize too strongly that Mitchells went into receivership solely as a result of their experience at Kariba. Had the British Government relented it could have been stopped. But we were living in a land where influence was more important than merit, and where there were facts to hide. Had the World Bank taken its initiative hours earlier, let alone the days, weeks or months that had been available to it, our torment could have been ended and the job could have been saved from the disaster that befell it. But they left no time and, in the end, Peppiat had to depend upon bad advice. Had Angus Paton acted honourably, even at the eleventh hour, all would have been saved and I have no doubt that solutions would have been found to the problems that he would have had to face. But he was not equal to it. Zambia was having a very bad time and, although not a cash economy, there was very little credit to

161

be had. We needed cash in Zambia to obtain supplies and to pay wages. The bank and the sureties were totally opposed to our sending money there and the bank would not make available funds to be used for this purpose. The events which followed were to lead inevitably to disaster.

But then, Kariba had been doomed from the start.

III

Receivership

Battening down the hatches

The calamity of 31 January 1973 had cast a long shadow before it and a brief account of some of the events that took place during the previous nine months, and particularly of the parts played by our bankers and merchant bankers, the sureties to the performance bond, and finally Coopers and Lybrand, is a necessary preliminary to the story of the receivership itself.

The most crucial fact we faced was that between October 1971 and April 1972 we had suffered an adverse cash flow at Kariba of £1 million and, at a time when we should really have been in our stride, work was almost at a standstill. In the previous October we had raised £1 million through the issue of a debenture stock, because it was considered prudent to augment the company's working capital; but in those few months the whole of that sum had disappeared down a large hole in Central Africa. Not only that, but the drain was continuing, and would go on unless and until the engineer acknowledged that the rock was treacherous and gave us some financial relief. Our reaction in April 1972, when the storm clouds had unmistakably gathered, was twofold. We stopped tendering for new projects, resisting invitations from valued clients and even from Gibbs, who, ironically, 'wanted new blood in South Africa'. At the same time we turned our attention to trying to collect some of the huge sums that were owing to us. We also made some internal reorganization in order to limit the disruption to the rest of our business. In cutting back on tendering we were, of course, taking the opposite action to a contractor who is seriously unstable. He is likely to seek his solution in a vastly inflated order-book, with a great deal of 'front-end loading', in the hope of gaining liquidity relief while putting his house in order. Our position was different. We had many assets to protect, and our biggest fear was that they would all be absorbed by this one disastrous contract.

Kariba presented an organizational problem, too. It had always been a fundamental belief in the company that 'indigestion', with consequent loss of efficiency all round, was the most fatal of all diseases in the construction industry. By closing off all new tendering and putting a stay on all new activities, we were containing the disruption caused by Kariba, which was making massive demands on our finances and on our senior executives' time. I decided that I should assume responsibility for dealing with Kariba and an arbitration relating to a contract at Peterborough Hospital which had surfaced after six years, thereby leaving the company to function otherwise as normally as possible. This was not just a matter of expediency, for by then Kariba posed a threat to the company's very survival.

We seek advice

On 19 April 1972 we began the first of a long series of meetings about Kariba with Keith Goodfellow QC, a trusted adviser who was now representing us in the Peterborough Hospital arbitration. His belief throughout was that on the face of it this was a case of fraud, but that it would be very difficult to prove. He consistently advised against withdrawal from the site because we would risk placing ourselves in the wrong and sacrificing sympathy.

To leave in such circumstances would have involved us in writing off all our losses on the contract, mounting at the end to £2.7 million, together with all the plant and equipment that was in Zambia. Our expatriate staff would have to be brought back and the bond of £2.4 million, entered into jointly by Mitchells, the Prudential and the Excess Insurance Companies, with counter guarantees from the group and the holding company to the Prudential and the Excess, would be forfeit. Relief from all these losses would only be obtainable if the company started arbitration proceedings in Zambia, which in practice would involve waiting for many years for a hearing, which in turn would take months and in which it would be almost impossible to obtain the services of counsel from the UK. In the meantime, the company's reputation and its credit, even if it were able to survive, would be largely destroyed.

Keith Goodfellow's reaction was undoubtedly further influenced by the fact that he knew that Gibbs and CAPCO had been over all this ground before on the south bank, and that if there had been any room for doubt as to the relative merit of schist and sound rock it had been finally resolved in a major arbitration on that contract. The insurance companies, too, had learned by bitter experience that the rock on the south bank had caused endless trouble. They had only been persuaded to provide cover on the north bank because the contract documents warranted that the rock was sound and that there would be no repetition of the immense losses they had suffered on the contract on the other side of the river. We knew of none of these things at that time. Alas, Goodfellow did not live to see this matter through to its conclusion; his death was a source of great personal sadness, and a tragedy for the company.

The outlines of a grim scenario were beginning to emerge by the end of April 1972 and, although its dreadful conclusion was as yet unthinkable, I feared that the company was becoming vulnerable.

I decided that it was time to call in the aid or advice of our merchant bankers. On 20 April I had a meeting with David Montagu, chairman of Samuel Montagu, at which I described our experiences at Kariba and my fears. Like many others, he could see no logic in it, and thought that a solution would be found. But there were many things none of us knew at that stage.

David Montagu was already aware of my views about reform in the industry and the hostility that they had aroused in some quarters, particularly with McAlpines. I told him of our increasing difficulty in securing payment for work, particularly in the public sector, and of my very real concern at the possibility of a long and unrelieved drain of resources into Kariba. There could be no doubt about the underlying stength of the company – Samuel Montagu had themselves carried out an investigation in connection with the debenture only six months previously; however, if Kariba continued indefinitely it was bound to create a serious liquidity problem and I suggested that we might move under a bigger umbrella. I knew there were companies within the industry which would be extremely interested in gaining access to our management capacity and our technical expertise, but Montagu thought it would be inappropriate for us to become involved in any negotiations with other contractors until the Kariba problem was solved. Instead, he suggested that I should inform the Midland Bank of the situation in order to retain their confidence and support. Himself a director of the bank he arranged a meeting for me that same afternoon with R. O. Barker, the chief general manager, to whom I explained the position.

This was to be the first of a number of meetings I had with Barker during the following nine months. The bank was particularly concerned because it had provided a counter guarantee to the sureties in respect of the performance bond in a sum of £630,000. Barker pointed out to me, on more than one occasion, that so far as the bank was concerned this was a demand bond which the sureties could call on them to pay at any time and therefore ranked, from the bank's point of view, as the equivalent of overdraft. As the months went by the bank became more and more insistent that some break in the Kariba situation was absolutely essential if it was not going to withdraw its support.

Montagu, meanwhile, was also concerned that Mitchells might appear already to have condoned the adverse rock conditions. He therefore recommended that steps should be taken to demand a renegotiation of the contract. He felt that if the main objective of the various authorities was to get the project completed in the quickest and most economical way, then, despite the risks involved in a confrontation, our position was reasonably strong. This view was shared by the Midland Bank and was, of course, our own belief. We were all proved wrong by the many months of abortive negotiations that were to follow, but then we had no knowledge of the political background to Kariba.

An unexpected development

May and June 1972 were months of very considerable activity and included tentative arrangements to visit the World Bank, which were eventually abandoned with the decision to set up the panel of inquiry.

However, on 9 May, just over two weeks from my meeting with David Montagu at which I had given him a full account of my anxieties and the particular problems we were encountering at Kariba, I was talking with a number of fellow members of the Federation of Civil Engineering Contractors at its annual dinner at the Dorchester Hotel when I was approached by Sir Robin McAlpine, at that time chairman of the family firm. He invited me back to his house for the talk, previously mentioned, at which he told me that 'they' – and here I assume that he was referring to the super-league – had a great admiration for my abilities, but were concerned by my refusal to 'join'. He said that what I was doing was 'beginning to hurt' and suggested that there might be ways of bridging the gap between us, and even that they might be able to help me. In particular, he mentioned that his brother, Edwin, had a large number of friends who went to him for advice, and he referred more than once to Edwin's close relationship with David Montagu. They were going to go public later in the year and Samuel Montagu were to be merchant bankers to the flotation. In this connection I had featured extensively in their discussions with their advisers, with particular reference to the treatment of the Anchor project in their prospectus. He admitted that they had already had over £30 million on the contract and still had a long way to go; if these figures were included in the prospectus I was going to be able to say, 'I told you so.'

Robin McAlpine himself might have been well-intentioned, but I was unsettled by the discussion, especially when he displayed an intimate knowledge of every move I had made to sort out problems which I knew had been deliberately contrived within the Federation to cause my company embarrassment. Although I was quite sure an invitation was being made, I was incapable of accepting it.

I told Robin McAlpine that I had no desire for conflict within the Federation, and was in fact anxious to work for the industry. My beliefs were, however, firmly held and could not be sacrificed. In my opinion the survival of our system and the way of life in which I believed was dependent upon industry learning to behave itself and showing, as it could not at the moment, that it produced the goods at the end of the line. In my view, the industry was not producing forty per cent of its potential output, and this was inexcusable. I made it clear to him that I knew about the campaign which Sir Edwin was waging against my company, and against me personally. Robin made no attempt to deny it; indeed he referred to it himself as a smear campaign but said that he had no control over Sir Edwin who was fascinated by the manipulation of people and situations.

I was very disturbed by this meeting and as I said goodnight at his front door at 1.40 a.m. I had no doubt that it had been a crucial moment in the company's affairs. Robin McAlpine's desire to help may have been genuine, and he may have been unable to understand why I could not compromise my beliefs, but they were more important to me than any other aspect of my business life and have continued to be so to this day. However, the gulf between us was by now very wide indeed. I was utterly opposed to Sir Edwin's philosophy, which was made all the more menacing by being backed by such extraordinary power. But I couldn't compromise my own views.

I have thought back to that meeting many times. Had I reacted differently the solution to the Kariba problem might well have been found, and perhaps some of the other pressures on Mitchells might have been relieved. Kariba was not mentioned, but I knew that was what we were talking about. To Robin McAlpine I may have appeared ungracious; but however often I review it, and in spite of all the wasted effort, the wasted years, the destruction of the Mitchell organization, and the hardship to so many that followed, I still know that if I had the choice to make again I would respond in the same way. There is no point in denying the trauma, the frustration, the loss of opportunity and the loss of my way of life that followed the receivership. I am sorry if others have suffered who might have been spared had I chosen differently, but I could not have lived with a compromise that was so fundamentally opposed to my basic beliefs.

I did not see David Montagu again after my meeting in April 1972. When I had first discussed with him the appointment of his firm as Mitchells' merchant bankers, he wanted to ensure that this would involve them in no conflicts of interest, and he cleared the matter with me by discussing other companies for whom they acted. He was a close friend of Sir Edwin McAlpine and well knew of his hostility towards us. I believe he had tried to make the peace, but had not succeeded. I was certainly not happy to learn through such a route that Samuel Montagu were going to handle the McAlpine flotation, which must have been a very big prize indeed. I was never able to develop with John Gillum, who handled the company's affairs thereafter, the close rapport I had appeared to enjoy with David Montagu. Much later I did ask the Midland Bank whether it might not be possible to change our merchant bankers because they no longer had my confidence, but I had to accept their advice that this was impracticable.

A few weeks after my talk with Robin McAlpine I had another significant encounter when in the company of mutual friends I met the late Ronald Dickinson, a former Head of Policy-making at the Exports Credit Guarantee Department and its Under-secretary until his retirement in 1970. He had immense experience of export finance and at the time of which I speak he had retired from public service and was practising as a consultant in this field in partnership with Lord Goodman. He knew something of our problems and told me that he was immensely anxious on our account. He told me that Gibbs were 'political animals' who had the capability of rapid manoeuvring and lobbying behind the scenes in order to protect their own position. There was no questioning his seriousness or the ominous note that he sounded, but he could go no further. And neither could I. How does one react in such circumstances – surrounded with threats which one cannot assess and dealing with people who acknowledge none of the accepted rules? Small wonder that for me the whole of 1972 was a period of growing unease.

Enter Coopers and Lybrand

In June 1971, twelve months after my appointment to the Civil Engineering EDC, I had received an invitation to chair a working party which was to be set up jointly by the Building and Civil Engineering EDCs to examine and report on the acquisition of construction by the public sector. It had come as a pleasant surprise, for I had not known that such an inquiry was contemplated. It was, however, very much a matter after my own heart and I was delighted at the opportunity. Its membership included the chairman of a major property company, the chief executive of one of our biggest national contractors, an under secretary from the Department of the Environment, the chairman of the Association of Municipal Corporations, the leaders of the two construction industry trades unions (one of them the chairman of the TUC), and Ian Andrew, a director of Cooper Brothers and Co., the management consultant arm of Coopers and Lybrand. The terms of reference of the working party provided for it to examine the various ways in which government bodies, both central and local, obtained the products of the construction industry, to consider different methods adopted and their effects on efficiency and output in the industry, to identify problem areas, and to advise on further studies where changes were recommended.

Progress on the working party was very encouraging and was enthusiastically supported by the NEDO secretariat when, in the spring of 1972, it became apparent that the question of slow payment in the public sector and its impact on efficiency and construction costs were bound to feature in our deliberations. As it was very unlikely that any members of the working party not directly involved would know how unpredictable the process of payment was, I spoke to Ian Andrew about the possibility of his firm undertaking an assignment for Mitchells.

At my invitation he came to see me at Bedford Square on 2 May 1972, and on 15 May he came to Peterborough with one of his consultants, George Gilbertson, for a full briefing. The intention was for Mitchells to make a complete financial reappraisal of its operations and, at the same time, to give Ian Andrew, as a management accountant and a member of the NEDO working party, an idea of the capricious attitude towards payment in the public sector. Matters for study would include the vast sums of money outstanding to the company in relation to the profits actually taken. There was also the problem of giving a true picture to the shareholders of the disproportionate bank of undisclosed profits. This in turn would lead to a reappraisal of the fields in which the company was operating, and of the justification or otherwise of continuing in a business where narrow margins, delays in payments and the effects of inflation meant that, while in accountancy terms the contract might show a profit, in real terms we were only subsidizing the client through enforced credit. Inflation accounting was still not widely adopted at that time, and in any case would have been virtually useless in the huge uncharted areas which were left in limbo by the payment policy in the public sector.

At the time this exercise was first discussed, Kariba was only reflecting, albeit in extreme form, a UK malaise which some consulting engineers were exporting abroad, thereby damaging the international standing of British engineers. Kariba differed from the general pattern only in degree, because its worst and most sustained abuses had not by then fully emerged.

Coopers' report: October 1972

Coopers' report, together with the investigation carried out by Samuel Montagu in connection with the placing of the debenture in October 1971, are of particular interest because they provide an authoritative and independent view of the company's affairs during this critical twelve-month period. They will have to be taken into account when judging the later report prepared by Coopers only three months after their first was received.

Andrew had informed me that before accepting any assignment his firm's standard practice was to advise clients that if they found any irregularity, financial weakness or other matter which might reflect on the stability of the company, they could not be a party to its suppression and would consider it their duty to make a full disclosure in their report. This was quite unexceptionable so far as I was concerned. In turn I made it equally clear to Andrew, and confirmed in writing, that the purpose of the report would be to prepare information for use in considering the direction of the company's policy. In particular I emphasized to him that his consultants were to have the fullest possible access to all information in the company, for without it there would be no point in undertaking the exercise. He would also have the closest cooperation of all our senior management. It has never been suggested that all these provisions were not subsequently respected to the letter by both sides.

Coopers started their assignment in July 1972. Although I did not see their final account, I was consulted about their penultimate one because I had given the instructions, and it was apparent that they were greatly exceeding estimates. It included charges in respect of 155 hours of director's time, 600 hours of supervising consultant's time and 16 weeks of consultant's time. I made no complaint because it was quite apparent that that time had been spent and I quote it now only to show that the exercise was a thorough one. Their report was submitted on 31 October and at a meeting that I had with George Gilbertson on 21 November, he volunteered the view that their researches had shown Mitchells to be a very sound operation, but he naturally thought it would be improved by incorporating his firm's proposals. I remember it very clearly because it was on 31 October that I had arrived back from the disastrous meeting in Lusaka where Gibbs and CAPCO had reneged on all the agreements so long and painfully arrived at for dealing with the Kariba contract. But this did not reflect on the accuracy of the report at the time that it was prepared and nowhere in the report was there any suggestion that the company was other than healthy, let alone that it was guilty of any impropriety.

This was in complete contrast to the report that was to be prepared by Coopers only three months later and passed to Samuel Montagu, but which was never published to the holding company board. This report, ill-balanced and containing the most astonishing inaccuracies, was used not only to undermine Mitchells at the time but was filtered into a general pool of misinformation where its most outrageous suggestion – a repetition of Gibbs' story that Mitchells had been overpaid at Kariba and was using Kariba money to finance its business – was used to attack Mitchells' credibility throughout the receivership and the Kariba litigation that followed. For good measure, and notwithstanding the excellent relationships which we as a company, and which I personally, had enjoyed with their two consultants, attacks were made on the competence of our board and extended to my personal integrity. Indeed Edward Walker Arnott of Herbert Smith and Co., Coopers' lawyers, told my solicitors, at a time when the receiver was trying to seize my pension, of allegations that I had been running the company to feather my own nest and that Coopers would be prepared to testify that my management had bordered on the brink of dishonesty because it had affected my commission and emoluments. As I had made a practice of waiving my entitlements from the company, and in 1971 alone had waived £43,000 in dividends and remuneration, it would appear that a charge of quixotry should have been added to the other allegations. It is my firm belief that Coopers'

173

hostility and their generation of prejudice, was intended to serve one purpose – to prevent my playing any further part in the company's affairs and in particular in relation to Kariba.

The record of Coopers' involvement with the company in 1972, and of the watershed in relationships which occurred with the introduction of the new representatives with whom we had to deal following the Kariba debacle, is part of the essential introduction to the receivership. If there was one group of accountants in the City who knew all about the Mitchell group of companies, and the situation in which they had been placed by their experience on the Kariba contract, it was Coopers and Lybrand. In the discussions leading up to the appointment of Paul Shewell as receiver, the fact that his firm possessed within its organization this unique knowledge, and that it would be available to us in the receivership, was for me a vital consideration. If the intention had been to serve the best interests of the company, the knowledge held by Ian Andrew and George Gilbertson would have been invaluable. The subsequent failure to involve them, mysterious as it was, is only one of the developments which have never been explained.

Kenneth Wright visits Kariba

In June 1972 I had been sufficiently concerned about Kariba to suggest to the holding company board that, in fairness to them and as background to the report I was making, I would welcome a visit to the site by one of the non-executive directors. As a result, Kenneth Wright, who, at the time, was president elect of the Institute of Chartered Accountants, went for three days (15–18 June), travelling to Salisbury afterwards to settle plans for a visit he was going to make during his year as president. Owing to other demands on my time I saw little of him except at meals and during the evening, but he made a complete tour of the works, including the workshops, quarry, offices, etc., and talked to many of the staff.

I quote from the last two paragraphs of an informal report he circulated to the other holding company directors on his return:

> During the visit I talked with more than twenty of the staff and got a most reassuring impression of their enthusiasm for the job and loyalty to the company. My judgement is that they are an outstanding team and that it is a considerable achievement to be able to build up such an organisation.
>
> I came away with one overriding impression: I am not qualified to express an opinion about the technical problems of the contract, but I

saw enough, and understood enough, to be entirely satisfied that we have every right to be proud of what we are doing at Kariba.

A meeting with the sureties

I have referred earlier to the meeting I had with the Prudential Assurance Company and the Excess Insurance Company who were the sureties to the performance bond – a standard requirement from all World Bank contracts. Under its terms they were bound with Mitchells in the sum of K4.1 (£2.4) million to be paid to the KNBC if Mitchells failed to carry out their obligations under the contract. The Prudential and the Excess had in turn received a counter guarantee in respect of £630,000 from the Midland Bank, with further counter guarantees from the group and from the holding company in respect of any sums which they might be called upon to pay out under the bond.

The brokers who negotiated the bond had been kept fully informed of developments at Kariba over a period of months. It will be recalled that when I returned from Washington on 8 December 1972, the auguries were not good. It had become clear that the Zambians were being forced into finding a solution, but that they were determined to take no action unless and until they could determine where responsibility for their predicament lay. Mitchells in turn could only obtain relief on the certification of the engineer. We did not at that time know that the engineer could not certify without the approval of CAPCO. Nor did we know that he was under threat of action from KNBC and that in giving an explanation for the issue of a certificate he would have to give KNBC precisely the ammunition which they sought. Finally, and overriding all other matters, was the fact that in the event of a certificate being issued there were no funds available with which to honour it. Even without this information there seemed little prospect, at least based on past performance, that Gibbs would give the explanation which would clear the way for the Zambians to agree to payment at the forthcoming meetings which, under pressure from the World Bank, were sheduled to start in London on 19 December. Nor did it seem likely that CAPCO, from their remote position in Rhodesia, would cease to exercise what we had come to regard as the 'Salisbury veto'.

This was the background, some of it known and some of it unknown, when, with my approval, the broker arranged a very important meeting between the sureties to the performance bond and myself, which took place at my office in Bedford Square on the morning of 14 December. Apart from myself and the broker, the meeting was attended by William Walker, the overseas accident manager of the Prudential, and Joseph Perry Mee, the bond under-writer for the Excess.

The meeting opened with the broker summarizing the information that had been given to the sureties to date. They had already been given copies of the report of the panel and a copy of the telex from Paton to CAPCO summarizing the engineer's recommendations for revision of the contract.

I then brought the meeting up to date with an account of my visit to Washington, the discussions with Paton and Sir Harold Harding following my return, and Paton's departure for Pakistan. I told them that Paton's partner, Norris, had said to me, 'We know you are entitled to additional payment; as to how long it takes us to decide how much, I would not like to forecast.' I referred to counsel's advice as to the strength of the Mitchells case and the dangers of withdrawal. The sureties were then asked to express their views.

Walker, for the Prudential, immediately and emphatically said that Mitchells should not put any more money into the contract. If Mitchells were forced out of business, the Prudential would sue Gibbs on the strength of the overwhelming evidence he had heard, and he was sure the Midland Bank would take the same view and action. Perry Mee, on behalf of the Excess, agreed completely and said that under no circumstances should Mitchells put more money into the project. He thought Mitchells had the strongest possible case for withdrawal. There was some general discussion during which Walker emphasized the need to keep the Midland Bank fully informed. The meeting concluded with both the sureties repeating their view that Mitchells should refuse to continue unless the promises they had received in the past were replaced by an immediate and substantial payment.

This meeting was crucial. For months I had been seeking some means which would enable me to contain what was happening at Kariba. I was no longer in any doubt that Gibbs were fighting for their lives and that they were quite prepared, if not determined, to sacrifice Mitchells in that cause. Until this meeting with the sureties, I had known that if we withdrew from the site we would be involved in crippling losses which would almost certainly ruin the company and destroy its ability to fight.

The situation was now changed. Walker had reminded me at our meeting that, apart from being sureties to its performance bond, the Prudential were trustees to the company's debenture stock and also held on their own account 168,000 ordinary shares. Paton had made more than one reference to our seeking a solution in arbitration, a course which he knew would provide no remedy because it would take many years, while in the meantime we could be forced over the brink. The results of receivership would be grievous, and for many, including myself, disastrous, but the company still had massive assets, of which the right of redress against Gibbs, KNBC, and possibly even CAPCO, was but one. With the backing we now had, there was every possibility that a rational approach would prevail if we were forced into receivership, and that in the long run redress would be bound to come, preventing both the creditors and the shareholders from suffering too grievously. Unhappy though the situation was, at least I now knew the worst and I could enter into the negotiations that lay ahead with the ground firmer under my feet.

A saviour?

It is appropriate here to enlarge on the role played by Ian Andrew of Coopers at the abortive meetings held in London with the Zambians during December 1972.

In their report, which had its origins in an examination of cash flow and contracts undertaken in the public sector, Coopers had been critical of the fact that the company did not charge to the contract executive time and other expenses incurred in the settlement of claims, nor interest outstanding on money which had not been paid at the proper time. It further noted that there was a tendency to cultivate goodwill at the expense of the vigorous prosecution of claims. It recommended that a group claims section should be established, that the group accountants should play a more prominent part in pressing claims and that a senior group executive should be appointed to develop close liaisons 'at the right level' in London to assist in resolving contract problems and in obtaining further work.

It will be noted how much these proposals are in conflict with the image, so assiduously promoted by those not well disposed to us, that we were 'claims merchants'. It was because of Coopers' obvious concern and surprise that we encountered so much difficulty in securing payment that, when I heard about the Zambians' proposed visit, I asked Ian Andrew and his consultant George Gilbertson to become involved.

Communications with the Zambians were not always as formal as they might be and it was in fact in the middle of a meeting of our

177

working party at the EDC headquarters in Millbank on 19 December, that I learned that they had arrived in London and I was asked if I could attend a meeting immediately. Ian Andrew accompanied me to the Zambian High Commission where we had our first meeting. It was not possible for me to attend the resumed meeting on 20 December. On Thursday 21 December, while these meetings with the Zambians and the consultants were continuing in London, a contingency meeting was held at Samuel Montagu's to decide on the course of action to be adopted if progress towards a meaningful payment was not made before the negotiations were concluded. Among those present were Kenneth Wright, who accompanied me, David Hobson of Coopers, and John Gillum of Samuel Montagu. John Gillum had been present at the board meeting of Mitchell Construction Holdings the previous afternoon when Ian Andrew had reported on his discussions with the Zambians and had said he felt confident that agreement would at least reach the point where an interim payment of between £1 million and £2 million would be made. Gillum took the view that no action was called for until the outcome of the negotiations was known. However, it was agreed that if the position remained unchanged after Christmas, Coopers would embark on a further report. But what we did not know was that Shepherd, who, it will be recalled, had been summoned in great haste from Salisbury, was actually in London the day of our meeting at Samuel Montagu. His arrival was to signal a distinctly new tone in negotiations with the Zambians, and was to lead to our fateful meeting on 27 December at four o'clock at which we realized that we had, after all, achieved no significant progress.

The meeting at Samuel Montagu's on 21 December was my first with David Hobson of Coopers. Bearing in mind that this meeting took place at the end of eight months during which Samuel Montagu had been kept fully informed, I had hoped that it would be fruitful and that a *modus operandi* would be decided upon should the worst befall. I was therefore very disappointed to find that Hobson was neither helpful nor encouraging. However, I put this down to the fact that he was ill-prepared and had no familiarity with the situation. I assumed that after some study, and consultations with George Gilbertson, he would be able to protect the Mitchells interests as well as anybody. I was greatly encouraged in this belief after the breakdown of the December meetings, when Ian Andrew told me that if there was one person who could steer us through the troubles that now lay ahead of us, it was David Hobson.

The second time I saw Hobson was at a meeting (19 January) at our

Peterborough office, which was attended by our various legal and financial advisers, and members of our holding company board. Following my exhaustive examination of the situation in Zambia, I was firmly convinced that I could not in any way modify my earlier assessment, which I had given to William Barker of the Midland Bank, that if we accepted the only offer open to us we would involve ourselves in additional losses of some £5–10 million. In fact, as has been seen, our additional losses might have been even greater because the Yugoslavs were eventually paid £20 million for work which Mitchells had been expected to do for little more than £5 million. On the other hand the money paid to them would have had to reflect the immense additional costs incurred as a result of forcing Mitchells off the site and therefore having to stop and restart the work. In this connection it is horrifying to think of the waste of resources which resulted from the failure of Samuel Montagu and Paul Shewell to respond to Freshfields' telephone call in 1973. The fate of Mitchells apart, a very high price was exacted from the international community to pay for running the World Bank as though it were a club.

This then was the situation when Hobson came to Mitchells' Peterborough office. Many months of negotiation, agreements that had been made and then broken and then an absolute determination to impose upon us a deal that bore no relation to reality, had led me to the conclusion that the company could take the matter no further and that our immediate salvation depended on the City's reaction. In these circumstances, and bearing in mind Ian Andrew's assurance that Hobson was the one person who could pull us through, I invited him to take the chair.

To invite another man to take the chair in my own boardroom was a hard decision, but it was realistic. There was nobody in that room whose knowledge of civil engineering contracting exceeded my own, but we were moving out of my sphere into those areas of finance and law which would apply in receivership – waters which for me were as yet uncharted. By my gesture, I wanted to leave Hobson in no doubt as to the extent of the cooperation he could expect from me, and from the company, should events follow what appeared by now to be their inevitable course. Had I known that Coopers were joint consultants with Gibbs on a number of projects and, more importantly, that with Gibbs they were advisers to CAPCO, and that they had been closely involved in the financial plan for Kariba which was now lying in ruins, I doubt I would have even allowed Hobson into the boardroom, let alone take the chair. As it was, I became increasingly disturbed as the meeting progressed. In spite of the clear exposition that counsel gave of the Kariba situation, Hobson displayed no sense of concern or even sympathy at what had been done to the company. Instead, he appeared critical and even censorious because we had allowed the company to get into this position so soon after the issue of the debenture stock.

It was abundantly clear there could be no solution once we withdrew from Kariba unless we were able to pursue redress. I pointed out that Mitchells had undoubtedly been the victims of fraud at the hands of Gibbs and of CAPCO and that any attempts to find a solution that ignored this would fail. Counsel had already stated on more than one occasion that, prima facie, there were grounds for initiating proceedings on the basis of fraud, but Hobson was apparently unwilling to give any weight to his view. I found this very disturbing, particularly as he was hostile when I tried to press the issue. Once again I had to assume that his attitude was due to a lack of familiarity with all the circumstances.

For those of us who live, or perish, outside the City establishment, the concept of conflict of interest must remain an impenetrable mystery. If I now believe that Hobson knew far more about Kariba than he acknowledged at that meeting, then he has only himself to blame. As it was, when he took my chair without disclosing Coopers' other interests, he committed his firm to a course of action from which there could be no turning back. I believe it is against this background that the future behaviour of Coopers' appointed receiver has to be examined.

Into receivership

If there has been some overlap in my introduction to the receivership, it is because it appears to me that the story would not be complete without the account I have given of how Samuel Montagu, the Midland Bank, Coopers and the sureties became involved, and were kept fully informed, during the long months that led up to the appointment of Paul Shewell.

At the board meeting (30 January) at which the decision had been taken to ask for the appointment of a receiver, it was agreed that John Gillum of Samuel Montagu should take the appropriate steps and that an announcement would be made to the Stock Exchange at 3.30 p.m. on Wednesday 31 January. The Mitchell board had favoured immediate suspension of dealings but had had to bow to the advice of the professionals. The meeting had started at 5 p.m. and by the time it was concluded there was no opportunity to take any further action that evening. The following morning, still without a word of advice or guidance from Samuel Montagu or from Coopers, I telephoned Sir Godfrey Mitchell, chairman of Wimpey, and made an appointment to see him. He was a man for whom I had a high regard and I thought that even at this eleventh hour, he might be able to assist us. My visit to him was of course virtually unheralded and while he gave me a sympathetic hearing he felt unable to intervene because Wimpeys traditionally had not been in the business of acquiring other companies. Added to this, of course, there had been no time to prepare and present our case.

I came away from this meeting to learn of Freshfields' call. There followed my telephone conversation with Peppiat, my call to John Gillum and his insistence that it was 'too late'. John Gillum made no attempt to enlarge upon this or indeed to continue the conversation in any way. It was in these circumstances that I got in touch with Peppiat again and had to leave him to make his approach – with the result that I have already recorded.

Following Freshfields' attempt at intervention and John Gillum's insistence that it was 'too late', I knew there was nothing further I could do in London, and so I drove north to Peterborough.

We had come to the end of a road down which we had been relentlessly driven over a period of many months, while those who could have helped had kept silent. Of course there had been a growing sense of impending disaster, but now the situation had to be faced, and my long experience made me confident of the magnificent spirit that had always existed within the group. The first shock would be quickly absorbed, and then everyone would face the challenge with unshakeable resolve.

There were comforts. Throughout the history of the company we had always kept our bankers and our financial advisers fully informed, and therefore we could reasonably expect to have both their sympathy and their confidence. Although there had been a liquidity crisis the company had maintained its goodwill. And although it had been drained mercilessly, at a speed which made it impossible to staunch the flow, it had gone down without as much as a writ, or even a threatening letter, from any creditor. At the same time it had immense assets in relation to its size, and to these had to be added the possibility of recovery in respect of the treatment we had suffered at Kariba. I knew that the Zambians would not lightly give up their right to recompense and that they would not abandon their claim to the performance bond.

181

I was therefore immensely comforted by the assurance the Prudential and the Excess had given me, and I was confident the truth would emerge, and with it our chance of redress. We would never be able to re-establish the company as it had been, but it was not going to be easy to run Mitchells ignominiously into the ground, without any redress for its creditors, or even its shareholders. Comforting too was the thought of the immense strength we would derive from the detailed knowledge of the company's operations possessed by Coopers, from whom we expected the closest cooperation. I recalled Andrew's and Gilbertson's astonishment as they witnessed the treatment we received at the December meetings. Now, after many months of grappling with the unknown, we would at last have one member of the establishment on our side.

Of course there were disappointments. During the long-drawn-out approach to receivership, we had been trying to formulate contingency plans so as to be ready if the worst befell us. But why had every attempt to penetrate the veil beyond the appointment of a receiver failed or been frustrated? It was as if one were entering into a secret society where each step had to be shrouded in mystery. Nevertheless the facts were there and would prevail.

Little did I know as I drove up to Peterborough that afternoon that we were about to exchange one game of blind man's buff played in Central Africa for another played in the City of London. Nor did I know that in the next 24 hours, following the appointment of the receiver, I was going to see the very heart and soul torn out of a magnificent company, that had hitherto withstood every onslaught.

Within days, one after another of our senior executives was to tell me, apologetically, that they had reluctantly come to the conclusion that it was 'every man for himself', and that their prime consideration from now on had to be their own interests and those of their families. It was out of character and distressing for me to witness, but I could not quarrel with their reasoning. Within two weeks the chairman of Tarmac Construction Limited, who had by that time taken over Mitchells, told me how worried he was by this disintegration and the appearance of rival factions within the company. I could have told him that if one wanted a textbook example of how to destroy the morale, and the very fibre, of a company, then I had witnessed it within the first 24 hours of the administration of the receivership. The physical assets had been grabbed before anyone else could get at them. But in the process the most valuable asset of all – the management which we had built together with such care and over so many years – was blown apart.

The receiver takes over

The announcement of the receivership was made at the close of business on the Stock Exchange on Wednesday 31 January 1973. This followed a suspension of the quotation at midday which was made necessary by the collapse of the share price as a result of the leakage of inside information. It was a pity that the directors' repeated request for an earlier suspension had been overruled, for this would have saved them from bearing a most unsavoury and hurtful additional burden, and one which I was apparently expected to explain.

That night I obviously felt dreadfully sad. We were a very closely knit company and had had a long and traumatic fight. It was almost beyond belief that after all our efforts a solution had not been found. Nevertheless, it had to be accepted. Everything possible had been done to save the company, but we had failed. Our consciences were clear, and now our task was to gather our strength, reinforce morale and do the best we could for the creditors and, if possible, for the shareholders. I had no doubt that the majority of the staff would rally round.

Many people telephoned my home that evening; some were sensitive and diffident, not wishing to disturb, but not wishing the moment to pass without expressing their concern and sympathy. Some, more realistically, were from chairmen of other companies who, while expressing their sympathy, felt it could not be too soon to register their interest. Amongst these was Bill Francis, chairman of Tarmac Construction Limited. He was a long-standing associate on the Midland section of the FCEC, and had often talked to me about his wish to acquire Mitchell Construction on behalf of Tarmac. Though such a proposition might have been superficially attractive to me personally on purely financial terms, it had always been quite out of the question. Mitchells had its own special quality and it would have been treachery of the highest order for me to have committed a loyal team to a different philosophy, regardless of its merits. Francis now suggested we might come to some arrangement and I told him, yes, I felt sure we could do a deal, but I was no longer free to discuss it: he would have to wait until the morning, when I would have a chance of discussing it with the receiver. I told him, as I told others, that if I were to enter into discussions with him on any other basis I would run the risk of losing the receiver's confidence.

He did not press the matter. How naïve can one be? My education had not started!

183

The receiver's inheritance

Once the gravity of the events at Kariba had become apparent, I had made it my business to keep our bankers, our merchant bank and finally the bondholders fully informed of every aspect of the company's business. I had sensed something very unusual at Kariba, without being able to identify it, and I had been extremely worried. The management situation that Paul Shewell, the receiver, inherited was this: that the companies were fully integrated with autonomous management of a high order, I had an intimate personal knowledge of two vitally important matters, namely, the history of the Kariba contract and of the Peterborough Hospital arbitration, and I had the loyalty of the staff. Furthermore, I had every right to expect the full cooperation of our bankers, our merchant bankers and the sureties to the performance bond. So, what was the financial position?

The group had not gone into receivership because it had been driven out of business at the behest of creditors: it had done so in response to advice. The company's assets had, therefore, in no way been exhausted and there were resources immediately available which could have been converted into cash. We had not done this because the economic situation in Zambia prevented credit from being available throughout industry. As a result, we could only remain in Zambia on a cash basis, and with losses continuing at £350,000 per month. Without the introduction of some machinery to give the company a breathing space, money generated elsewhere in the group was bound to go down the Zambian drain. It was also the case that even had we been able to see prospects of a change, the bank had placed a veto on the disposal of any assets, the proceeds of which might go to Central Africa, unless and until we could find a solution to the Kariba problem. If this had not been the case there were many immediate sources of funds. By settling outstanding accounts at a massive discount we could have raised over £2 million from outstanding contract settlements (in fact, over £3 million was raised after the receivership in respect of contracts which had been fully completed before 1973 while a similar sum was received in respect of work already executed, and for which payment was outstanding, on existing contracts). Apart from those companies within the group which were involved in construction, with their fine headquarters and their regional offices, all of them free of debt, there were plant, manufacturing, property and development companies, all with fully autonomous managements, which with their related properties had a minimum going-concern value in excess of £5 million.

With the appointment of a receiver the directors are stripped of all their powers and have no control over the company or its assets. All authority is vested in the receiver and can be delegated solely by him. Obviously vital and urgent appraisal was necessary and, with it, the formulation of the policy to be pursued. And yet, beyond Gillum's 'too late' I could not find out what was going on and there was no attempt to contact me.

Where was the receiver?

On 1 February – the first day of Shewell's receivership – I arrived early in the office. The trickle of mail, which was to become a flood, had already started to arrive.

But where was the receiver?

The letters I received then were a source of strength. They came from public authorities, from companies and other organizations whose names were household words, from presidents and past presidents of institutions, from leading QCs, from journalists, and finally from all levels of the staff, both past and present. They were encouraging beyond belief as one after another they acknowledged what Mitchells and its standards had stood for. From overseas, from Hong Kong, from Singapore, from central and southern Africa, where Mitchell men who had left the company had still kept in touch, and from all over the United Kingdom, came messages of affection for and pride in its achievements. All expressed dismay and disbelief at what had been allowed to happen, and recorded a sad sense of personal loss. One of the principal trade union leaders wrote: 'You must feel all the world is anti. We are not and have confidence. I have taken more beatings than you ever will – smile, that really annoys them!'

But where were the faceless ones and the 'Yours evers' from the City? And where was the receiver?

There was a general bewilderment among the staff. What could they do next? Most just carried on with their jobs as usual, and out on sites urgent programmes of construction continued.

But who could give a lead or any reassurance about the future? Were the staff, like me, expected to get the only news of their plight from the newspapers – the only source from which I had myself learned the name of the receiver? Who could bring confidence and purpose into what was now to be done?

And where was the receiver?

What was happening to the men on site in Zambia? What could we tell them? Who, indeed, was going to pay their wages or even their fares home? Rumours started to come through. They had been surrounded by the army, turned out of their offices, barred from their cars, brought up from underground by troops. Meanwhile, by some fortunate piece of timing given only to a very few, Angus Paton and his partner, Paul Back, were on the site at the time. Indeed, Paton, who, following a meeting with Barlow Lyde on Saturday 27 January, had arrived on the site the afternoon before receivership was announced, told David Harries he just 'happened to know' that any further moves to save the situation were too late.

But while all this agonizing was going on, where was the receiver?

I was not surprised, and was even gratified, to hear later that after the staff in Zambia had been ejected, every piece of paper in their offices, whether company business or not, was commandeered, examined and microfilmed, and only returned to Mitchells many months later. My pleasure came from knowing that there were on site notes of many of the conferences which had taken place with counsel over the previous nine months at which he had expressed himself with very considerable clarity. As these documents would no longer be privileged, I was looking forward to some of them being revealed at the trial.

The newspapers had, of course, been busy, and the morning editions contained numerous quotations and speculations, supported by comments from John Gillum of Samuel Montagu.

I found some of these singularly ill-balanced and wondered at their purpose. Were they going to strengthen the receiver's hand? Were they going to inspire confidence and prevent things from disintegrating into total disorder? Were they intended to help anybody? And, if so, who?

And where was the receiver?

The newspapers were also reporting on the share dealings and on a request by John Gillum that the Stock Exchange should make an inquiry, as rightly it should have done. As expected, the inquiries initiated by the committee set up by the Stock Exchange Council were primarily directed to me. I was able to satisfy myself, and I assume the Council, that whatever else had caused the collapse of the Stock Exchange price, it had nothing to do with dealings emanating from Mitchells. I did, however, note some of the names from the list of dealings that was sent to me, and in due course was able to identify transactions that had resulted directly from holders being advised that a receiver was about to be appointed. I was also able to identify the City sources from which this information came. But try as I might, I could not arouse any interest at the Council. Had the Council applied its resources to the matter, I would also have liked to know more about what lay behind an article published in *The Times* of 21 December – just in the middle of discussions which we were having in the City. After referring to the fact that Mitchells was 'once again in the backwash of reports of serious difficulties at Kariba' it noted the drop in the share price that had taken place steadily since the beginning of November (i.e. following our abortive Lusaka meetings). More significantly it noted that a 'big put option' had been arranged on 18 December. A put option is a reasonably sophisticated operation even today, when the market in options has been widened and made far more popular. In December 1972 it was a much rarer bird and a transaction such as that in Mitchell shares could hardly have passed unnoticed – as indeed *The Times* report testifies – in City circles. It would not be unreasonable to suspect that it was one of those occasions when sophistication had been accompanied by at least considerable erudition, if not inside knowledge. If Mitchells had succeeded in solving its Kariba problem it might well have fulfilled the London Business School forecast as to its growth prospects, in which case the put option would have been a very expensive speculation. As it was it would certainly have been of interest to us to have known who it was who had acquired such a vested interest in our failure. In the event an enigmatic statement was issued to the effect that a list of share dealings had been sent to me, but that I had indicated that I was unable to help. Perhaps I was unduly sensitive, but it seemed to me to be an announcement that was calculated to raise eyebrows and I have been conscious of a reaction ever since. If the Stock Exchange is serious in its desire to root out insider dealing, then it must not allow its curiosity to wane when it approaches hallowed ground.

There were indeed many things going through my mind that morning. But above all I was frustrated, knowing that the whole organization was waiting for the lead it desperately needed, but which without the receiver no one could give.

Rumours started coming through from the City. Mitchells were to be the subject of a swift and total annihilation. Why? And how did people know?

It was also rumoured that the receiver was tied up with Kinnear Moodie Concrete Limited. Why? What conceivable plan would lead a receiver of a group of companies to start his assessment with one of them? Of course, it did not require genius to know that the 12½ acres of industrial land which the company owned adjacent to London

187

airport was a very valuable asset. But that was not going to run away. What about the rest of the business? What about the management, which was waiting for decisions and for a reassertion of authority which had been so dramatically removed?

So that first morning went on. There were SOSs from Zambia and from the wives and relatives of staff. Everyone wanted guidance and there was no one to give it. Bewilderment began to give way to anxiety and then to resentment. Were we too busy to worry about them? It would have been so easy to reassure and to rally. But pious statements to the press expressing concern for the welfare of the staff did little for the company where the needs of the moment were simply not being met.

Where was the receiver? At last the answer came. He was in the building.

There had been no courtesies, no telephone calls, no communications to me of any kind. Apparently he had just installed himself in the office which Coopers had already been using.

To make sure that there was no room for misunderstanding, I made my way to this office. My skill, knowledge and management capacity were at the disposal of anyone who needed them. In the interests of the creditors and shareholders I was willing to work in any capacity.

This was my first encounter with Paul Shewell. He paid scant attention to what I had to say. He got up, walked out of his office, and as he went down the corridor told me that he would see me the following Wednesday. It was obvious that for some unknown reason I was being deliberately isolated.

I returned to my office with the realization that we had a fight on our hands. I had numerous calls from the press, one of which was from Sidney Lenssen, the editor of *New Civil Engineer* – the journal of the Institution of Civil Engineers with a world-wide circulation. Lenssen previously built up *Construction News* from what was virtually a labour sheet – known irreverently within the industry as the 'Jackers Journal' – to being a powerful voice and almost required reading within the industry. He had taken up his post with the *New Civil Engineer* on the understanding that he would transform the Institution's existing journal from a constant drain on resources into a profitable enterprise and had received in return an absolute assurance that there would be no editorial influence.

I invited Lenssen to come to Peterborough where I had assembled an outline of the story with all the supporting documents. I left him alone with them. After four hours he emerged, shattered by what he had read, and determined to write it up in his journal. Under the heading 'The Story of Borehole Number 4', and featured on the cover, his account appeared in the following week's issue. (Borehole Number 4 was part of the original programme upon which the 1961 report was supposed to be based. It was the one nearest the centre of the underground machine hall.) His courageous and essentially comprehensive story constituted a devastating indictment of the guilty men at Kariba. And yet they didn't raise their heads above the parapets. A story of waste, inefficiency, corruption and a complete disregard for all moral values evoked no reaction. Once again the establishment had woven a protective cocoon around one of its number.

This is the sort of luxury that the Third World should not be called upon to subsidize.

On Friday, the second day of the receivership, I sent a circular letter to the staff, feeling that they deserved some message, and knowing they were hurt at being ignored. It was not the rallying call I would have liked to have given, but it was the best I could do in the circumstances. However, even the draft had to be submitted to the receiver, through accredited channels. Adjusted, it went out as follows:

> I am sorry that it has not been possible for me to write to you with any certainty regarding your own future or that of the company because, as you will realise, this matter is now entirely out of my hands. At the end of a very sad week, however, I feel that I must write and say that I have been proud of the standards that we have preserved in this company and proud of the team that helped to build it up. None of us is blameless, we all make mistakes, and there are always better ways of doing things, but as a company there is no cause for any of us to be ashamed. Not least, my admiration goes to all those at Kariba who have put up an incredible show in the face of most appalling adversity.
>
> The failure of the group will affect many people in many ways, some of them more sad and even tragic than others. *As chairman I am conscious of all of them and of the responsibility which I must bear.*
>
> At Kariba I have seen the staff close to the project exerting an almost superhuman effort in which they have not spared themselves for a moment and this has been reflected elsewhere in the group. My admiration and gratitude for the spirit that has been shown is unbounded and it would be wrong of me not to pay tribute to all concerned, even in the present unhappy circumstances, but as long as geological information given to contractors, even under warranty,

189

contains so little that relates to the facts, it is difficult to see how repetitions of such unhappy situations as we have run into are ever going to be avoided.

I wish I could give more help to you all, but unfortunately it is no longer within my power. What limited advice I may be able to give, however, will certainly be at the disposal of anybody who asks for it.

The words in italics were the receiver's contribution: my own draft had mentioned a shared responsibility, with myself bearing the major burden. To me the important thing was that a message should go out.

What was happening?

In the days that followed the receiver's appointment, the atmosphere was heavy with secrecy. In an organization where free communication had been the essence of our management philosophy, suddenly there were only rumours, and most of those were picked up from the press. What was happening?

To find out one has to go back to the insistence of John Gillum that the announcement of the appointment of a receiver should be delayed until the close of business on the Stock Exchange at 3.30 p.m. on 31 January. If the reasons behind that decision remain obscure, the consequences do not. It was clear from Peppiatt's call that the information had gone to Washington. And it could be inferred from Paton's presence at Kariba that it didn't come as a surprise to him. If it was already 'too late' when I phoned John Gillum in the morning, how many more people were in the know? Obviously it was known in the City where share dealings were suspended at midday following the collapse in the share price.

But during the day there was a series of events of the greatest importance. I subsequently learned that notwithstanding Francis's telephone call to me on the evening of 31 January, he had already been very active. I do not pretend to understand what took place between the decision taken by the Board on the evening of 30 January and my first meeting with the receiver on 1 February. I do, however, know that Francis received a call from the City, whether before the announcement had been made or after is unclear, to the effect that a receiver had been appointed and that within hours he was able to tell his host at a cocktail party that Tarmac had acquired Mitchells. Long before I met Shewell, or even knew his name, the matter appears to have been all over.

Secrecy was paramount and by the Sunday morning Shewell and

Francis shook hands on a deal whereby the bulk of our assets were to pass into a new company which would be under Tarmac's control and Shewell was given an assurance that he would receive at least £3 million, i.e. enough to meet the requirements of the secured creditors – the actual consideration being dependent upon the trading results of the company. The subsequent complex agreement whereby Tarmac secured these assets was drawn up by Tarmac and signed by Shewell ten days later. From the point of view of Francis and Tarmac, who were well experienced in this type of operation, it was a superb deal. From the point of view of the receiver it was absurd, and nobody with knowledge of the industry and working in the interests of the creditors and the shareholders would have put a signature to it. In due course, as will be seen, it was to be the subject of the most severe strictures on the part of the liquidator to the Group, but by that time it was too late.

To think that I had worried for months about the company's duty to preserve assets!

Not surprisingly, it took a very long time for the liquidator to obtain a copy of this agreement, and then it was only given to him on condition that I should not be allowed to see it. Anybody familiar with the industry would have seen that the outcome of the agreement would be substantially a matter for Tarmac's discretion. However, there were a number of other features which were even worse. The first of these was that the agreement provided that the consideration to be paid by Tarmac should be based on trading results for the period ending 31 December 1975. This meant that the liquidator was kept out of funds for over five years.

Typical of the attitude adopted by the receiver was that he included a company in the Tarmac agreement which had a shareholders' surplus of nearly £600,000, even though this company was neither a charging subsidiary under the Prudential trust deed, nor a cross guarantor of the group's indebtedness to the Midland Bank. By the time this company had been through the sausage machine provided by the Tarmac agreement, the shareholders' surplus of £574,836 was reduced to a yield to the liquidator of £156,628. I do not yet know how this matter was finally resolved between the liquidator and the receiver.

According to calculations made by the liquidator in 1977, the losses resulting from what he described as the 'receiver's action in selling the assets of the group with unnecessary haste and at gross undervalue' amounted to some £4.6–5 million. The liquidator's figures were, however, accountant's figures. As a contractor, and one who was

191

familiar with the assets which were so precipitately sold, I would assess the loss to be very much higher.

As an example of the treatment of assets under the Tarmac deal, our plant company, Anglo Scottish Plant, was typical. With modern, well equipped plant and workshops standing on twenty acres of ground at Peterborough, and with further depots at Leeds and Glasgow, the company had two hundred employees and a very successful, fully integrated and autonomous management. There had been an instant rush of enquiries about it from plant hire companies when the receivership was announced – but they were never considered. This very successful operation was included in the Tarmac deal purely on the basis of a discount to the already heavily written down book values of the plant. In fact, Shewell gave Anglo Scottish Plant an instruction to stop trading in the first few hours of his appointment and their managing director, Keith Lawson, virtually refused. When Shewell said that he could have no money, he replied that he didn't need any. With so many other things to be sorted out, Lawson was left on his own for some months and the company, now operating as part of the Tarmac group, had amassed £700,000 on deposit and was earning interest before the end of the year. Thereafter, as Anglo Scottish Plant was run down and integrated with Tarmac's plant department, Lawson, discouraged, left and set up his own plant consultancy – to return to Tarmac four years later as Plant Director in charge of their international operation. At the time of writing he is Director and General Manager of their UK and International Operations, including their hire subsidiary controlling some £40 million plant.

Assets not mentioned in the Tarmac deal were treated no better: Kinnear Moodie Concrete, which specialized in the manufacture of precast concrete tunnel linings and was internationally recognized as being pre-eminent in this field, had superb modern plant and equipment standing on a twelve and a half acre industrial site at Feltham, adjacent to London Airport. With £600,000 worth of stock, £650,000 worth of debtors and a £2 million order book, it too, had a first class autonomous management who had grown up within the company. On the night of Shewell's appointment – and at a time when, as chairman of the company, I still had not even learned his name – Shewell phoned the managing director, Rupert McBean and instructed him to be at his, Shewell's, office in the morning. McBean refused and, as it was Thursday, told him that all he wanted from him was a £14,000 cheque to meet an immediate demand for wages. Shewell tried to get very rough but McBean stood his ground and, in the face of implied threats, he told him that as far as he and his team were concerned, they would not have the slightest difficulty in getting themselves relocated if that's what they decided to do. In the event, Shewell sent down one of his acolytes with a £14,000 cheque and a demand for the keys of McBean's car. As the company policy was that staff should own their own cars, he was disappointed. The staff at Feltham derived some satisfaction from seeing him having to find his own way back to London by public transport. Ken Roberts, then chairman of Dowmac (now chairman of the Norcross Group) – one of the biggest precast concrete manufacturers in the world – telephoned me to say that he would come over to see Shewell 'at the drop of a hat'. Neither he nor I found it possible to arrange for him to see Shewell – the only response he got to his inquiries being a formal notice to the effect that all bids had to be in within seven days. Given that Kinnear Moodie Concrete was a very large business with big stocks and order books and was sitting on a valuable site, and with about thirty asset strippers hovering around, Shewell's response to Roberts's enquiry was absurd. As it turned out, he had to extend the seven days because the management demanded the right to approve the purchaser, otherwise Shewell would have only a site for sale as all the staff would have gone. By that time they were legitimately more concerned to protect their own welfare and that of the company than they were to maximize the yield to Shewell. There was even a hold up on the disposal of the company because Shewell had virtually committed the land in the Tarmac deal and he had to disentangle it with Francis before he could complete the sale. Finally, Charterhouse took the business over paying only a sum equal to the massively discounted value of its assets. In the first eight months trading to the end of their financial year the company made a profit of £170,000 with a turnover of just over £2 million. Within six months the Feltham site which had been included in the sale at £500,000 was sold to Bovis for £800,000 with a lease back arrangement, and Kinnear Moodie Concrete stayed there until 1976, at which time the whole area was developed as a light industrial estate and the company, now renamed Charcon, moved to a new site in the Midlands.

I will conclude this brief insight into Shewell's stewardship by referring to our overseas operation in Canada. Here he departed from his normal practice of not consulting the management, with the result that the Canadian companies were purchased by their own management at a figure that was effectively fixed by them. I knew there was a major land deal in the offing and wrote to the receiver asking to be involved, but my request was ignored. Meanwhile, the Canadian directors were concerned to acquire the company before the deal was consummated and were having a struggle to keep the potential purchaser from their door. Putting up virtually no capital, but supported by the company's Canadian bankers, they acquired all the Canadian companies together with their Caribbean subsidiaries, including a ready mix plant and a concrete block-making factory. The chief executive, who had joined Mitchells in this country as a graduate engineer, took fifty-two per cent of the equity and the four other directors took twelve per cent each. They then quickly wound up the company and its subsidiaries, and the chief executive, still young and by now a very rich man, retired to Vancouver to pursue a new way of life. A sidelight on this business was that immediately on the announcement of the receivership, two of the Caribbean executives flew to this country to see Shewell to try to buy the manufacturing plants in Barbados. They were kept waiting and eventually saw him for ten minutes but were given no hearing. They did, however, succeed in getting the companies: they paid BWI$450,000 for them to their new masters in Toronto.

Each of these companies was started personally by me. The young managers had been selected and had grown up with me. I knew them all intimately. Had Shewell, who had no idea of their value, handled them reasonably, or intelligently, there would have been some chance of realizing their true value. Once again, on the evidence, it seems inescapable that my exclusion from the company's affairs had been a fundamental policy decision, imposed on him for reasons that still have to be explained.

I have already described why, in spite of all the resources available, Mitchells had no alternative to receivership as a result of Kariba. It is possible that even before my meeting with the sureties on 14 December, they and the Midland Bank knew more about the financial background to Kariba than we did because I have since learned the Prudential had been seeking information as to where the money to pay us for our work was to come from. It is even possible that this is why the Midland Bank insisted that we should not dispose of any assets in the months running up to receivership, and that if we did, the proceeds would have to be devoted to reducing or eliminating our overdraft. As long as the City is run as a secret society one can only conjecture. I am, however, entitled to be deeply critical of the fact that, although our bankers and our financial advisers had a full eight months notice, they failed to assist us in any way in preparing the

194

contingency programme for which I had persistently canvassed in case the worst should happen.

There are at least three other counts on which I regard Shewell's behaviour and performance as inexcusable. First, why did he not immediately follow up Freshfields' call to the effect that the World Bank had instructed the receivership to be stopped? If that approach had been too late to stop the formal appointment, it was certainly not too late to put before the Bank a balanced account of the company's affairs which, had it been available, would have shown that even a partial payment of the sums due to us at Kariba would have been sufficient to eliminate the company's operating overdraft with its principal bankers. Second, the difference between success and failure in the Peterborough Hospital arbitration would amount to £2 million. I will comment on this matter later, but with such a sum at issue, why was it that the receiver attended a conference with counsel without me or any other representative of Mitchell Construction?

The third item relates to the Kariba contract itself. Mitchells had ploughed a tremendous amount of money into Kariba, which was waiting to be dug up. It was only necessary to survive. Bill Francis was, above all, a contractor, and Tarmac had the necessary resources. A round-the-table discussion would have established its potential yield. Why was this potential never explained or discussed? If Tarmac didn't want it why was no effort made to find someone else who did?

As for the main group of construction companies, there were many people who would have been interested. Those who visited Peterborough were fobbed off with comparatively junior staff, while the chairman of one large group of public companies complained to me bitterly that he had been out of the country for only two days, but by the time he got back it was too late. Michael Jordan was to tell me in discussion, before his appointment as liquidator, that when Shewell arrived in his office on the 31 January (I understood from overseas) there were instructions on his desk as to how the receivership should be dealt with down to the last detail. It was this that made Michael Jordan's early appointment so vital. These instructions are among papers that I have requested which relate to the affairs of the holding company while Shewell acted as receiver and manager. I am advised that they are the company's property and that we are entitled to them. As will be seen, he has so far (May 1987) refused to surrender them.

Following the liquidator's appointment there was one final farce. The company had a flat at Abbey Lodge overlooking Regents Park which I occupied. As a result of personal connections I had been able to buy it for the company, redecorate it and equip it at minimal cost. With the growth of the property market it represented a very considerable asset, not least because much of the work had been done by Dudley Poplack who went on to refurbish the American Embassy and, thereafter, Highgrove House and Kensington Palace for the Prince and Princess of Wales. I recommended to Shewell that it should be sold as it stood. Instead he got an agent's valuation and then instructed Sotheby's to remove what they wanted allowing what was left to be sold to a dealer who took it away on a lorry. As regards what was left after this destruction – the sale of the flat itself – this proved to be the one instance in which the liquidator was able to act before it was completed. He insisted on a far higher figure than that at which it had been sold by Shewell. In view of the millions of pounds worth of assets which had already gone beyond recall, this was truly ironical.

I get the sack

Shewell, it will be recalled, had said that he would see me on Wednesday 7 February, and, sure enough, he did. I telephoned to remind him that we had an appointment at midday, and he met me to let me know that after twenty-four years with the company my services were no longer required.

What were his instructions? Had there been a call for a ritual sacrifice? Certainly nobody in the industry, not even suppliers who were bound to suffer, had demanded such a gesture. Was there some more personal reason behind his behaviour, or did receivers always behave like that? It certainly appeared to me then, and subsequently, that my personal destruction ranked high on his list of priorities, and was part of his instructions. But if so, where did they originate and why? Certainly my exclusion from Mitchell matters would be good news to CAPCO and Paton, but who else would benefit?

I had, of course, made it clear at the penultimate meeting with Coopers, at which Hobson took the chair, that the responsibility for our demise rested not with KNBC, but with CAPCO and Gibbs, whom I suspected were jointly implicated in fraud. Even if Hobson did not immediately recognize that this should have barred his firm from further involvement, one would at least have expected that Coopers would have realized that they had a special responsibility to protect Mitchells' avenues of redress and ensure that the one person who by this time knew more about the Kariba contract than any other – myself – should be kept available to help. They must have known how important it was for those with whom they were associated that the facts about Kariba should not emerge: surely they would have been wise to recognize the need to act impartially and so avoid doing anything that could be interpreted harshly if the truth came out?

Kariba apart, I had a unique knowledge of the group's activities and of its worth. What was to be gained by my dismissal? What was the reason for the hostility shown to me afterwards? I had made my services available to the liquidator, but why were staff, who were ready to help, warned that they might be in breach of duty by assisting me with the Kariba proceedings? There was, perhaps, no reason why Shewell should have accepted my opinions or my advice, but there would be few in the industry who would have suggested that they were not worth listening to.

Immeasurable and irretrievable damage was done in those first few days and many questions remain to be answered.

A meeting with the receiver and the liquidator

It was not until 13 February 1975, two years after the receivership, that at my request I had my first full discussion with Shewell following his appointment. The meeting took place at Cork Gully's * in the presence of Michael Jordan, who had been appointed liquidator.

I had asked for this meeting because at every turn, and especially over Kariba, the liquidator was being held up through a lack of funds, which was entirely due to Shewell's handling of the receivership. I wanted to know from Shewell why this was the first occasion he and I had discussed the affairs of Mitchell Construction.

He replied that he had thought I was in need of a holiday and would not have been able to assist him in 1973. This was too absurd. He had not seen me, he had not spoken to me, and he had made his decisions without reference to me. I told Shewell that it was well known in the City that he had been given instructions as to how he was to deal with the company, and I wanted to know whence these instructions had come. I detailed many of the instances where I considered he had not taken reasonable care to ascertain the value of assets before he had disposed of them, and I explained the difficulty that was being created even now by his lack of interest in Kariba. I told him it was obvious that his quite disastrous agreement with Tarmac had been drawn up

---

*Sir Kenneth Cork's well-known accountancy firm, which specializes in receivership and liquidation.

without the benefit of any expertise on his side and that it would be clear to anyone with knowledge of the industry that he would only get out of the new Mitchells 1973 company what Tarmac decided to give him.

Eventually, Shewell asked me, 'albeit late in the day', if I was prepared to assist him. I replied that my services had always been available and remained so, but that I did not see how I could help him in his discussions with Bill Francis. The agreement existed, Francis and Tarmac had behaved properly, and it seemed to me that Shewell was more likely to win concessions from a position of weakness, hoping for Tarmac's goodwill, than by trying to bring pressure to bear.

Francis was to tell me later that Tarmac made a lot more money out of the deal than he had anticipated – though this was only to be expected given the way it was handled by Shewell and, in particular, his reliance upon Coopers' highly prejudiced second report. To Francis it must have seemed like taking sweets from children and notwithstanding his satisfaction with the eventual outcome, it was still many million pounds short of what could have been accomplished had Shewell not acted in secrecy. Millions of pounds which even on the basis of the deal that was entered into, and about which Jordan complained so bitterly, would have been shared between Tarmac and the receiver if the company and its management had been retained as an integrated unit, rather than being broken up and destroyed as it was.

Bill Francis and I had had a close association over many years, both within the Federation and on other bodies, including a private discussion group. He had made no secret of his interest in acquiring Mitchell Construction for the Tarmac Group and, in particular, how it could fit into Tarmac's plans. After the agreement with Mitchells was signed, Bill asked me to meet him in London, where he apologized for the way the negotiations had been conducted, but explained that it was 'a commercial opportunity he could not afford to miss'. I told him that I had no criticism whatsoever of his behaviour: his duty was to Tarmac and it was for others to protect Mitchells. My good personal relationship with him has continued to this day and I have never felt any resentment towards him or Tarmac. But the fact remains that a very different deal would have been negotiated if we had had expertise on our side. As it was, the Tarmac agreement was a disaster.

After Shewell had left, Jordan was very scathing about his performance, and told me that the Tarmac deal had aroused great bitterness among the trade creditors. In his opinion at least £2.5 million had already been lost to the creditors and he believed they would be looking for redress from Coopers, probably through their professional indemnity insurers. Nearly three years later, when he was suffering great frustration and had had a better opportunity of assessing the consequences of Shewell's receivership, Jordan asked his solicitors, Messrs Oppenheimer, Nathan and Vandyk to obtain counsel's opinion as to whether there could be any redress. Accordingly, instructions were sent to Allan Heyman QC. These recorded the liquidator's concern at the receiver's actions in selling the assets of the group with 'unnecessary haste and at gross undervalue'. While recognizing the difficulty of challenging a receiver's actions, the instructions repeated the allegation that the receiver had 'blatantly failed to sell the assets at anything near their proper value' and concluded by saying that 'In the circumstances of this case, and having regard to the substantial losses involved,' the instructing solicitors felt the liquidator 'might indeed have adequate grounds for challenging the receiver's actions'. I do not know what advice was received or whether it would have been varied had the relationship between Coopers, Gibbs and CAPCO been known.

The disposal of such a large body of the company's assets and the way it was done, closed the door to the possibility of an early conclusion to the receivership.

The Peterborough Hospital arbitration

I am extremely sorry that despite all your efforts and those of your colleagues, the Kariba contract has necessitated the appointment of the receiver. I have greatly admired your fortitude over the past months and the way you have borne the burdens placed upon you as chairman. I trust you will not hesitate to get in touch with me if there is any way I may be of help.

Keith Goodfellow QC,
counsel for Mitchell Construction,
February 1973

It has been a great tragedy. You have always had my unbounded admiration for your enormous ability and you now have my total sympathy. We hope the arbitration will continue as we regard ourselves as committed – and committed to a worthy cause. Meanwhile you are at the forefront of our minds and hearts and will remain so.

Michael Chevasse QC,
counsel for Mitchell Construction,
February 1973

An account of the Peterborough Hospital arbitration – in progress at the time of the receiver's appointment and whose findings were finally published on 3 December 1973 – provides a pertinent detour at this point in the story.

The case was important for a number of reasons. From the liquidator's point of view, success would have meant that notwithstanding Shewell's actions in tying up so much of the group's resources in the Tarmac agreement, there would have been funds available to pursue the Kariba litigation. From a personal point of view, it had other special significance. It was one of the tenets of my management philosophy that any fool could disagree and therefore the fact that the arbitration took place at all was a sign of some failure. On the other hand, the climate had changed since my early professional days. At that time any suggestion that one should resort to arbitration was considered an extreme affront. More recently, and particularly with the increased incidence of the public sector client, arbitration or its threat seems to be regarded as just one more step in the negotiating procedure. But for me Peterborough Hospital represented a first. It remains the only occasion on which I have ever appeared in any litigation involving a construction contract. Peterborough Hospital, however, had a further special significance for me, because I was well known locally and had been deeply concerned about the troubles that arose while the contract was in progress. I had followed the arbitration closely and had read through every bit of evidence that had been given in the 226 days since its inception, and I was grateful for the two manuscript letters I received from counsel which seemed to offer at least some confirmation that my confidence in my judgement was not misplaced.

The contract and the subsequent arbitration were significant for one other thing. I accepted that my views about reform were unpalatable amongst some of the industry's establishment, but it was none the less disturbing to learn from many quarters that both I and the company were the target of constant attack – and even that a decision had been taken that we were to be destroyed. For most of us such threats and boasts don't seem to belong to the real world. But as the years went by I found good reason to know otherwise. Among so many other inexplicable happenings, the Peterborough Hospital arbitration brought to the surface a great deal of evidence and at least one irrefutable example of the campaign that was going on behind the scenes.

Mitchells and their international activities had attracted strong local interest in Peterborough. We took pride in having opened up a whole range of new opportunities for the young people of the city. We had initiated sophisticated training schemes within the company, and many of our Peterborough trainees are now very successful in their own right.

Because we had such a strong local image, to say nothing of a large staff, many of whom were intimately involved in Peterborough affairs, I was concerned that apart from having built Peterborough power station, our own offices and those of Mitchell Engineering Limited, we had done very little work locally and we had no major projects in prospect. And so Peterborough Hospital was chosen as our showpiece.

The first contract at the hospital had been for the nurses' home, which was secured by George Wimpey. Although we were unaware of it at the time, the experience had led the chairman of Wimpey, Sir Godfrey Mitchell, that grand old man of British construction, to decide never to work on a Ministry of Health project again – a decision which was certainly maintained for many years.

Mitchells were awarded the second contract, for the workshop and boilerhouse, which was successfully completed, and then we were awarded the contract for the main hospital building. It later emerged that the lowest tender, which was from a very well-known public group, was rejected in favour of our own. This would seem to have been a vote of confidence in Mitchells; however, although the chairman of the lowest tenderer felt aggrieved at first, he later congratulated himself that their offer had been rejected.

The problem that arose at Peterborough had a simple root. As so often happens in contracts that are incompetently administered, the design had not been finalized, and it was not until after the contract was let that the architect ordered a revised, and very complex, window design directly with the subcontractor. The construction involved a whole series of interrelated operations by different trades, each waiting upon the other, and all having to work to extraordinary tolerances in order to assemble the whole. It would have made an interesting architectural forerunner to the Rubik cube, but as an exercise in practical construction it was a disaster.

The magnitude of the problem can be judged by the fact that the subcontractor, a very large company and one of the leaders in the field, lost £250,000 merely trying to fix the windows. More serious from our point of view was the fact that progress on the whole contract became dependent on the windows being fixed and many interrelated operations being dovetailed. In the meantime, the fact that the building was not wind- and weather-proof resulted in terrible disruption, and loss of control over all the other subcontracted trades.

Those responsible for the design took every possible step to avoid being blamed, either for the extra costs involved or for the delay, and it was soon our turn to learn about the treatment suffered by others who had worked under their direction. We tried hard to maintain reasonable relationships and secure what progress we could. We could hardly do otherwise: Peterborough Hospital was the principal landmark to be seen from my office window and it became a permanent challenge. Not only did I visit the site regularly, but head office personnel gave it the best possible attention. We allocated to it some of our very best foremen.

Half-way through our time on the project we had done just about everything we could to cope with the difficulties and cultivate a better atmosphere on the site. At that stage, we appointed one of our most senior agents as a full-time manager, resident on the contract. Nearing retirement, he had an extremely impressive record, having been agent on many major contracts, including the Chapelcross nuclear power station and the nuclear chemical separation plant at Windscale. He came to Peterborough in response to an appeal made personally by me. It was my view that his experience and tact would enable him to convey to the hospital board's representatives a better understanding of the problems that beset the site.

As the situation became more serious, criticism of Mitchells became indiscriminate; the clerk of works led the attack on the standard of our workmanship. In response, the director in charge invited, at my request, the heads of the various trades at the Brixton School of Building, none of whom was known to me, to make a report. At the same time I asked a retired ex-director of works from the Atomic Energy Authority to visit the site and report on what he found. I was confident that I was not mistaken in my own assessment of the workmanship. It was as good as, if not better than, any that could be found in the country – a view endorsed by all the reports when they were received. But nothing we could do could secure acknowledgement of this on the site.

A chance meeting between one of our directors and William Tatton-Brown, the chief architect of the Ministry of Health, led to my inviting him to meet me and to visit the site. He accepted but then it appeared that he was being put under considerable pressure to cancel the visit. However, I pressed him very hard and eventually he came to Peterborough.

He visited our offices, but I was astonished when told that he was under direct instructions not to visit the site. We stood at my office window, looking out at the hospital, and I said how absurd this was. There were major problems on the site, which were being attributed to our supervision and the quality of our workmanship. He was obviously well briefed about the contract, and I was concerned because he spoke as though it had been established that we were at fault. We were both experienced, and I considered that the work was not merely good, but really first-class. I was willing to go round to the hospital there and then to show him the workmanship and put an end to the argument. I told him he was free to interview each of the senior staff, the trades foremen, the engineers and in fact anyone he wished to talk to, in order to satisfy himself whether or not they were an excellent team, dedicated to overcoming all the difficulties. We could not have orchestrated such an examination and he could therefore have settled the matter by making a five-minute journey. But he was immovable.

There was clearly something wrong, and when a mutual friend suggested that I might meet Brian Walden, then First Secretary of the Treasury, I was grateful for the opportunity. The chaotic state of construction throughout the country was in the news and I told him of our experience. He expressed interest and undertook to make some inquiries. He attempted to let some light into the matter, and even tried to organize a joint high-level inspection by representatives of the company and the ministry, but in the end he had to admit defeat. He told me he was mystified, because this resistance was quite unusual, and he came to the conclusion there was some influence at work which he could neither identify nor penetrate.

The contract was becoming a nightmare for the company, though this element of the inexplicable was becoming familiar. In the meantime the question of progress was becoming a matter of public concern. The labour on the site objected to the hospital board's behaviour and particularly to the conduct of the clerk of works who was audibly critical of everything they did. As a result, the MP for Peterborough, Sir Harmer Nichols, himself a former Parliamentary Secretary of the Ministry of Works, took the matter up with the Minister of Health. The usual pattern emerged, and I can do no more than quote from an account he gave much later to the press.

Apparently, he accused the Minister, Kenneth Robinson, of a 'grave dereliction of duty, for not becoming involved. I have warned him by letter, by private conversation, and finally by parliamentary questions, of the deteriorating relations between the hospital board and the contractors but he preferred to do nothing.'

We, as a company, could do no more than press towards our own solution. The vital thing was to re-establish a sound programme and with it the confidence of our subcontractors. Subcontractors who have been continually disrupted through no fault of their own not only lose interest and establish priorities elsewhere, but can no longer be tied to their commitments. It was decided that the whole works should be replanned, and all possible resources devoted to the completion of the shell, i.e. overcoming the window problems and those of the associated trades. In order to re-establish confidence and goodwill, all the subcontractors were invited to a full-day conference in Coventry so they would know exactly what was required of them and could raise any queries. It was an exceptional step, to which the subcontractors responded well by pledging their full cooperation and support. We had, incidentally, sought and failed to get the involvement of the board's architectural department in the preparation of the programme, but they seemed to be completely ignorant of computerized methods of programming which were standard throughout the company.

Our contract provided that 'if the contractor fails to proceed with the works with reasonable diligence and if he should continue such default for fourteen days after a notice of such default has been given to him by the architect', then the employer could terminate the contract. The contract further provided that a notice under this clause should not be given unreasonably or vexatiously and that it would in any case be void if the employer was in breach of the contract at the time it was given.

In July 1966, as soon as we had solved all the cladding and window problems and got the building sealed, we received notice of default. Though we made the job an absolute priority over the next two weeks, we felt increasingly helpless, as we realized there was no intention on the other side of doing anything but terminate the contract. Promptly at the end of fourteen days we received notice to this effect.

In view of the immense damage done to the company both locally and nationally, we immediately initiated proceedings alleging wrongful dismissal. At a hearing in the High Court, the hospital board's application for a stay in the proceedings until after the hospital was completed by another contractor was rejected. However, the hospital board appealed on the grounds that the contract provided that disputes should be settled by arbitration after the works were completed. The hospital board's appeal was allowed and thus it was that more than five years elapsed before the matter came in front of an arbitrator.

The matter before the arbitrator was the company's claim that the contract had been wrongfully determined, and it appeared there were three issues to be decided: first, whether or not the company was proceeding with reasonable diligence at the time the notice was given; second, if this was decided against the company, whether or not the resultant default continued for fourteen days during which the notice was effective; and, finally, whether the notice had been given unreasonably or vexatiously, or whether the hospital board was in breach of the contract at the time the notice was given. There was nothing in this to suggest we were about to embark upon an arbitration that was to last for a record 239 days. After 137 days, when all Mitchells' witnesses had been examined and cross-examined, both Queen's counsel appearing for Mitchells expressed themselves bewildered. They had never understood how the contract had come to be terminated in the first place, nor how the hospital board could defend the action, but they had assumed that there must be some deficiency in their brief and that evidence would emerge which would account for the hospital board's behaviour. But no such evidence had emerged. In addition, they said that the hearing was being spun out with what appeared to be endless irrelevancies. They both assured us that a judge would not have allowed a court's time to be so wasted: however, an arbitrator was in a far more difficult position when it came to challenging the way that counsel chose to present their case.

It would be pointless to try to summarize the hearing, but significantly there did emerge during our examination of the hospital board's documents an interesting report from the unfortunate Tatton-Brown. Although I had failed to get him to visit the site, he had apparently reported back that he had been impressed by my sincerity and my wish to get on with the contract. He also noted that I was very sensitive to adverse publicity, particularly in Peterborough. Against this it appeared that he had had highly defamatory accounts of what purported to be Mitchells' behaviour on contracts carried out under the direction of two different consultants. The important thing was, as was brought out in evidence, that although Mitchells had at one time employed these consultants on work carried out within the group and for the group, our relationships with them had never been other than cordial, and we had never carried out work for others under their direction.

I knew of some of their close and profitable associations and had no doubt that, wittingly or otherwise, they had been caught up in a smear campaign, with which we had long been familiar. There are circumstances in which people can become very susceptible to suggestion if it is made to them in suitably impressive and influential surroundings. Thus are myths – those most formidable weapons – created.

Many people were mystified by the Peterborough Hospital arbitration, but I have no doubt that this brief cameo encompassed what it was all about.

The arbitration had lasted 226 days when the receiver was appointed and he arranged a conference with the company's legal advisers for 5 February 1973. I opened this account of the Peterborough Hospital arbitration with quotations from letters I received from the two Queen's counsel who had represented Mitchells. It will be recalled that as part of the process of battening down and containing the disruption caused by Kariba I had assumed responsibility for the coordination of the hospital arbitration. I had attended the hearings when they appeared to be of particular importance, but every night the transcripts of the evidence given during the day had been delivered to me and I had read them and commented on them, even though it frequently had to be done in the early hours of the morning. There is no question that my presence at the conference with counsel would have been helpful, and certainly could not have done harm, and yet this conference went ahead without my knowledge. What was at the root of this extraordinary behaviour by Shewell?

The record of the conference is illuminating. Counsel spoke with unaccustomed forthrightness. On matters of law he was confident of his view, but even if the contract was to be interpreted the way the hospital board's counsel contended, it would make no difference. Mitchells, he declared, would win. He maintained that Mitchells' case had got stronger throughout, while the evidence of the board's witnesses had shown how inept they were. He added that the respondents knew they were going to lose, and that they were applying for security for costs. If they did not get that security, they would drop their counterclaim and walk away. As for the motive behind the whole proceedings, he had a strong suspicion that it was to 'grind Mitchells into the ground'. Indeed, this was the widely held belief within the industry.

The successful outcome of the arbitration would have resulted in at least £1 million flowing into receivership, which would have been enough to put the liquidator in funds. Apart from our counsel's confidence of an award on the basis of the facts, the hospital board was in clear breach on a number of legal issues which we were entitled to put to the courts for a ruling. A ruling on any one of them in our favour would have invalidated the notice of determination and thereby ensured our success in the action. From my knowledge of the background influences at work, and even without regard to the sums involved, I would have advised most strongly in favour of this, but it was not done.

The reaction of both Mitchells' counsel to the injustice that was being done can be judged by their offer to carry on with the arbitration for whatever the receiver felt he could pay them. They even went so far as to offer to continue for nothing. And yet with the case virtually complete, and with so much at stake, Shewell appears to have had no concern, other than to find the shortest possible route to conclusion. This provided yet another occasion when he failed to consult or inform himself, and therefore the responsibility for what followed was entirely his.

It had been confidently expected on our side that once the hearing was completed the arbitrator's decision would not be long delayed, but this was not to be. In the event it was not until 3 December 1973, seven months after the completion of the hearing, that the arbitrator published his award. It was simple and quite devastating. He found that 'the claim is dismissed and the counterclaim succeeds'. The award included seven years' interest and costs against Mitchells.

Keith Goodfellow spoke to me on the telephone when the award was handed to me. None of those involved during the arbitration or since have ever questioned the good faith of the arbitrator, but Goodfellow said that the only way that such a decision could have been arrived at was 'by constant whispering in the arbitrator's ear that it was time to teach somebody a lesson'. Later, Goodfellow advised the liquidator in a written opinion, 'Although I adhere to the view that the award constitutes a grave miscarriage of justice, unfortunately it exhibits no defect in law.'

The law is now changed: if a similar award was published by an arbitrator today he would be required to give a reasoned award, but in the case of Peterborough Hospital no explanation was ever forthcoming.

By way of postscript, I would add that leaks from the ministry and elsewhere indicated from a very early stage that the board's case was considered to be hopeless, and Goodfellow maintained that they only persisted because the financial burden was carried by public funds.

Goodfellow's opinions were confirmed some years later in an unexpected quarter when I wrote to Perry Mee in July 1981. The only other time I had had any communication with him was when he attended the Kariba meeting in my office at Bedford Square on 14 December 1972, representing the Excess Insurance Company. I needed some information and he was kind enough to provide it. By that time he had returned to America where he practised as an attorney at law. After saying that in his view there were more than sufficient grounds in the Kariba case for Mitchells to obtain relief, he wrote:

> At this point, I should tell you that I consider the role of the receiver to be grossly unfair to unsecured creditors. Mitchells should have won a substantial sum in the arbitration proceedings against the Peterborough Hospital. I say this because, while I was lunching with someone in the City, my companion held a brief conversation with a passer-by in the restaurant. That individual, to whom I was not introduced, in reply to my companion's query as to what he was doing, stated that he was involved in the Peterborough Hospital arbitration proceedings. He went on to say that Mitchells continued to produce evidence against which 'we had no defence'. I gather that the proceedings had been under way for several months. You can imagine my shock when I saw the decision was for the hospital. Is there no duty to prosecute claims vigorously? It would seem receivers are not so obliged in the UK.

Our failure to get an award in the Peterborough Hospital arbitration represented a personal nadir. Through most of 1972 we had been at the mercy of seemingly uncontrollable forces. It had seemed that with the appointment of the receiver the bottom must have been reached, and from there we should be fighting back. But not even the experience of ten months of Shewell's stewardship had prepared me for the trauma and disillusionment of the Peterborough Hospital award.

Sadly, Keith Goodfellow was taken ill and was unable to deliver the final speech in the hospital case; he died soon after and we were deprived of his invaluable advice and detailed knowledge of the contract during the preparation of the Kariba case. But I understand that right up to the time of his death, when relaxing at the end of the day, he would hark back to the 239 days of the Peterborough Hospital arbitration and its extraordinary outcome.

The liquidator

It was soon after the appointment of the receiver that I learned from the press of the formation of an unofficial committee of creditors under the aegis of Cork Gully. Frustrated and unable to prevent what I regarded as the reckless dissipation of the company's assets I immediately telephoned Cork Gully to let them know that I was entirely at their disposal and that I would help them in any way that I could in the interests of the creditors. Thereafter I had meetings with Norman Cork and Michael Jordan, the liquidator-to-be, and I became aware of a most bizarre situation which, whether or not it applies generally, certainly had not been anticipated in relation to the Mitchells receivership.

It appeared that they knew in some detail the instructions that had been given to Shewell and they were convinced that he was going to do everything he could to get rid of assets before the liquidator's appointment. It was necessary for them to act quickly and they were anxious to get into a position where they could look over his shoulder before all was lost.

I was particularly impressed by Michael Jordan's forceful approach and I sought only one assurance before committing myself completely to his aid. I asked him quite directly whether he or his firm had any involvement with McAlpine. If this were the case I would not continue. I explained my reasons to him and only on receiving his categorical reply that his firm had no such involvement did I commit myself. Much later, during a meeting at which I was seeking from him an explanation of how things had gone wrong, he was to tell me, as I thought somewhat shamefacedly, that he had now been admitted to Edwin McAlpine's list of friendships.

As a result of Cork Gully's initiative, a statement of affairs was prepared and presented to a meeting of the creditors at the Chartered Insurance Institute on 27 April 1973 by Michael Jordan, whose appointment as liquidator was now confirmed.

Unfortunately, the receiver had by now beaten Michael Jordan to it by disposing so quickly and so recklessly of so many assets. Most worrying of all was the fact that the settlement under the Tarmac agreement would not be made until after the production of the accounts for the new company for the period ending 31 December 1975. This meant not only that most of the group's assets had been locked up for years ahead but that, in the meantime, the receiver was appropriating the proceeds from all other assets too, on behalf of the secured creditors. He was also retaining £630,000 on behalf of the Midland Bank against any possible liability in respect of the counter guarantee they had given to the sureties for the performance bond. In this way, in spite of the huge potential surplus available, the liquidator was kept out of funds for over five years. Meanwhile he was entirely dependent upon the Prudential and Excess Insurance Companies to finance the Kariba litigation. There was never any doubt in Jordan's mind that, if it had not been for the Kariba contract, Mitchells would still be in business and, recognizing as he did that the company's right of redress in relation to Kariba represented an extremely valuable asset, he repeatedly expressed his bitterness at the five-year delay forced on him before he could come to grips with the litigation in his own right. Against this background the loss of expected funds from the Peterborough arbitration was a particularly savage blow.

IV

The Kariba Litigation

KNBC calls the bond

On 10 July 1973 KNBC called upon each of the sureties for payment of the performance bond. In reply, both the Prudential and the Excess said they were aware that Mitchells were alleging repudiation against KNBC and that it would therefore be more appropriate to leave the matter until that dispute was settled. They went on to point out that they had been induced to enter into the bond by representations as to the rock conditions given in Gibbs' site inspection report, which they had since been advised were inaccurate. They reserved the right to contend that they were entitled to avoid liability under the bond. At the same time, and true to their word, both insurance companies wrote to Gibbs advising them that they would, in the event of KNBC pursuing payment, claim to be indemnified by Gibbs against any liability and expense in which they might be involved. Following these exchanges and their failure to secure payment under the performance bond, KNBC issued a writ in the Queen's Bench Division of the High Court in September 1974.

There had been virtually no market in contractors' performance bonds in the United Kingdom when the Kariba contract was let, and Perry Mee had come to this country to assist Excess in the development of a market in this field. It was he who had taken the lead in the underwriting of Mitchells' Kariba bond. He had already informed KNBC that, in the event of any proceedings being instituted to recover the bond, they would be strenuously defended and it was refreshing to find that, led by him, the sureties now embarked upon a spirited defence. They argued that, contractual matters apart, Gibbs owed a duty of care to any who might be expected to rely upon the accuracy of their geological report. Mee and Walker had both relied on the report, and the expert advice that had been given to their companies resulting from it. They were ready to testify that, bearing in mind the insurer's experience on the earlier, south bank, project, they would not have

213

entered into the bond without the reassurance given in the report.

As the bonding agreement provided that the sureties had recourse to the company if they incurred liability under it, the sureties joined Mitchells in the action as they, too, were at risk. Mitchells, once involved, completed the circle by counterclaiming against KNBC and against Gibbs.

Although this case is apparently complex, owing to the number of parties involved, it was in fact rather more simple than most disputes which arise under civil engineering contracts. There were basically two issues: first, whether or not the site investigation report was indeed accurate, and whether it had been prepared with reasonable care, and, second, if the report was incorrect, whether Gibbs had attempted to renegotiate in good faith and to certify the necessary amounts to restore Mitchells to the position they would have been in had they not run into unforeseen rock conditions. There remained the problem of the receiver keeping Jordan out of funds; however, since there was no conflict in the interests of the sureties and the liquidator, and as one solicitor was acting for all three, the sureties were meanwhile supporting the action.

Fortunately, it was possible for Mitchells to prepare for the litigation on a shoestring. Charles Greenwood, an old family friend and a very capable provincial lawyer, had provided the company with guidance and legal advice since its inception and had joined the board of the holding company when it was floated in 1963. Unfortunately Charles's health had forced him to retire at a crucial time, but one of his junior partners, John Hardwick, who had been involved in his general practice and had assisted him in relation to Mitchells' affairs, was retained by the sureties. Pitched as we were against the serried ranks of London lawyers (KNBC had been granted a moratorium on their right of action against Gibbs and CAPCO, to extend until the completion of the present case, but had insisted on retaining their own lawyers) it was an uneven battle but, with my commitment, and aided by the willing help of a number of ex-Mitchells employees, we were able to hold our own with the minimum of cost. In our circumstances, this was particularly important because it was already clear that the receiver was not inclined to assist with any of the funds at his disposal, and I was particularly anxious not to strain the loyalty of the Prudential and the Excess.

KNBC appointed Beale and Co. with Desmond Wright QC and John Blackburn as their counsel, while Gibbs appointed Barlow, Lyde and Gilbert with David Gardam QC and John Tackaberry as their counsel. The Prudential, the Excess and Mitchells were represented by Hardwick of Greenwoods with K. S. Rokison QC and M. J. Moore-Bick as counsel.

In view of the suggestion made later that costs were a major factor in the decision to abandon the proceedings, it is interesting to note that, at what proved to be the last hearing, Mr Justice Donaldson was informed, in response to his questions, that Mitchells' costs to that date amounted to £55,000. The figure surprised him as much as it did the numerous lawyers appearing on the other side. As that modest sum covered a period of some four and a half years, during which there had been five preliminary hearings in the Queen's Bench Division and one appearance before the Court of Appeal, it suggests that the law does not necessarily have to be ruinously expensive. We had also by that time prepared practically the whole of our case, supported by proofs of evidence from all the most important experts and witnesses. Of course the costs on the other side would have been very much higher: given the possibility of future litigation between them, they had to be represented independently of each other.

The hearing in the Court of Appeal had resulted from attempts by the other side to obtain a ruling that Mitchells' counterclaim should be referred to arbitration in Zambia rather than being decided at the same time as the remainder of the action. As the issues to be decided were virtually identical we had been relieved when Mr Justice Donaldson had rejected the application on the grounds that the proposed change of course had come too late. We were still more relieved when an appeal against his decision was dismissed by Lord Justice Ormerod and Lord Justice Roskill in the Court of Appeal with costs against the Kariba North Bank Company.

Abandoning a job before it is completed is foreign to my nature, but as the years dragged on I wondered whether I might not have to make an exception. I had asked repeatedly when the case was likely to come to trial, but had been told that this would be decided only when all preparations were completed: at that stage an application would be made for a hearing date and then there would be a delay of at least eighteen months. On making further inquiries I found that there was in fact no reason why the date should not be fixed beforehand, and on my insistence an application for a hearing date was included in matters to be heard before Mr Justice Donaldson on 14 March 1979. I was very pleasantly surprised when he fixed a date in October 1980 immediately following the long vacation. The effect of this pronouncement was electric: laywers, on all sides, seemed to leap to life as if they had springs in their bottoms. Too soon! Too soon! All the work that had to be done! And this over six years after the event. Mr Justice Donaldson yielded ground, but slowly, and when he finally fixed the date for April 1981, just over two years ahead, I was immensely relieved.

Refreshing, too, was the way he dealt with the question of the disclosure of documents required from CAPCO. The other side were pleading that, because of the status of the illegal Smith regime, it would not be possible to compel cooperation from CAPCO. I was intrigued by the suggestion that the World Bank and others felt it appropriate to agree to the appointment as agents on such an important project an organization that could not be called to account, and I had expected at least some lengthy submission on this subject. Not so. Mr Justice Donaldson dealt with it crisply and in one sentence: all who were familiar with the real world knew of the many transactions which were taking place in Rhodesia, and he was quite sure that lawyers would not find the difficulty insuperable.

In the long, tortuous history of the Kariba experience, the two hearings before Mr Justice Donaldson and the one before the Court of Appeal were among the few occasions when I felt in touch with reality.

Progress

The hearings before the courts – the preliminary hearings, the hearing before the Court of Appeal, and the hearing at which Mr Justice Donaldson fixed the trial date – were of course procedural, and were conducted quite independently of our preparation for the case. I have dealt with them here for the sake of convenience but will now return to the circumstances following the decision of the Court of Appeal in November 1977 which ensured that the Kariba dispute would be heard in England, and thereby cleared the way for us to assemble all the necessary information to fight our case.

A great deal of work had been done and proofs of evidence had been taken, but I was conscious of being the only person on our side with a technical background, and I was therefore anxious that independent experts should be appointed by the liquidator. I already knew that the other side were to be advised by a firm of quantity surveyors, and one for whom, incidentally, I had a very high regard. In my view, Gibbs' transgressions in the matter of certification were not occasional, marginal or technical, but were blatant and part of a deliberate and sustained policy. In the circumstances I believed it extremely unlikely that the firm they had retained would be prepared to defend their position in court. But it was obviously necessary to provide against this possibility. It might also be necessary to reinforce the resolve of the liquidator and the sureties. I was being given unstinting help by many ex-Mitchells personnel who worked in the evenings and at weekends, at their own expense and without any prospect of reward, and the evidence we now had was overwhelming, but as the sum at issue was clearly going to be in excess of £10 million, it was obviously desirable that our evidence should be submitted to independent experts for evaluation and a report.

In December 1977, realizing how dependent the creditors would be on me, and recognizing the possibility of their concern as to costs, I suggested to Jordan that I should make a contribution to the costs in return for an equivalent percentage of any realization. This was not directed towards my personal gain, but I thought it the best way to convey to the creditors, not only my conviction as to the outcome, but to give them an assurance that I would not lose interest. Jordan, whose approach had always been aggressive towards Kariba, was enthusiastic, but after a meeting between myself and the creditors' committee, at which the proposal was endorsed, it foundered on counsel's advice that my retention on such a basis would be champertous.

However, 1978 did see one major step forward: after five years of frustration, Jordan received funds as a result of the partial settlement of the receiver's agreement with Tarmac. This was a very welcome development because it meant that at last we might have more freedom of action. Kariba had long since become a burden to me, but the coordination of our case was a task which I alone could perform. Originally I had thought of it as an assignment of three to four years but I could not turn my back on it. Little did I realize that even then, in 1978, many years of effort still lay ahead.

Although we had to contend with setbacks, good progress was being made when, in the summer of 1978, arrangements were in hand for a further inspection of the rock cores in Rhodesia.

A reunion, and I meet P. L. Smith

During 1978 I learned that Mee's place at the Excess had been taken by a Peter Smith. I had had no contact with Smith but such reports as I had from Hardwick were not encouraging. Over the previous months I had had a series of meetings with ex-Mitchells executives, but in August 1978 I had been able to arrange a meeting attended by all the key men. This meeting proved important for two reasons: first, it was heartening for me to have a reunion with ex-colleagues, some of whom I had not seen for five and half years, and to find that the spirit of the company survived – they were more than ready to give their time and effort to the Kariba cause. Second, Smith had learned of the conference and had asked to attend. I regarded this as something of an intrusion at that stage but agreed, even so, and it therefore became the occasion of my introduction to Smith.

The impression of Smith that I had gained from Hardwick had not been unjustified. His participation in this meeting was illuminating, if not helpful: I sensed his hostility and I could also tell that he had been in very close contact with the other side. I had lived with Gibbs' words too long not to recognize them, no matter who said them. Gibbs' assertion that we were using Kariba money to finance our business surfaced again, and was only one of the things that caused me disquiet. I emerged from the meeting convinced that Smith had interests inimical to Mitchells, which had not been disclosed.

I spoke to him after the meeting, and felt still more uneasy, for he insisted that the case would have to be abandoned as the sureties were proceeding on a false premise. They were claiming that in underwriting the bond they had been influenced by the geological report, but this, he said, was not true. Underwriters of contractors' bonds were only interested in the financial standing and security of the contractor, and did not concern themselves with technical and contractual issues, which were the contractors' business. In these circumstances, they could not proceed on the basis that Gibbs owed them a duty of care.

I was puzzled by Smith's apparent eagerness to abandon the case without even a fight. His firm had, after all, rejected Gibbs' claim and put up a defence. Both Perry Mee, the underwriter of the Excess, and Walker, the overseas general manager of the Prudential, had by this time provided proofs of evidence they had describing the researches made before they underwrote the bond, and the reliance they had put on the geological reports. Why should he now argue so strongly that they hadn't got a case, and, above all, how had he come to be so obviously in contact with the other side? Was he putting forward his argument in ignorance of the facts, or was he assuming that I had no knowledge of them?

Smith's argument was quite untenable. Had he not read any of the reports or Mee's proof of evidence? Or, if he had, why was he so ready, and indeed anxious, to forfeit £2.4 million without putting up a defence?

Nor was I at all reassured by what followed.

A joint inspection of the rock?

As part of the consolidation of the Mitchells case I had for a long time been pressing for a further and more detailed study of the rock cores which were stored on the Rhodesian side of the Zambezi. If I was right in my firm belief that we had been the victims of a major political fraud, then the proof must lie in the rock cores.

We had already assembled overwhelming confirmation of the inaccuracies in the report; however, examination of the rock samples themselves had necessarily been restricted, because of border restrictions and the fact that the cores were all contained in steel boxes in a wire-fenced enclosure on the Rhodesian side. Although these limited examinations had yielded sufficient information to show that the logs were wrong, it was obviously desirable to relog in great detail a wider sample for the benefit of the court.

In our researches during the course of the contract, our concern had been to obtain the best possible expertise in order to know the facts. Consistent with this, none of the experts we had nominated or retained in the fields of geology or of rock mechanics had been known to us personally before we invited them to act, and no attempt had been made to influence them. Even now, in 1978, I had met Professor Anderson only once and Professor Shackleton not at all. It was decided to ask Professor Shackleton whether he would make a further visit to Kariba for the purpose of a more detailed study of the cores, which would involve a number of days in the compound, and to our delight he accepted.

In ensuing discussions between Hardwick, Gibbs' solicitors and those of KNBC, it was agreed in principle that a joint inspection should be made. The purpose of this would be to assist the court by establishing what measure of agreement there was concerning the engineering qualities of the rock, and identifying any differences, thereby saving time and cost. Gibbs' solicitors asked for the proposal to be put in writing so that they could refer it back to their clients. Hardwick duly did this, and his letter included the following:

It is, we feel, encumbent upon the parties and their advisers to adduce evidence as to the accuracy of the borehole records and, if possible, to submit to the court an agreed logging record of the cores recovered from the boreholes, such cores being now and for many years past maintained in a locked compound on the south bank at Kariba.

In addition to agreeing, or attempting to agree, a common record

219

of these cores, we are also advised that evidence should be adduced as to the engineering qualities of the different types of rock encountered underground on the north bank at Kariba, and that preferably such evidence should be in an agreed form. Whilst there may well be room for argument as to the correct interpretation of the respective engineering qualities of the rock concerned when set out in a descriptive format, we are advised that the scope for argument would be substantially reduced, if not removed altogether, if the engineering qualities of the different types of rock are analysed and set out in an agreed engineering formula.

Unfortunately, at this point Gibbs apparently realized that a very unfavourable situation – for them – was developing – a situation made all the more alarming because the Zambian Government also wished to be independently represented. Their solicitors had already been informed that Gibbs' site staff was critical of the borehole records and the report generally, and it was now decided that joint inspection was a most dangerous prospect. In an undignified scramble to extricate themselves, everyone seems to have blamed everyone else and in the event the joint inspection was vetoed. Hardwick was advised that it would not be possible to undertake the joint exercise 'during July or August' when Professor Shackleton was known to be available.

In view of the fact that Professor Shackleton and Gibbs' expert, Professor Knill, had already agreed that they would both travel to the site on 14 August, Hardwick wrote to the solicitors for KNBC and for Gibbs asking whether they would reconsider the matter, since provisional arrangements had been made. However, they would not change their decision.

Although the proposal that Dr Knill should accompany Professor Shackleton had been vetoed, the Zambians, undoubtedly deeply suspicious, had by now instructed two experts of their own, Professors Coolray and Turner, to join the inspection. Not surprisingly, this caused alarm in Gibbs' camp. The fear was expressed that if such a joint inspection took place Professor Shackleton and I might put words into the mouths of the Zambians' experts. As I do not claim to be a geologist, I find it hard to imagine how I could have influenced two learned professors, and indeed I would have expected any attempt to do so on my part to be counter-productive. However, Barlow, Lyde and Gilbert reported to Gibbs' underwriters that KNBC were 'effectively under the control of CAPCO' and that pressure had been brought to bear to see that neither of them would attend the site inspection. This provides an interesting sidelight on the relationship that CAPCO, who had started out as 'agents for construction', had by now established with KNBC who were supposed to be their employers.

Another visit to Kariba

Once this fiasco was behind us, Professor Shackleton and I went ahead with preparations for our own visit. In this we had the full support of Jordan, although Smith reacted in the most extraordinary way. I had planned to use the period between 11 August (when Smith and I had met for the first time) and 17 August, when Shackleton and I were due to depart, collecting drawings and other data and generally preparing for the trip. In the event, however, these days were overtaken by unrelieved chaos. It became clear that Smith, for reasons best known to himself, was intent on stopping our visit at almost any price. With only a few days to accomplish his purpose, he threw discretion to the winds. He brought incessant pressure to bear on Hardwick, with whom I had a series of meetings which were constantly disrupted. Things finally reached the point of absurdity when, on 16 August, I was informed that he was going to apply for an injunction to prevent our travelling. I pointed out to Hardwick that, although not a lawyer, the idea that Smith, or anyone else, could go to court and obtain an injunction to prevent Shackleton and me from going to Central Africa to look at some pieces of rock was plainly ludicrous.

I knew that Shackleton was suffering similar harassment, but in spite of everything we did meet at London airport and flew to Salisbury, as arranged.

I needed to accompany Professor Shackleton, partly because I had not been to the site since 1972, and there were certain matters I wanted to verify, but more importantly because I was familiar with the location of the rock cores and the way they were stored. I had in mind that when it was first proposed, during the course of the contract, that the cores should be examined, Dr Back had said that such an examination would serve no useful purpose. He had said that the cores had originally been stored in wooden boxes, but that 'some Africans' had got into the compound and broken up the boxes for firewood. The result was that the cores had become mixed and no longer presented an accurate record. After a long experience of the hazards associated with trying to establish facts at Kariba, I thought it was advisable that someone familiar with the site should accompany Professor Shackleton. It emerged that the cores were in the care of the engineer in charge of the power station – as they had been since the beginning. He denied all knowledge of the wooden box story and assured us that they had remained in the original steel boxes from the time they were drilled. Furthermore, Professor Shackleton was able to satisfy himself that there was no discontinuity in the cores themselves.

Once in Central Africa, we were able to accomplish most of what we intended. Professor Shackleton spent three very full days examining and logging cores. I made a number of inquiries in Salisbury and elsewhere. The visit was, however, marred by one extremely inconvenient interruption. There was regular communication across the dam by agreement between the authorities, and through our lawyers and those of KNBC and Gibbs in London we had made all the necessary arrangements to examine the cores on the Rhodesian side and then to cross the dam in order to make further inspection of the works on the Zambian side. From there we were to proceed to Lusaka. On our arrival at Kariba, however, we found that Gibbs had sent a man from London with instructions that he should stay with us every minute that we were on site. This man informed us at the eleventh hour that he had instructions 'from above' that we were not to be allowed to cross over and visit the north bank station. I made inquiries with the Rhodesian authorities at the frontier, and they assured me that as far as they were concerned we could cross, but that we would need CAPCO's cooperation, which they were withholding.

A series of telex messages and intensive efforts by Hardwick in England proved fruitless, and eventually we had to return to Salisbury and then fly south to Johannesburg, north to Blantyre, and from there to Lusaka, a distance of some 2,000 miles, involving considerable expense as well as loss of time. Professor Shackleton did not plan to accompany me to the north bank station, and since I could not be sure of my reception I had to abandon this visit altogether. As Professor Shackleton recorded on his return, he 'never expected honour from that quarter and was therefore not surprised' by our treatment, but it was difficult to believe that so much trouble had been taken to prevent our visit to the north bank for merely petty and obstructive reasons. There were after all things I wished to see, and it is reasonable to assume that there was either something to hide or that Gibbs and CAPCO wanted to avoid our having contact with the Zambians.

Immediately upon my return to England I wrote to Jordan referring to the terrible shambles to which our affairs had been reduced before my departure, and suggested that we should find an early opportunity to discuss how we intended to proceed. Jordan replied that he personally had been very concerned to ensure that the visit to Kariba took place despite the efforts that had been made by Smith to prevent it. He was aware of the frustrations which we had encountered, both before and during our visit, and he welcomed my suggestion. As a result a meeting was arranged at Cork Gully's office on 24 October. I was told that the Prudential would be present and Smith, accompanied by a legal adviser and an engineer, would represent the Excess. The solicitors proved to be Hewitt, Woollacott and Chown, and the engineer to be from a company called Engineering and Power Development Consultants Limited (EPD). The meeting itself seemed to be mainly devoted to inconsequential fishing around for bits of information, but I was curious about EPD because all the recognized consulting engineers associated with tunnelling were extremely familiar to me and I had never heard of them. The tunnelling world is fairly small, and I was unable to find anyone else who knew anything about them either. Eventually I learned that they were a subsidiary of Balfour Beatty, who had been one of our competitors when tendering for the Kariba project. Later still I discovered that there was a close association between EPD and Gibbs, and indeed that they sometimes acted together as joint consultants, with EPD playing a more entrepreneurial role, on overseas projects.

The role of Excess and of P. L. Smith

We really never learned whether or not Excess had any direct or indirect interest in Gibbs as their insurers or re-insurers.

Michael Jordan to me in a letter
dated 3 September 1980.

We have heard that Excess Insurance Company Limited appear to have lines of a substantial nature on each layer of assured's [Gibbs'] professional indemnity insurance.

We are sure that it would be embarrassing to Excess Insurance Company Limited in these circumstances to have access to our report in view of the obvious conflict of interest and we would suggest that with leading underwriter's approval you should seek agreement with Excess not to be shown our reports and to abide by the decision of the remainder of the market involved.

Messrs Barlow, Lyde and Gilbert
to the brokers, 21 November 1973

On 22 January 1979, Jordan wrote to me saying that he was very disturbed that Excess had apparently still not completed their review of the position. On 24 January Hardwick wrote to me too but saying that he understood that Excess had now completed their review, but he did not know the results.

If Michael Jordan and John Hardwick did not know of the intentions of Smith and of Excess, there were others who did.

I do not recall when I first realized that Excess were so fully involved with Gibbs' professional indemnity insurance, but my first record of it was after my meeting with the ex-Mitchells personnel on 11 August, which Smith had insisted on attending. From that time onwards, I had no doubt that Smith was operating against Mitchells' interests, and I tried to bring this out into the open, only to meet with evasion and equivocation. As will be seen from the extract from Jordan's letter, no admission was ever made.

By the summer of 1978 Barlow, Lyde and Gilbert were singing a very different tune to the one they had sung in 1973, when they made their commendable pronouncement of principle quoted at the head of this section. They were under instructions that any way of settling the case prior to trial had to be pursued, but while confirming that this instruction was uppermost in their minds they had come to the conclusion that there was no alternative, as matters stood, to fighting the action out to the full. They were also concerned at the inadequacy of Gibbs' professional indemnity cover which was limited to £1 million against a potential liability that they had already assessed to be at least £3 million. In the circumstances, they were advising their under-writers that a reserve of the full amount of the policy exposure would not be unwarranted.

Would there then be an equivalent exposure in relation to a subsequent action by KNBC?

On 9 August 1978, two days before the meeting at Cork Gully's offices, Barlow Lyde sent the underwriters a remarkable document setting out some of their misgivings. In particular they were concerned that they had so far found no way of preventing the case going to trial. They were, however, able to mitigate the bad news with a report of recent developments, which might have 'heartening consequences'. Quite simply, Barlow, Lyde and Gilbert were incensed at the role I was playing and by the fact that the liquidator, 'supported by the vast resources of the Prudential and the Excess', appeared to have 'very little else to do with the remaining funds at his disposal but to invest them in a gamble for fairly high stakes'. They had, however, 'learned that Mr Smith had been somewhat unhappy at the situation for some time', and had as a result consulted his solicitor, Mr Wadsworth of

Hewitt, Woollacott and Chown, with whom they had had a series of discussions. The outcome of these discussions had been that 'moves have been made to entice the Prudential and the Excess away from the influence of Mr Morrell and Messrs Greenwoods'. Barlow, Lyde and Gilbert were at pains to emphasize that the use of the word 'entice' did not imply that there was 'any form of conspiracy'. Apparently, what they were doing was merely responding to an initiative that had come from Smith.

The document went on to lay out some details of the plan they had developed. This started with the vetoing of the joint inspection, the fruits of which we have already seen, and went on to propose that the Prudential and the Excess should carry through a plan to rid themselves of Greenwoods, 'even though they may stay on the record'. There was no need to look further for the reasons behind Hardwick's obvious distress during those summer months, his appeals to his partners for guidance, and the warnings I know he received that there was a danger of his being forced beyond the bounds of propriety. But that was not all; for Barlow Lyde had more to offer: 'In particular, we feel it would be useful for Excess and Prudential to appoint their own expert to assess the rock conditions . . . we feel that such an inspection should be made without either Mr Morrell or his adviser looking over the expert's shoulder.'

That solicitors for one side might decide it was too dangerous to cooperate in a joint inspection was one thing, but it must be a little unusual for them to join in a decision to unseat the solicitors representing the other side, and then lay down conditions to be atttached to the way their opponent's expert witnesses carry out their task.

What had happened to the principles enunciated in their letter of 21 November 1973? If it would have been embarrassing for Excess to have access to the professional indemnity insurer's report 'in view of the obvious conflict of interest' even though those conflicts were known and declared, why was it not an embarrassment for them to collaborate in the reverse relationship? What steps did they take to confirm Smith's motives? Did they not have some fear that they might be becoming involved in someone else's conspiracy? Assuming that Barlow Lyde were entitled to exercise wide discretion in securing advantages for their client, and even accepting that they were justified in overlooking Smith's behaviour, was there no impropriety in planning with Smith and his lawyer, both of whom were privy to the innermost councils of our side, to remove or neutralize our solicitors?

It is certain that neither Smith nor Mr Wadsworth of Hewitt, Woollacott and Chown revealed their schemes to the liquidator.

I have always understood that solicitors have very strict rules regarding even *potential* conflicts of interest but presumably these can be waived provided those concerned have been persuaded that the other side does not deserve protection.

Why should Smith, and the lawyers of Excess, be negotiating behind the scenes to weaken or destroy their own case? Why should they destroy their own negotiating position by indulging in intrigue with the other side? Even if they acknowledged no duty arising out of the understanding given at the meeting on 14 December 1972, did they not have a duty, both moral and legal, in their role as guarantors to the Mitchells performance bond? Since they would have recourse to Mitchells' assets, and therefore a claim in the liquidation, in respect of any payment under the terms of the bond, did they not have a duty to act in the matter only within the terms of this relationship and to keep Mitchells fully informed? No doubt these were all questions to which Barlow Lyde addressed themselves before deciding that in pursuing their chosen path they would neither be initiating nor participating in a conspiracy.

One has to be diffident about challenging the judgement of such eminent experts in the law, but they themselves, by their very denial, had posed the question. Is it not possible that their answer was more than a little subjective? Would it survive a wider and more dispassionate examination? I would like to think that a court might take a different view.

More frustration, but some progress, and some anxieties

When, on 14 March 1979, Mr Justice Donaldson fixed the trial date I determined to press very hard for a proper programme of preparation and for the appointment of experts. There had been no lack of effort on the part of myself, Hardwick and my ex-colleagues. All the evidence for the prosecution of our case had been assembled. What was now needed was the appointment of a professional consulting engineer experienced in tunnelling and underground work and a professional quantity surveyor with experience on multi-million pound projects to provide the liquidator and the sureties with an independent assessment of the strength of our case.

After Jordan had proposed a most unsuitable candidate, I wrote to him outlining the sort of qualifications and experience we would require in our consultant, and gave him a list of consultants whom I considered qualified to act. I was quite sure that in a case which now had at least £10 million at stake, this was not an appointment to be made without the most careful appraisal.

As I was about to go to Canada and then on to New Zealand for an extended period, I obtained approval to approach Charles Haswell, the senior partner in Charles Haswell and Partners, who expressed his willingness to act. In my opinion we were very fortunate to have his services, not only because he was an internationally recognized expert in underground works, but also because he had considerable experience as an arbitrator in major disputes.

Two hurdles were now cleared – we had a hearing date, and a first-class engineer prepared to represent our interest. This was progress indeed, even if I had had to wait over six years to see it achieved. But I was still not altogether at ease. My anxiety stemmed from two sources: first, the still unexplained behaviour of Coopers, and second, the behaviour of Smith and Excess. At that time, I had no idea of the involvement of either with the other side.

As regards Coopers, I wrote to Hardwick recalling the help that we had had from Ian Andrew and George Gilbertson, which Hardwick himself had witnessed at the meetings in 1972. I reminded him that there appeared to have been a watershed in our relationship at the time of David Hobson's appearance, and added that I had a clear impression of extreme hostility, particularly when we had been critical of Gibbs. In the circumstances a clarification of Coopers' position was desirable, together with a direct approach to ensure that Ian Andrew would be available to us at the time of trial.

We had never seen Coopers' report, but a summary of the draft had indicated that it was a hatchet job, whose findings had been completely discredited since their appointment. I thought it desirable that we should have a meeting with Coopers and especially with Andrew to clarify their attitude and assure ourselves of his availability. Failing that, I wanted to bring their report out into the open where it could do no harm. I had, in fact, learned that there had been a 'leak' of a confidential report which had reached Samuel Montagu, but had not been seen by our holding company board, and there was evidence that this leak was being used continuously behind the scenes in an effort to damage Mitchells' credibility. This leak contained one particularly damaging statement, an endorsement of Gibbs' oft-repeated allegation that Kariba funds had been used to finance the rest of our business and I was curious to know by what route Coopers had come to adopt it.

Coopers had taken the lead in the financial subcommittee of December 1972, which had shown that there was a massive shortfall of income against costs at Kariba, and in their draft report to Samuel Montagu they had recommended that a reserve of £2.7 million should be made against losses, or, as described in the 1972 account, 'unrelieved costs', incurred at Kariba up to that time. Under the circumstances, I thought they should be asked face-to-face, if Kariba was financing the company's business, who was financing Kariba?

As regards Smith, I decided that I should make a direct approach to ascertain his position and that of Excess. I had been disturbed by his apparently uncooperative, even hostile, attitude and more recently I had heard murmurings from Hardwick about an 'honourable settlement'. Remembering the obligations his predecessor had freely entered into in December 1972, I needed some indication of his future intentions. However, when Hardwick learnt of my intentions, he wrote saying there had been a considerable turn for the better and that Smith had telephoned to express the desire that there should be no disunity and, significantly, that Hardwick and his firm Greenwoods would continue to act for all the parties. Hardwick's letter was generally reassuring: he said he was satisfied there was now no risk of Excess starting discussions with the Zambians on their own initiative, a possibility of which I was not previously aware nor of their taking any other action which might provoke a 'repeat of the traumas of last August'. Finally, Hardwick felt he ought to alert me to the 'new climate presently prevailing', which I took to mean that Smith was being more cooperative. In my reply, I accepted that on the strength of what he had said it appeared that I need not take direct action with Smith, but I asked to be informed of any change.

Enter Engineering and Power Development Consultants Limited

On 3 April 1979, having made it clear that Kariba had complete priority and that I would maintain constant communication, returning at any time I was needed, I left for New Zealand to visit my daughter and bring back my boat, which had been in the care of my son-in-law for two years. I told Hardwick that I was particularly anxious to be informed when Charles Haswell's appointment had been confirmed. I was satisfied that a completely independent report was necessary in order to establish the strength of our case, though from experience I knew we were not in a grey, but a 'black-and-white' area, to echo

Paton's words. Apart from the one meeting with Haswell when he had agreed to act, I had not seen him in ten years, but this was of no importance. Nor did it matter that I would be on the other side of the world while he studied the case and submitted his report. I was in no doubt that an expert studying the documentation could come to only one conclusion. However, I was very shocked to receive from Hardwick a letter, dated 6 June 1979, in which he informed me that it had not proved possible to instruct anyone on the list I had submitted, because the sureties 'led as you would have anticipated by Excess, were anxious for instructions to be given to Engineering & Power Development Consultants Limited'.

When I had written to Jordan outlining the principal considerations when appointing an expert witness, I had in mind the following:

1 All the names should be internationally recognized professional firms of consulting engineers, specializing in underground works, and if of UK origin they should be members of the Association of Consulting Engineers.
2 The firms should all be of at least equal standing to Sir Alexander Gibb and Partners.
3 The individual partners, and particularly the one who would act as the expert witness, should have qualifications and experience at least equal to those who might give evidence for Sir Alexander Gibb and Partners and, in particular, Angus Paton.
4 The chosen expert should have no known close association with either party to the litigation such as would be prejudicial to his independence and judgement.

What was the rationale behind the appointment of EPD? And why was it Excess who insisted on the appointment of their nominee as a condition of a common approach?

EPD did not enjoy any of the attributes I had considered essential in an expert witness, but there were other reasons which made them unacceptable. In his letter, Hardwick put forward two arguments in their favour, which struck me as having the opposite effect. The first of these was that a Mr Moorhead, who had been Gibbs' resident engineer on the south bank at Kariba, would lead their team, and the second was that EPD had considerable experience on World Bank work. In any trial we would undoubtedly be attacking Gibbs' reckless approach to geology and safety, and would therefore be expecting Moorhead, as an expert witness, to condemn on the north bank practices which he had accepted on the south bank, where more than a hundred men had been killed.

On the second point, namely EPD's involvement with the World Bank, this would be a questionable advantage. Anyone who acted on our behalf would have to be prepared to incur the disfavour of the World Bank, as if the matter went to trial they would be the one organization that was going to finish up with 'egg on its face'.

However, there was a further and overriding reason why EPD were totally unacceptable as witnesses appearing for the sureties – a reason which makes it inescapably clear that neither Excess, nor EPD, nor indeed by this time Hardwick, had any intention of allowing the case ever to go to trial.

The experience of underwriters on the south bank project, which had been carried out for CAPCO under Gibbs' direction, had been extremely bad, and we have it from Dr Olivier that Gibbs had sided with the contractor and the employer in the advancement of claims against the insurance companies. The results were that the insurance market had been soured and a great deal of reassurance was required before underwriters would participate in the new project. Some had been provided by the warranty in the contract documents, but the insurers still insisted on a technical report before proceeding. This report was prepared by Mr Coxon of EPD after he had visited our office with the brokers and had had a long discussion with the director under whose control the contract would be executed. Coxon had then produced an eighteen-page report on which the brokers and insurers relied when underwriting the risks. I may say I knew nothing of EPD's role at the time of their initial visit: neither our broker nor our contracts director was impressed by Coxon, and both regarded his visit as a non-event, not worth mentioning. In fact, I did not know this previous history when I first learned of EPD's appointment as our own 'experts', but it is clear that if there was one firm in the industry who could not appear as an independent expert witness on behalf of the Prudential and the Excess, then that firm was Engineering and Power Development Consultants Limited.

I withdraw

I read Hardwick's letter with astonishment and dismay. The implications were all too clear and only one course of action was open to me: I could no longer be involved, thereby lending credibility to an exercise which I had become convinced was disreputable. Accordingly I wrote to Hardwick and Jordan advising them that I had no confidence in the arrangements that had been made, and that in the circumstances my services would no longer be available. Hardwick replied asking me to place my decision 'on ice', and I then wrote at far greater length telling him exactly why I considered EPD to be entirely inappropriate and why I was not prepared to reconsider the matter. I took the opportunity of recording the extreme unhappiness I had felt for some time at the way the proceedings had been handled, and I reiterated my belief that Smith and Excess had been suborned. In conclusion, I wrote, 'My determination that the Kariba story will be told is, of course, unaffected.'

In the meantime I had received notes of the first conference with counsel following the appointment of EPD, and at which the representatives of that company, headed by Mr Coxon, were present. I commented in my letter on the unsatisfactory way this conference appeared to have been conducted.

If Barlow Lyde and their associates had set out upon a course of enticement some twelve months earlier, it was clear that in Smith they had found a veritable Pied Piper. I had long complained that all initiative seemed to have passed to Smith, and now our side had followed him, apparently quite blindly, in appointing the 'expert', and were prepared to leave this vital first conference with counsel entirely in his hands – for neither Prudential nor the liquidator were represented. If Prudential were satisfied that their obligation as guarantors, as well as their undertaking given to me in December 1972, were not going to be compromised, then there was no reason for them to attend. But it is difficult to accept that this was the case. With such a huge sum at issue, the liquidator's failure to participate, or even to have any competent representation, was both inexplicable and inexcusable.

As it was, only the Excess, accompanied by representatives of EPD and Hardwick, who had survived the plan to remove him, were present. EPD's performance more than confirmed my earlier view that they had neither the experience, the status, nor the independence necessary for the successful discharge of their role, and from my reading of the conference notes, it appeared that counsel shared my view. Apart from anything else, they repeatedly expressed the need to call in other experts, and Coxon admitted that they had no one who could match the experience of Paton. Why, then, had they been retained?

The task of EPD was confirmed at the conference as being

1 to give an objective and dispassionate view of the material
   investigated and to advise whether, in technical terms, those on

whose behalf they had been instructed had a good arguable case;

2 to prepare a detailed report, which report would form the basis of the evidence they would give at the trial.

During the conference, counsel kept returning to one theme, namely, that the sureties' and the liquidator's best argument would be to demonstrate that the contractor should have been paid a very large sum of money in respect of additional costs. We shall see in due course how EPD discharged their duty with regard to this, their principal, task.

The report of the conference reinforced my view that counsel was being involved in a charade. In particular, counsel had referred to Moorhead's status as a witness, for Moorhead himself was apparently uneasy on this account. Counsel had pointed out the importance of impartiality and said that it could be both damaging and dangerous for Moorhead to give evidence, and so it was agreed that Coxon should give evidence on EPD's findings instead. But why did he not emulate Moorhead and inform counsel that he had advised insurers at the tender stage? For that matter, why didn't Smith seek advice? Finally, since Hardwick had prepared no less than three proofs of evidence – those of Perry Mee of Excess, Walker of Prudential and Rattray of Bartlett and Co. – each of which referred specifically to Coxon's involvement with the insurers at the time the bond was entered into, why did he not sound a warning? Surely these three, who seemed to have assumed control between them, could not all have suffered an aberration of memory on such a vital point? Why did they keep silent? Could it be that following counsel's unequivocal statement regarding Moorhead they realized that disclosure of the earlier involvement of Coxon and EPD would have destroyed the last vestige of credibility in EPD's appointment?

Michael Jordan has since told me that counsel was in fact kept informed of all the many relationships involved in these proceedings, but there is no mention of it in the conference notes. If counsel was in the know, then it would appear that he too was participating in what he knew to be a charade, a proposition which I still consider unthinkable.

A final attempt

My decision to withdraw had been made when I received Hardwick's letter advising me of the appointment of EPD. The report of the conference with counsel arrived later. Meanwhile, I had become

232

disturbed by Jordan's apparent lack of resolve, for he had been so enthusiastic and determined in earlier days. His abdication in favour of Smith and his acquiescence in the appointment of EPD, which had resulted in Mitchells' interest being virtually unrepresented at the vital conference with counsel, seemed to suggest that a decision had been made not to prosecute the action, and no attempt was being made even to secure our negotiating position. Was there, even now, a possibility that I had misjudged the situation?

I felt so disturbed that, notwithstanding my earlier resolution to withdraw, I telephened my son, Paul, from Indonesia. He is a chartered quantity surveyor with wide experience of major building and civil engineering contracts. Paul agreed to arrange a meeting with Michael Jordan to make sure there could be no misunderstanding between us. The scenario that I could see unfolding, as I presented it to Paul, and as he subsequently presented it to Jordan, was as follows:

1 EPD would make a confused report, which would underrate the strength of Mitchells' case, fall short of clearly condemning Gibbs' conduct, and introduce a number of irrelevant issues to create confusion.
2 It would then be suggested that the case was not sufficiently clear-cut to justify an all-out defence, and that the sureties' interest would be best served by compromise.
3 Gibbs would readily agree to such a compromise and it would be sold to their client on the grounds that the EPD report was less than fair, but that it contained the seeds of a case against KNBC.
4 The liquidator would agree to the compromise so long as it released the £630,000 which was currently held by the receiver against the Midland Bank counter guarantee in relation to the performance bond.

Jordan told Paul I was wrong to have drawn these conclusions but that since he was convinced that Smith would insist on having EPD's report, he thought it was best to have it prepared, which would allow him to have sight of it. This was preferable to isolating himself from it, in case it turned out to be necessary to dissuade the committee of inspection from making a compromise based on its findings.

Jordan was leaving shortly for Australia and suggested that if I could meet him in Singapore we could discuss the situation. This was arranged and I met him in the luxury of the Mandarin Hotel, Singapore, on 3 November. (I refer to the luxury because I had left

Wellington some six months earlier, and had not slept ashore since. I can warmly commend sailing around the world to any who are involved in the complexities of the law in England, for the time scale of such an expedition will be found to fit in extremely well with the judicial pace!) It was an extended and very relaxed talk, and it was a source of great satisfaction to me that we were completely in agreement. The cat had been slipping out of the bag for a very long time and with the appointment of EPD at Smith's insistence there was little but the tail left undisclosed. We both realized that the inevitable consequence of Mitchells' succeeding in the action would be litigation by the Zambians to seek redress from Gibbs and from CAPCO and, as a result, the World Bank and the British Government would be exposed to publicity with unwelcome political repercussions. There were, therefore, bound to be very powerful influences at work which would seek to stop the action. Jordan himself was still short of funds and wanted the continued cooperation and support of the Prudential and Excess. In reality, the battle seemed to be over the soul of the Prudential. According to Jordan Smith and Excess were certainly going to insist on the production of the EPD report and in his view it was necessary to give 'Master Smith' enough rope to hang himself, by allow the EPD report to be produced. Then, 'if it followed the lines that we anticipated, we would be able to attack it and expose it for what it was'.

In order to do this he needed assistance. If I would not cooperate it would be a severe handicap, for there would be nobody else able to examine and expose the report. In the circumstances I agreed to make myself available, without in any way compromising the position as I had already recorded it. I would continue to do everything I could to help, but on a strictly honorary basis. For his part, Jordan said that as soon as the report was to hand he would forward it to me for my examination and report.

We were also able to discuss the administration on our side including our legal representation. Again we were in unison. By retaining a Peterborough solicitor we had kept down costs, but the job had grown too big for one man, working single-handed and heavily involved in a local practice. Also it was obviously going to be impossible for Hardwick to attend a long trial in London. Jordan agreed that it was time to reinforce our legal side with leading London advisers, while retaining the local solicitor to assist.

I was immensely encouraged by our discussions which had covered every aspect of my earlier uneasiness. It seemed to me that at long last Kariba was going to get the attention it deserved.

The EPD report is flushed out

Jordan now knew that I was waiting for further signs that a real sea change had taken place. In order to ensure good communications I maintained regular telephone contact with my son Paul. I began to feel anxious again when there was no sign of the EPD report and when Paul's constant efforts to make contact with the liquidator met with very little success. Sailing up the west coast of Malaysia I was able to maintain contact until I left Penang on 26 December. Thereafter I knew that I would be out of touch for nearly two weeks while sailing further north. I visited the islands of Lankawi near the Thailand border, then the Island of Sebang off northern Sumatra and, finally, on 8 January, I arrived at Galle, Sri Lanka, to find an urgent message waiting for me from Paul. When I telephoned, he told me that he had learned through some careless social gossip that the EPD report had been prepared and submitted to counsel with whom a conference had been scheduled to take place on 10 January. It was not unreasonable to infer that somewhere pressure was being applied to rush the thing through before the report could be challenged and to use it to secure counsel's endorsement that the best interests of the liquidator and the creditors would be served by a negotiated settlement.

Paul had taken immediate steps with Cork Gully and the solicitors to obtain a copy of the report and had in fact collected it from Hardwick on 3 January. The cover revealed that it had been presented in November. There was, of course, no longer any possibility of my examining it before the crucial conference and Paul, who had no detailed acquaintanceship with the contract, was left with very little time to forestall any precipitate decisions that might be made at the conference on the 10th. However, it emerged that the report was so conspicuously and seriously flawed that this did not in the event present any difficulty.

The earlier passages were reassuring in that they confirmed the substance of Mitchells' case against KNBC and Gibbs. It confirmed that the 1961 investigation report was inaccurate and misleading, that the consultants had failed to pass on to Mitchells the important information contained in the Matheson report of June 1971, and furthermore had failed to take cognizance of that information in their own actions. It also confirmed that Gibbs had either been incompetent or had failed properly to discharge their responsibilities in the technical directions given to Mitchells, and that Gibbs' responses to Mitchells' applications for additional payment were at odds with the terms of the contract. Finally, it noted that the terms of Gibbs' consultancy agreement with the employers were such that the employer had reserved rights and powers to himself which amounted to unwarranted interference with the engineer's duties to certify in accordance with the main contract.

On the basis of these categorical conclusions on the technical aspects of the case, there could be no decision other than to proceed with the action. However, having proceeded thus far, the report came to an astonishing and quite irreconcilable conclusion, namely, that in spite of all these circumstances there was at the end of January 1973 no substantial sum of money due to Mitchells. In view of counsel's repeated emphasis that the question of under-certification went to the root of the repudiation issue, this finding was, of course, potentially fatal to any resolve to pursue the case.

Paul was able to show that the basis adopted by EPD had been quite misconceived and inept. Using their own figures, extracted from the report, he demonstrated that Mitchells' true shortfall was of the order of K6.3 million. Paul's suggestion that he might attend the conference with counsel was refused but in a letter of 9 January, advising Jordan of these figures, he pointed out that this vital section of EPD's report should not be taken as a basis for any decisions about the strength of the Mitchells case and that none should be made until I had had an opportunity to comment on the report as had been agreed with Michael Jordan in Singapore.

Notwithstanding Paul's warning, the conference with counsel on 10 January, which the sureties and the liquidator attended, proceeded solely on the basis of the EPD report. Counsel opened by saying that the report was encouraging on issues other than finance. In a long conference he returned repeatedly to the same theme: if, as EPD maintained, there had been little or no under-certification then there was not much in the litigation for the liquidator, and the defence of the sureties that there had been financial repudiation of the contract on the part of KNBC would fail. On the other hand, if EPD's investigations had shown something like K5 million under-certification then this would support the allegation that Gibbs had failed properly to certify monies that were due. Nowhere in the notes of the conference is there any indication that Paul had advised that the EPD report was flawed and that in fact the true shortfall was of the order of K6.3 million – a figure that was subsequently, and very reluctantly, accepted by EPD as correct.

The notes show that EPD were extremely unhelpful and even

hostile at the conference. Any determination to continue the case must have been further undermined by EPD's statement that they had been obstructed by a lack of information and documentation in Mitchells' records, which meant that they had been forced to base much of their work on theories, broad assumptions and approximate calculations. Although counsel was unimpressed by some of the arguments put forward and dealt with them appropriately, this allegation about records was bound further to undermine confidence. The fact that it was subsequently shown to be quite untrue could not repair the damage done at this conference, which was to be the last held with counsel. The notes of the meeting show that Jordan was in effect the only representative on our side. Referring later to Hardwick's contribution, he said, 'We just didn't have a solicitor on our side.'

At the end of the meeting, counsel stressed once more that the figures were of vital importance to the sureties and to the liquidator and *were essential tools for him when it came to giving definitive advice*. Jordan told him he wanted me to have the opportunity to comment on the EPD figures, and that arrangements were already under way for me to return to England. The fact remains that this exercise would have been entirely unnecessary had the report been forwarded to me in accordance with arrangements made in Singapore. A most important conference with counsel had been compromised because it had centred on the entirely inaccurate representations in the EPD report. Smith and Excess were to apply great pressure as a result of which no further conference with counsel was to take place – not even when EPD were compelled to agree that the under-certification was in excess even of Paul's figure of K6.3 million. Indeed nowhere in the documentation is there any indication that the real shortfall was ever advised to counsel – not even when he was asked, at a much later date, to endorse a secret settlement, the details of which were transmitted to him only over the telephone.

Another look at the EPD report

I arranged to return to England on 22 January. Meanwhile a meeting between Paul, Hardwick and representatives of EPD took place at the latter's offices at Sidcup (21 January) for the purpose of reviewing their figures. It might reasonably have been expected that our 'experts' would have set about putting their house in order. But this did not prove to be the case, and it was a reluctant and unhelpful EPD who had to admit that their figures were wrong and that they would have to do the exercise again. By the end of the meeting it was quite clear that the figures which would emerge would certainly substantiate the allegation of repudiation and, when added to the technical evidence already adduced, would make our case overwhelming. Yet Paul could detect no sign of enthusiasm from either EPD or from Hardwick, and this caused him some disquiet. No doubt he would have been still more concerned had he known that at this juncture a covert campaign to reach a settlement had begun to intensify, and that Hardwick was already involved with the other side. On 17 January Hardwick had in fact met KNBC's solicitors, Beale & Co., to examine possible terms of the settlement. On what basis was he negotiating? If the figures hitherto tabled by EPD were right, then Mitchells were entitled to no damages at all; on the other hand, if the figures being put forward by Paul were right, then the amount of damages, loss of profit and interest would amount to £13 million. What stance does one take in negotiations when one doesn't know whether the sum at issue is nil or £13 million? And this disregarding the damage done by forcing the company into receivership. It would seem to be fairly obvious that for those immediately involved in the negotiations the merits of the case had ceased to be of importance. Even though there were fifteen months to go before the trial date, there was an urgency about this operation which was only consistent with someone wanting to prevent the emergence of the facts.

Neither Paul nor I was to find out about these negotiations until months afterwards. At best this was inconsiderate, and inexplicable – unless there was something to hide.

Another meeting was arranged for 28 January to be attended by myself, Paul and the liquidator at which EPD would table their revised conclusions. Having returned to the UK I had seen Jordan at his office with Paul on 24 January, and he had expressed his concern at the lack of support Hardwick had given him at the 10 January conference, and was critical of the performance of EPD. We agreed we needed improved representation, but we decided to review this after the meeting on 28 January.

At that meeting EPD produced a revised figure of K3.263 million 'that might potentially be claimed as additional expense'. It did appear that EPD were being dragged reluctantly along the path, but these figures were just as flawed and insupportable as their earlier ones. After their inadequacy had been pointed out to them once again, they embarked on the exercise for a third time with the provision that there should be another meeting, this time with the sureties present, on 5

February. Following the meeting on 28 January Paul and I met Jordan and I repeated my belief that Smith was involved in a conflict of interests, and I told him I thought the matter should be clarified. Jordan agreed and addressed a telex to Excess specifically asking whether or not they were involved with Gibbs' professional indemnity insurance. I do not know whether he received a reply, but it will be recalled that in a letter to me, he stated, 'We really never learned whether or not Excess had any direct or indirect interest in Gibbs as their insurers or re-insurers . . .'

I also discussed with him the degree of commitment on the part of Prudential and Excess. I suddenly thought that Jordan might not have been made aware of the assurances given by Prudential and Excess at the meeting held on 14 December 1972. As the debate had for some time centred around whether or not Prudential and Excess were going to support Jordan, this was a matter that Hardwick should certainly have brought to his attention. When I showed Jordan the memorandum of that meeting he expressed surprise: he had not seen it before, he didn't know it existed, and now he was aware of it he considered it helpful. It was extraordinary to me that in spite of my referring to the document on innumerable occasions, Jordan could remain ignorant of it. As EPD's performance had confirmed the worst fears we had expressed at Singapore, it was now agreed that Paul's firm, Davis, Belfield and Everest, would examine and report on the contract as a whole and obtain advice where necessary. Jordan said that in view of EPD's extremely poor performance, he was not prepared to pay his share of their fees and that if necessary he would as liquidator assume responsibility for the payment of Davis, Belfield and Everest's fees.

Once more there appeared to be some daylight. It was therefore with even greater interest that I looked forward to the meeting to be held on 5 February.

It was unfortunate that at the last minute Jordan was unable to be present, because it was then that EPD were finally compelled to admit that their figures had been completely wrong and that the revised shortfall in payments to Mitchells had been of the order of K6.398 million. Again they were extremely ungracious about it and, in Jordan's absence and without any help from Hardwick, the meeting became very difficult. At Smith's prompting, EPD volunteered that in their view the figures did not make any difference and that Mitchells' case would fail anyway. Paul expressed astonishment that they could sit through a series of meetings and see their figures discredited again and again, as they were upgraded from a negligible figure to a deficit to

Mitchells of K6.398 million, and still say that Mitchells would not succeed. It was difficult to believe that EPD had been commissioned to make an independent investigation and were not acting under instructions to prepare the way for terminating the litigation: otherwise their performance had been so inept that one would have expected little notice to have been taken of anything further they had to say. The one thing that did remain, however, was that Davis, Belfield and Everest were now getting instructions to prepare an independent report, predicted to cost about £20,000, which would be underwitten by Jordan alone if necessary. With £13 million at issue, based on figures which had now been accepted by all, £20,000 became a negligible figure and for the first time we were going to get a competent report about Kariba from which the other side, for that is where Smith and EPD clearly stood by now, would find it extremely difficult to dissociate themselves.

Had I but known it, this was to be the last meeting I was to attend in connection with Kariba prior to the secret settlement, for unrelenting pressure was being applied behind the scenes to secure a cover-up. It is a comment on the way these affairs were being conducted that neither Jordan nor any of those present thought it necessary or courteous to tell me that the negotiations for settlement were going on between solicitors. Their probity can be judged by the fact that they were being undertaken by people who still made no effort to assess the amount at issue.

On 12 February, unaware of these moves, Paul wrote to Jordan confirming his understanding of Davis, Belfield and Everest's brief, and I returned to Sri Lanka in a more optimistic frame of mind. After over seven years of frustration, intrigue and incompetence, the machinery was now established which would enable us to put before counsel figures he had described as 'the essential tools which he needed in order to give definitive advice' – tools which should have been available to him months, if not years, before.

The optimism I felt must have been the triumph of hope over experience. Davis, Belfield and Everest's instructions were not confirmed for a month, and then only in severely truncated form. Meanwhile Smith, far from being contained, was taking the lead even more aggressively and negotiations between solicitors had given way to direct discussions between himself and the other underwriters of Gibbs' professional indemnity insurance. He was urging that now was the time to get a settlement agreed.

Were Excess, in their capacity as sureties for Mitchells' performance bond, so anxious to make payment under that bond that they preferred to negotiate from a position of ignorance, rather than strength, without the benefit of a confirmed report and without the benefit of counsel's advice? And since they were in effect guarantors, had they no duty to keep the custodian of Mitchells' affairs informed having regard to the fact that whatever money they paid out they would be claiming back, together with costs and expenses in the liquidation? Or had they discharged that duty and was Michael Jordan by now a party to everything that was going on?

The subterfuge continued. By 2 April, while Davis, Belfield and Everest were still preparing their report, draft proposals were agreed with the other side, which were to be submitted by Beale and Co., KNBC's lawyers, to KNBC, the Zambian Government and the World Bank for their approval.

Rumours that a settlement might be imminent reached Paul through a chance social contact. On 7 May he wrote to Jordan advising him that having now had the opportunity to review the case in greater detail, he could see no basis upon which the other side could defend against Mitchells' claim and, in view of the rumours he had heard, he added that his opinion was that the Kariba action represented a sizeable asset, and that 'any settlement which does not include a realistic assessment of that asset would have no merit'.

Whether or not there was any combination of facts or circumstances which could have affected the issue, his letter was too late: on that very day the various parties agreed the terms of the settlement.

The settlement

The settlement reached between all the parties at a meeting at Cork Gully's offices on 7 May had its genesis in the earlier meetings between Smith and Gibbs' professional indemnity underwriters – meetings, incidentally, which did not feature on the timetable of events given to me by Jordan at a much later date. Rules regarding propriety seem to have been waived completely at these meetings where proposals for terminating the action were cobbled together. Substantially unchanged, these provided the basis for the final settlement. Thereafter Jordan, so he told me, came under intense pressure to go along with Smith's proposals, and as a result the all-party meeting was held in London on 2 April. The proposals before that meeting provided for the creation of a pool into which both the sureties and Gibbs' professional indemnity insurers would make contributions, and out of which the claims and counterclaims of KNBC and Mitchells would be settled.

Interestingly, adoption of the proposals depended first on Beale and Co., who had not hitherto consulted KNBC or the World Bank, contacting them urgently to find out whether or not the proposals would have their approval. Second, it was necessary for Jordan to take the advice of leading counsel as to 'whether it would be proper' for him to settle on the basis proposed.

At that stage Jordan appears to have taken no steps in the matter. As agreed, however, Barratt of Beale and Co. did relay the proposals to Zambia and to the World Bank, and as a result KNBC, who were not at all happy, decided to send representatives to London. This was perhaps not surprising in the light of their unexpected costs and their earlier determination, expressed to me by Angus Paton, that they would 'get one of us'. Tremendous pressure was brought to bear upon the Zambians and eventually and very reluctantly they agreed to a settlement, but only if they received a minimum of £1.2 million. I learned subsequently from the Zambian High Commissioner and the Zambian Trade Commissioner that even this payment was only accepted because they had been advised that if the case went ahead they 'wouldn't have a leg to stand on'. So far as the action against Mitchells was concerned, this was of course true, because with the compliance of the World Bank officials they had been led into a trap in the October 1972 meetings.

It was agreed between all the parties that in view of the interest shown in the litigation by the engineering and construction journals, a press notice should be issued in order to avoid speculation. At the same time it was agreed that all the figures involved in the settlement should remain secret. The need to maintain secrecy was vital because publication of the figures would have shown that there, in the heart of the City, 200 yards from its Guildhall and 6,000 miles away from where it all started, the rape of Mitchell Construction and its creditors and its shareholders had been completed.

The press announcement

It was in fact through the press that I heard of the settlement.

The various parties had been singularly naïve if they imagined that by issuing a press notice they could quell speculation, and one can only assume that they had so isolated themselves from the industry that they did not realize how much international interest surrounded the events at Kariba. The disappearance of a contractor from the world scene might not normally arouse great interest, but the Kariba experience had wider implications.

The provision and accuracy of geological information is a matter of vital importance to contractors everywhere and indeed to clients. Inadequate and inaccurate information causes tremendous disruption, dispute and escalation of costs. In the 1960s significant moves were being made to ensure that as much information as possible was obtained before a contract was put out to tender, and similar efforts were being made to define the limits of a contractor's risks. In this way, keen tenders can be obtained and the genuine can be sorted out from the opportunist. Kariba had appeared to mark a great step forward because the information given in the contract documents was warranted, and yet here was a contractor who had been forced into receivership as a result of unforeseen rock conditions, and the question of responsibility had not been resolved. Beale and Co., KNBC's lawyers, were to go on record as saying, 'At the time, we lawyers understood from the engineers that borehole records could be regarded as "facts" and they were therefore warranted. Of course, we have now recognised from the Kariba case that a borehole record is not a fact, because all the descriptions are opinions. In those circumstances we certainly wouldn't recommend that a similar clause should be included again.' Had the matter proceeded to trial, this lawyer and others might have been disabused of the idea that distinctions in geology and rock mechanics are necessarily and always questions of opinion and not of fact. As it was, the Kariba experience had set back progress by at least a generation. Had these matters been better understood, the parties would not have been so surprised by the reaction to their press release.

I learned of the settlement on my arrival in Malta from Port Said in the middle of May. I was sitting in an office in Malta when a telephone call came through from someone asking if I could be traced. It was from a journalist on the *New Civil Engineer* who, by dint of great initiative and not a little luck, had tracked me down. He and other members of the technical press gave me what information was available about the settlement details. The terms were to be kept private, but the impression was given that the liquidator would receive about £1 million. The press greeted the information with considerable cynicism, and one journal commented that there appeared to have been a remarkable turnaround because the liquidator was believed originally to have had a strong case. The press also commented on the involvement of EPD, noting that the suggestion of a conflict of interest

243

due to their association with Gibbs was dismissed by a spokesman from the Excess.

The continued interest of the press resulted in some very remarkable revelations, so much so that the parties were driven to consider how to prevent further publicity. Not surprisingly, it was decided that any action or protest would be counter-productive, and as discussion was the last thing they wanted, an embargo was put on all future communication with the press. Since these matters were of vital significance to the industry and had important implications for the efficient deployment of international funds on civil engineering projects generally, the press continued to insist that the issues had never been properly ventilated or satisfactorily concluded. The explanation given to them was that legal costs were prohibitive, but in fact no proper exercise was ever done to estimate them. The figure previously quoted had been doubled during discussions at the final settlement, and multiplied by six by the time it was issued to the press: presumably then it owed more to politics than to careful analysis and forecasting.

I was extremely disturbed by everything I learned from the press. If the liquidator was to get £1 million on behalf of Mitchells, this was nothing compared with the damage the company had suffered. Indeed, when they were eventually obtained, the figures which had been on the table at the settlement meeting showed that the amount due to Mitchells in respect of work done up to January 1973 had increased to K7.55 million. The amount at issue at the trial would have been that sum plus a minimum of eight years' interest, plus damages for breach of contract (i.e. the loss of profit on the work that was done by the Yugoslavs), a total figure which might be conservatively estimated at £13 million. And this still without any allowance for the enormous damages resulting from having deliberately forced the group into liquidation.

On my return I sought an explanation from Jordan. It is hard to see why, apparently without a fight, he should have acceded to the pressure which he claimed was exerted by the sureties. He undoubtedly had adequate grounds for resisting it. Indeed, there were a number of factors that should have sharpened his resolve. First, he was about to get a report which he must have known was going to strengthen his hand immensely, providing counsel with the essential information he had said he required in order to give definitive advice. Second, with over twelve months to go before the trial, there was no great pressure on him to bring the matter to a conclusion. Third, he

244

knew from 'without prejudice' discussions with Beale and Co. that they were interested in a negotiated settlement, 'although it wasn't known how such a suggestion would be received by their clients'.

There were indeed so many factors which might have been expected to encourage Jordan to take his time that, in spite of his assurance that the committee of inspection had accepted the settlement upon the advice of counsel, I was by no means convinced as to the propriety of what had happened. I was also concerned to know why, if the settlement was genuine, it should be surrounded by secrecy. In view of my long involvement I asked for copies of the agreement so that I could satisfy myself that the liquidator had been justified in agreeing to it, but I was informed that I could have copies only on the understanding that I too became a party to the secrecy. I was not prepared to be bound by such terms. I remained especially intrigued by the oft-repeated statement that the settlement had been arrived at 'on commercial grounds rather than on the merits of the case'. The phrase is superficially persuasive, though it might not be unfair to describe it as glib. But the one thing that could not be said of it was that it was informative. Whose commercial interest had been served? Had all interests been equally represented at the final settlement?

The fact is that they were not. In my inquiries as to how the settlement came to be agreed, I found, notwithstanding that Mitchell Construction Holdings was a party to the dispute, that neither the receiver nor anyone authorized to act on behalf of the company was in attendance at the meeting. Although the agreement subsequently put before Mr Justice Donaldson, on the basis of which he entered judgment, had Hardwick's signature on it, apparently made on behalf of MCH, no one had had a mandate to sign it. This in itself epitomizes the cavalier attitude of those who rushed through this travesty of a settlement. So far as they were concerned MCH need not have existed.

KNBC's plight was understandable: they had been manipulated into an impossible situation, in which they could not defend themselves, for, encouraged by Gibbs and CAPCO, and with the World Bank representative failing to give proper advice, they had at the October 1972 meetings, and thereafter, taken initiatives which led to the breaching and, ultimately, the repudiation of the contract. Their commercial position was therefore unattractive and a settlement that gave them anything must eventually have proved acceptable, especially since they could not protect themselves without the support of Gibbs and CAPCO. The alternative of fighting on alone, and thereafter seeking redress from Gibbs and CAPCO, meanwhile exposing to public view the part they had played in providing Ian Smith's Rhodesia with such a valuable facility, must have been singularly unattractive.

As for the insurance companies, what commercial consideration could have weighed with them? And how could the propriety of their behaviour be measured? They were guarantors to the Mitchells bond and as such owed a special duty to Mitchells, irrespective of the assurance that had been given to me in December 1972. I would categorically refute that they had the right in any circumstances to lump together liabilities under Gibbs' professional indemnity and Mitchells' performance bond in order to achieve some compromise settlement which suited their purpose. It might be suggested that all such obligations, moral or otherwise, could be satisfied providing they had the approval of the liquidator, but in this case the liquidator was not to claim that the arrangements had his approval, but rather that he was compelled into them through pressure applied by the sureties.

So far as Gibbs were concerned, the issue at stake was indeed precisely the one Paton had confronted me with in June 1972, i.e. 'them or us', because it was clear that their professional indemnity insurance would nowhere near cover their potential liability should the Kariba action go against them. To avoid public examination, and what the *New Civil Engineer* described as 'embarrassing courtroom revelations', would certainly have been commercially attractive to them. But Gibbs are not a commercial firm: they are a professional firm, and I am reminded of the passage in *Power From Water*,* written by Paton and his partner, Guthrie Brown, in which they write, 'The consulting engineers do all they can to make sure the contract is so drawn up that their clients do not carry an undue or avoidable risk, while at the same time the contractor gets a fair deal. It is a big responsibility, the consulting engineer acting in a quasi-judicial capacity between his client and the contractor.' I also recall Sir Harold Harding's reminder to Paton that 'in the matter of certifying additional monies he had to act 100 per cent as a professional consulting engineer and not be concerned to protect himself and his partners'.

I was to learn later that the settlement agreement contained a paragraph specifically designed to protect Gibbs and their underwriters from any action which might have arisen before the date of the agreement (i.e. against any action brought by KNBC). One recalls the

---

*Published by Leonard Hill Books, 1960.

deed of release that was placed before Mitchells in 1972, whereby, in return for Gibbs recommending to KNBC that they enter into the revised form of contract, Mitchells had to give an undertaking not to seek redress against Gibbs. There is no precedent so far as I am aware in professional practice for a consulting engineer making the issue of a certificate conditional upon a bargain affecting his own position. Will it become fashionable one day for a consulting engineer to issue a certificate only on receipt of a deed of release from both his client and the contractor, so he cannot be held responsible for his actions?

More facts emerge

I was extremely frustrated at the refusal to let me see the terms of the settlement. The press rumour that the liquidator had secured £1 million appeared to be confirmed when, in a letter to the creditors of 2 June 1982 the liquidator advised

> Following protracted negotiations with all parties involved, including in particular the sureties under the contract bond, the compromise settlement was reached in May of last year [sic] which provided for a sum of approximately £1 million payable to me as liquidator. This settlement was agreed by counsel acting on my behalf and has also received the approval of the committee of inspection.

From all this one might assume that £1 million had been received by the liquidator and that the deficiency in the liquidation had been reduced accordingly. One might also assume that counsel had given studied consideration to the proposed settlement and that, having regard to the very large sum of money involved, the committee of inspection would have received a full report.

A great deal of information has come to light since 1980 which shows that all three assumptions were wrong.

The terms of the settlement are now known to me. They provided that:

1 A fund was created into which Excess and Prudential each paid £675,000, Gibbs' insurers paid £500,000, and Gibbs paid £25,000 (the amount of the excess under their professional indemnity policy).
2 Out of this fund KNBC received £1,200,000 and the liquidator on behalf of the group received £675,000.

At first sight it would appear, therefore, that the liquidator got not £1 million, but £675,000. However, a clause in the settlement provided

247

that it was 'without prejudice to any rights of indemnity in respect of their respective contributions which Prudential and Excess had against Holdings or the group'. As Excess and Prudential had each paid £675,000 into the fund, they would therefore be claiming a total of £1,350,000 in the liquidation. Where, then, was the liquidator's £1 million? How was it that counsel gave his approval to such a settlement, and how was the 'remarkable turnaround' referred to in the *New Civil Engineer* immediately following the settlement explained to the committee of inspection? And in particular, how had counsel been able to give an opinion without having yet received the figures which were the 'essential tools' he needed? It emerged that, unlike Beale and Co., Jordan did not go back to counsel until after the final settlement was reached on 7 May. In a letter to me of 4 June 1981, and in reply to my specific query, the liquidator, while still refusing to give me any details of the settlement, told me that on 8 May Hardwick spoke to Rokison (counsel for the Mitchell side) on the telephone and secured his endorsement of the settlement. The 'essential tools' were apparently no longer required and Jordan informed me in his letter that he had a fee note for £50 as evidence of advice given by counsel in telephone conference. Various members of the committee were approached on the telephone and a majority gave their approval.

One must be in very big business indeed when one sacrifices a £13 million claim on the basis of a £50 telephone conference in which counsel has been compelled to give advice without the benefit of 'essential' information.

Michael Jordan has since suggested that, even if he had been better informed, he would still have settled the Kariba litigation on the same basis. This was because it had been made known to him that Gibbs had only £1 million of professional indemnity cover. This argument will not stand up to even the most superficial examination.

The fact is that Gibbs were introduced into the action by the sureties on the basis that they owed a duty of care to all who might rely upon their geological report. This was because there was no contractual relationship between Gibbs and the sureties.

Mitchells' position was very different for it was primarily to their client KNBC, and not to Gibbs, to whom they were entitled to look for redress. In this contractual relationship KNBC had to be responsible for the actions of their agents. Why did Gibbs and their professional indemnity insurers contribute £525,000 to the settlement if it wasn't in respect of professional negligence of a very high order? And in what field did this negligence occur if it wasn't in relation to the geological report and the costs and disruption that flowed from it? It is difficult, and even impossible, to envisage circumstances in which Gibbs' admitted liability didn't in turn give Mitchells the right of redress against KNBC.

But the Zambians were deeply aggrieved. They had been trapped. Nevertheless there is no record of them ever having behaved other than correctly. KNBC had a power station.They also had the overt and covert support of the British Government and the World Bank. If a judgment had been made against them it would have been met. They would then have sued Gibbs and CAPCO and the whole plot would have been revealed.

In the event, the Zambians demanded their minumum of £1.2 million as the price of their acquiescence. There was no logic to the way in which it was raised. It was a gross injustice to Mitchells, to its shareholders and to its creditors – which is why, of course, it all had to be done so secretly. The expediency behind the Kariba settlement can be readily understood: the cynicism is much harder to take.

The moment of truth: January 1980

What was it in January 1980 that led to such frenetic activity on Smith's part to obtain a quick settlement? In May 1979 Barlow Lyde had, like our own counsel, decided that the whole issue turned upon certification and that it was essential for the defence to nevertheless attempt to renegotiate in good faith and to certify the necessary amounts to restore Mitchells to the position that they would have been in had they not run into unforeseen circumstances. Accordingly Gordon Worrell, of E. C. Harris and Partners, chartered quantity surveyors, was commissioned to make a report.

Worrell must have discovered a number of irrefutable facts in the course of his researches which he could hardly have found reassuring. He would, of course, have learned that the terms of Gibbs' engagement interfered with their freedom to certify and were therefore in conflict with a fundamental provision of the contract. This would not have provided him with a very encouraging point from which to embark upon his task of demonstrating that they had acted in good faith. But he would soon have found further evidence that was both damning and unanswerable. There was full and detailed documentation on the files that Gibbs had accepted that the only reasonable basis on which to proceed was that Mitchells should be paid their costs plus a management fee. There was Gibbs' own telex to CAPCO advising them of the agreed amendments to the contract. There was the document incorporating the proposals for revisions to the contract which had been agreed and signed by Paton and myself in Lusaka on 27 October 1972. Then there was the report of the independent panel of inquiry. Finally, Worrell would have discovered the history of the December 1972 meetings in London where it had been insisted that Mitchells had to sign the infamous 'deed of release' as a condition of their receiving any contribution to the losses they had already suffered – and this was accompanied by the ultimate condition, confirmed and reconfirmed in the documents, that the only basis on which further negotiation would be entered into was if the company undertook to complete the whole of the work within a total price of £15 million.

It is clear that Worrell, who is a Fellow of the Royal Institution of Chartered Surveyors and of the Institute of Arbitrators, must have found himself in some difficulty. He would have been well aware of the nature of the report which was going to be produced by Davis, Belfield and Everest. Additionally we in Mitchells had known and worked with E. C. Harris and Partners and Worrell for over twenty-five years when, in happier circumstances and with different partners involved, we had without difficulty settled with them numerous accounts for major contracts where they had acted for Sir Alexander Gibb and Partners.

I have no doubt that it was all these factors, and not the complexity of the task, that resulted in a series of deferments in the presentation of Worrell's report, during which time he was having consultations with Gibbs and their lawyers.

There was of course another difficulty: the fact that, in the incredible tangle of conflicts that enmeshed the unhappy Kariba story, Worrell had been jointly instructed by Beale and Co. and Barlow, Lyde and Gilbert, notwithstanding that they in turn owed their appointments to the fact that their respective clients were in conflict.

The position at the beginning of 1980 was that Smith and the other parties to the enticement plan must have known of Worrell's draft reports and, as they were at the same time attending the meetings held on our side, they knew of the inevitable findings of the report about to be submitted by Davis, Belfield and Everest. In fact Paul's interception of the EPD report and his letter to Jordan of 9 January must have come as a rude shock to their plans.

It is known that although that letter was very conveniently not tabled at the conference with counsel on 10 January, it was nevertheless the subject of discussion outside the meeting.

It was in these circumstances that, in complete disregard of counsel's insistence that he needed an accurate statement of the shortfall in certification before he could give definitive advice, Hardwick, acting on instructions and aided and pressurized by Smith, entered into the settlement discussions with Beale and Co. during the following week. At the same time Smith pursued similar discussions with the leader of Excess's fellow underwriters to Gibbs' professional indemnity insurance. In this way the panic, and very secret, settlement was arrived at while those responsible, knowing the substance of the reports they were about to receive from Worrell and from Davis, Belfield and Everest, were spared the embarrassment of having them on the record.

Smith's role in this matter is clear, but how he persuaded Jordan to adopt the same attitude is yet to be explained. Certainly there is no logic in the terms of the settlement, the way it was presented to the creditors, the secrecy that surrounded it, or the speed with which it was completed. There were others, apart from Smith, who must have breathed a sigh of relief at the cover-up, including Coopers, the World Bank and the Foreign Office.

I had never expected to see one of E. C. Harris' partners appear as an expert witness on the subject of certification at Kariba, though Worrell's evidence would certainly have been most fascinating. However, the association of E. C. Harris and Worrell with the various people involved did not end, as might have been expected, with the submission of his report, nor with the secret settlement. Immediately after the settlement, Smith, his task accomplished, left Excess and joined E. C. Harris and Partners at their offices in Basildon and, following a short period of training, he set up in practice as senior partner in the Construction Risk Partnership at 3 London Wall Buildings. Mr G. W. Worrell joined him in the partnership.

There is little more to tell. On 1 June the amalgamation between Coopers and Cork Gully, which had first been announced in early April, was consummated. For those who would seek a modicum of justice, the world is depressingly small at the top.

Epilogue

In 1984, all the secured creditors having been paid in full, Paul Shewell was required by law to hand Mitchell Construction Holdings back to its directors. It was a moment for which I had been waiting. In the years of receivership I had been compelled to watch helplessly as the company was destroyed and its assets squandered. Now, for the first time since 1973, I had authority to act. Shareholders and creditors had been deprived of what was rightfully theirs and my name and that of others had been besmirched.

Those who had suffered were entitled to know the truth and there were at least two other matters that still required answers: Who had forced the farcical settlement of the Kariba litigation? And how was Kariba financed between the time that CAPCO notified KNBC that they were running out of money in July 1972 and new loans were negotiated, something that was not effected until August 1974. There would, of course, remain the question of what action could be taken by shareholders or creditors to secure the redress to which I had been assured they were entitled.

These matters were considered at an Extraordinary General Meeting of shareholders held at the Chartered Insurance Institute on 27 March 1985. Michael Jordan attended the meeting, as the nominee of a trust which holds shares in the company. During discussions he told those present that the Prudential and the Excess had presented him with an ultimatum, the burden of which was that if he did not agree to an immediate settlement on terms which were virtually dictated to him, they would pay the whole of the sum involved in the performance bond into a trust from which half would immediately be paid to KNBC, withholding the other half unless and until the liquidator abandoned his action. He protested that this action had left him 'absolutely high and dry' and that he had had no alternative but to submit to the pressure. Having regard to the very powerful arguments available to him, it is still not clear why this was so, nor why he had had to be a party to so much secrecy.

255

Jordan suggested that the shareholders' best interests would be served by placing the company in the hands of the official receiver, who would have a duty to look into allegations of conspiracy and, if it had occurred, to send his report to the Director of Public Prosecutions. However, after some discussion, the meeting decided that an approach should first be made to shareholders holding 30,000 or more shares with a proposal that they should subscribe a halfpenny per share to pay for definitive advice from leading counsel as to the best course for the company to follow. The sum raised would be more than adequate and, as the subscription from the holder of 30,000 shares would be only £150, to involve the smaller shareholders would not be economic. If any of the major shareholders concerned did not wish to subscribe, it was suggested that they might be invited to place their holdings at the disposal of the company.

The Prudential

Before approaching the major shareholders I had a conference with leading and junior counsel and was advised that in counsel's opinion the circumstances eminently justified the cost of proceeding.

I had already had an unsatisfactory encounter with the Prudential at which an executive – apparently holding a senior position, but certainly without authority – could only transmit the decision which had been made 'by the people upstairs' that the Prudential was not prepared to support the company.

The Prudential, with 168,000 shares, was our fourth largest shareholder; they were trustees to our debenture stock; they were underwriters to our performance bond at Kariba; and, finally, I had had from their assistant general manager a personal assurance of their support should we be forced into receivership. In presenting its public image the Prudential proclaims a basic philosophy: it is that as the largest shareholder in a company, which it frequently is, it does not consider that its sole responsibility is to buy and sell as profitably as possible, but rather to accept that it is actually part of that company with all the responsibilities which flow from that.

And yet, pressed for an explanation, the Prudential representative insisted that they had acted on purely commercial considerations. Although I attempted to break down barriers at that meeting and subsequently in correspondence up to the level of chairman, it became clear that I was wasting my time.

Obviously discouraged, I nevertheless wrote to all the institutional shareholders asking them in turn for their support. The response, with some exceptions, was disappointing. One reply, however, was of particular interest. It was from one of Britain's oldest and most highly respected institutions. In it I was informed that, although a prima facie case appeared to have been made, they regretted that they found it difficult to commit themselves because the investment committee of the Association of British Insurers had firmly advised against their becoming involved and had added that this attitude had the backing of other insurance companies concerned. Notwithstanding the Association's denials, I had a meeting with the institution concerned and was left in no doubt that the information they had given me was accurate – and indeed there could have been no possible motive for it being otherwise.

It appeared that I had come across yet another club in which all members are equal but some are more equal than others. The Prudential is undoubtedly its most powerful member.

What commercial considerations prevented them from supporting the company? It could hardly have been the £840 which would have been the amount of their contribution. It is not as if they considered their shares valueless because, when asked whether they would surrender their share certificates for cancellation, as proposed at the Extraordinary General Meeting, they refused on the grounds that if the company were successful in its action they were entitled, as shareholders, to participate in any resultant proceeds. It would appear, in their case, that commercialism went hand in hand with cynicism.

In my youth, and indeed over the years, I have always known the Prudential as 'The Rock'. Among my souvenirs I have one remaining piece of biotite schist which was excavated from the machine hall at Kariba. I will be happy to present it to them, perhaps to display in their foyer, where it might serve to remind them that with rock, as with other things, it is quality and integrity that count.

The liquidator and the committee of inspection

I might by now have abandoned any hope that the company might escape from the sinister and cabalistic influences that had dogged it for so long; but there remained the possibility of recourse to the committee of inspection, appointed as a watchdog to protect the creditors' interests. I asked for a meeting but it was refused. In his letter advising me of this refusal, Michael Jordan told me that a majority of the members of the committee had been consulted and of those who had replied a majority had indicated that the proper channel for communication was through himself. With a committee of thirteen, a majority would comprise seven members and a majority of that seven would be four – not a difficult target for a forceful chairman, who knows the strengths and weaknesses of the members of his committee, to achieve on the telephone. It was the same intriguing formula that had been used to obtain approval of the Kariba settlement. By this time many of the leading accountancy firms specializing in insolvency were expressing views. Some considered it extremely unusual that barriers should be erected to prevent the chairman of a company having meetings with the committee of inspection. Ernst and Whinney's insolvency partner was reported as saying that in nearly all cases it was impossible to get the chairman anywhere near the committee. Others, having regard to the amalgamation that had taken place between Cork Gully and Coopers, whose failure to disclose interests and subsequent performance were the subject of criticism, considered that Jordan should have ceased to act or, at the very least, that a co-liquidator should be appointed. Notwithstanding this, Jordan took a very positive role and effectively and continuously barred my having a meeting with the committee. Even refusing to let me have the names and addresses of the members so that I could write to them direct. Only by channelling all my communications and evidence through him could I make contact with them. In spite of all my other experiences, I was amazed that with all the evidence available I was unable to arouse any reaction. Was the committee of inspection no more than a very expensive rubber stamp?

Paul Shewell and Coopers

Meanwhile, having taken over the company, I was anxious to complete certain documentation. I already had in store a huge cache of papers – several tons in weight – from Kariba. I now wished to discover further information concerning the conduct of the company's affairs during Shewell's receivership. Communication had been made difficult and frustrating because Shewell had left Coopers in England to take up a post with the firm's Hong Kong branch. In the circumstances I asked that all papers relating to the company's affairs while he acted as its general manager should be forwarded to me or made available for collection. I added that I was particularly concerned to have a copy of the brief which formed part of his initial instructions, details of which had been given to me by Michael Jordan at the time. After some correspondence, during which Shewell contested the company's right to this documentation and I in turn was advised by lawyers that the company was so entitled, I received a letter from him saying that he considered that grounds were being sought for mounting a claim against him and that, in any case, in his opinion, any such claim would be statute barred. He continues to deny the company access to this documentation.

Her Majesty's Government

Deep Throat is alleged to have advised Woodward and Bernstein in the Watergate affair to 'follow the money'. In the case of Kariba it was a question of 'trace the money'. The problem of financing the civil engineering work at Kariba once CAPCO ran out of funds had been partially resolved by forcing Mitchells into receivership. But there remained the question of how the Yugoslav contractor was paid possibly $20 million for work completed before finance became officially available as a result of the revised loan agreements not entered into until August 1974. It is known that there was considerable concern and dispute involving Her Majesty's Government, the World Bank and the Zambian Government as to how this work was to be financed. When the revised funding arrangements were agreed, they were notable for the fact that, taken at their face value, Zambia was for the first time forced to make a major contribution – indeed one that was greater than CAPCO's own original contribution – to the local costs. In other words the position appeared to have moved from one in which Zambia was acting as a conduit which facilitated Ian Smith's Government acquiring an invaluable facility, to one in which they were actually providing funds for the privilege.

As the British Government were guaranteeing loans in respect of both the original Kariba scheme and Kariba Stage 2 it was reasonable to assume that details of all the loan arrangements were known in this country. Through Mitchells' Member of Parliament, Dr Brian Mawhinney, Timothy Raison, then Minister for Overseas Development (the Overseas Development Administration), was asked how this finance was provided. It would be tedious to go through the mass of correspondence that has accumulated during the two years following that initial request. First I was informed that no bridging finance was necessary and thereafter that finance was always available from the World Bank. For obvious reasons the World Bank does not provide finance for local costs, under which the majority of the civil engineering work falls, but confines its aid to the provision of external finance required for plant, equipment and other services not available in the country concerned. This explanation was therefore not acceptable. It was only after very extended correspondence that Timothy Raison at last acknowledged that the finance necessary to pay Mitchells had to come from CAPCO. This, of course, brought us back to the fact that CAPCO neither had the money itself nor access to financial markets. At this stage Timothy Raison insisted that his ministry had no knowledge of how the local funding was brought about and referred me to the World Bank.

In due course I was told by the World Bank that all the necessary information had been passed to the UK Executive Director at the Bank and that they had nothing they could add.

This led back, inevitably, to the Overseas Development Administration (ODA) and further correspondence – again more notable for its evasion, equivocation and downright mis-statement than it was for enlightenment. The only change was that Timothy Raison had been replaced as Minister by Christopher Patten. At this juncture it occurred to me that there had been one omission in the correspondence that had come from the Minister – nowhere had mention been made of an agreement which, on the face of it, seemed to deal only with UK Government guarantees. On closer scrutiny, however, it emerged that it was not merely an updating of an earlier guarantee, but it referred, in a long and complex clause, to various amounts 'deemed to have been released' and also 'special payments' that had been made by the United Kingdom relative to the works. This document was of special significance because it was signed on the day that Zambia assumed responsibilities for financing these local costs which, it was originally intended, should be borne entirely by CAPCO.

At my request and, as he put it, at the risk of incurring the considerable ire of his ministerial colleagues, Brian Mawhinney on my behalf asked Christopher Patten the following:

- For what specific expenses were the payments intended?
- What was the total amount paid by the United Kingdom?
- What were the dates and amounts of each separate payment?
- Under what obligations were the payments made?
- What was the consideration received by the United Kingdom for the payments?

I had suggested to Brian Mawhinney that like me, the Minister might temper his ire with discretion, but I was not altogether surprised that my request was denied. Instead Dr Mawhinney was informed that, as it appeared that I had known about the agreement all along, 'nothing would be gained if I were to answer . . . his questions'. Dr Mawhinney then advised that no purpose would be served in pursuing the correspondence with the ODA. I have accepted his advice. Indeed, in the light of my experience, I could no longer have any confidence in any information emanating from that source.

All the evidence now suggests that it was pressure from the British Government that was responsible for the initiation of the Kariba North Bank Scheme and for the involvement of Zambia in an arrangement which must at best have been very disagreeable to them. When the financial package broke down, Zambia had to be accommodated and appeased. In a game of bluff and counter-bluff the Zambians refused to yield. In the search for a solution Mitchells, who had had the courage to respond to government exhortations to secure overseas work, were deliberately sacrificed and the evidence points to the United Kingdom having effectively subsidized the Yugoslav contractor who then completed the work on a cost-plus basis.

Much has been made of the damage to UK prestige and reputation arising from the Kariba contract and attempts have been made to lay the blame at Mitchells' door. I see no virtue in allowing my company to remain a scapegoat.

The professionals

This account, long and detailed as it is, leaves many questions unanswered. What is the reaction of the Association of Consulting Engineers to one of their number who deliberately conceals geological information, who enters into an agreement with a client which is in direct conflict with his duties to act independently, and who knowingly and deliberately countenances the destruction of a contractor? What is the reaction of the Institute of Chartered Accountants to a member who fails to disclose a vital conflict of interest and then produces a report that contains unsustainable allegations, appoints one of its partners to preside over the annihilation of a company and the disposal of its assets in a manner so eloquently described by Michael Jordan? What has the Law Society got to say about a gathering of solicitors and counsel who draw up and, disregarding conflicts of interest, sponsor a plan to entice all support away from any potential victim? A plan which, with whatever legal nicety it is presented, will to the layman exhibit all the hallmarks of conspiracy.

NEDO

It was with some sadness that I decided to resign from the Civil Engineering EDC and more particularly from the chairmanship of the joint working party which was examining public sector purchasing in the construction industry. I was asked to stay but, having regard to the circumstances, I felt that if the report was other than anodyne my chairmanship would provide a weapon in the hands of any who might seek to undermine its findings. Had I known what was to ensue I might have acted differently.

Bobby McAlpine, now chairman of Sir Alfred McAlpine, filled the vacancy occasioned by my resignation from the EDC itself. At the time of writing, Ian McAlpine, a director of Sir Robert McAlpine, is lined up for membership. But two other developments make me wonder whether what I regarded as the main virtue of the EDCs – their independence from sectional interests and their ability to focus on the wider scene – retain their validity.

First, Sir Kenneth Wood, chairman of Concrete Limited, was appointed as my successor to the chairmanship of the working party. I would like to have seen someone less committed to negotiation. It could be said that if the fact that I was known to favour competition had not been an obstacle to my chairmanship, there was no reason why the same principle should not apply to those who were known to favour negotiation. On the other hand they had been well represented in the past – and indeed one of Sir Kenneth's co-directors had been among the three industrial members on the Banwell committee. It was perhaps unfortunate that one of Sir Kenneth's companies, Northern Concrete Limited, had attracted some criticism when it was awarded a negotiated contract worth £2.5 million, which in the opinion of the district auditor of the authority concerned, 'lacked the discipline inherent in competitive prices'.* It is similarly unfortunate that Sir Kenneth has since had devoted to him a full-length programme of television's *World in Action* which few of us would envy. Whether or not these things arose out of anything but bad luck they would not seem to have provided an ideal background for an appointment of such significance in the area of public policy. The report of the working party, when it was received, certainly didn't break new ground and within the industry generally was regarded as a non-event.

The second appointment of which I would not have approved was

---

*See *Web of Corruption* by Raymond Fitzwalter and David Taylor, Granada, p. 197.

Gordon Brunton's to the chairmanship of the Civil Engineering EDC following the death of Professor Jock Campbell who previously occupied the post. At the time, Brunton was chief executive of the Thomson organization which owned numerous of the industry's principal publications including *Construction News* and the *Consulting Engineer*. *Construction News*, in particular, had under its previous editor built up a great reputation in the industry and had become required reading. However, there had been a long history of interference with the editors in the group and a number of reports that Gordon Brunton had personally intervened in editorial policy. In a series of well-reported incidents it had been stated that editors had been instructed as to what should and should not be included in their papers which had resulted in resignations and, in one case, it was reported there had been a stormy two-hour interview between Brunton and a reporter on the *Sunday Times*, who, with others, refused to accept what was regarded as unwarranted inference.

I have no doubt that Gordon Brunton is a man of considerable administrative ability, but the papers over which he exercised control were of great importance to the industry. I am very doubtful whether, in these circumstances, he was not already in a position to exercise sufficient influence in the construction industry without his EDC appointment. In the event Gordon Brunton served as chairman of the Civil Engineering EDC from 1978 to 1984 and, his name having been put forward by the industry, he was knighted in 1985.

One thing is certain – it is a far cry from the days when attempts were made to stop my own appointment and, subsequently, when efforts were made to have the Civil Engineering EDC wound up. It would now appear that it is being absorbed into the establishment. Whether this is a good thing, and whether in the circumstances it is likely to make an effective contribution to the overall health of the industry and of the economy, must now be a matter for conjecture.

I have explored the anatomy of the Mitchells experience and recorded the details in an effort better to understand it myself and, if appropriate, to make its lessons known. In the company's dilemma the law could provide no answer. For all practical purposes, both as regards protection and redress, it need not have existed. No matter how clear and how well defined the issues, the law is all too often available only to those with access to almost unlimited resources. Nor are public scorn or fear of exposure weapons in the hands of victims. The laws which rightly exist to protect the virtuous from defamation have become a shield behind which any amount of iniquity can be perpetrated without fear. Mitchells' experience following the findings of the independent panel of inquiry illustrates both the possibilities and limitations of such procedures under the law and its practice as it is at the moment. Similarly, I am bound to recall again my only court involvement in a contractual dispute – the Peterborough Hospital arbitration which went on for 239 days and at the end of which two leading counsel could detect no other reason except harassment for it having been brought. It is not for me as an industrialist to suggest how the absurd and archaic procedures which I observed during that experience could be improved in order to make the law a conduit for, rather than a barrier to, justice and the approaching requirements of the twenty-first century. What is beyond doubt is that for many of us the law is not working and cannot work. Ironically, my proposals for participating in the Kariba action were barred because they would be champertous; out of all the people who have paraded through these pages, with their multiple and conflicting interests, I would be the one, whose colours were firmly nailed to the mast, who could not be relied upon to tell the truth in the witness box. How often have I looked enviously across the Atlantic at the much despised contingency fee procedures, under which lawyers are paid a percentage of any damages recovered while conducting the case for nothing if it fails. I have been assured that Mitchells would not have lacked a good lawyer, or even competition for the brief, had we been in America.

One of the most depressing things about the whole affair is the number of people who could have spoken but who kept silent and, more important, those who would have liked to speak but were frightened to do so. The casualty rates among those who ignore warnings is high and there is nowhere for them to turn.

As I have been writing this book I have thought repeatedly of others who have tried and failed; of the Alan Grimshaws and the Eddie Milnes,* whose efforts and whose sacrifices should be on the consciences of all who witnessed their struggles. The eyes of a large part of

---

*Alan Grimshaw: 'In the 1970s a Coal Board employee and a brilliant administrator, Alan Grimshaw, went to the House of Commons with allegations of overcharging by pit prop firms on the Coal Board. His allegations led to savings for the tax-payer of some £7m. Soon after the savings were made, Alan Grimshaw was sacked by the Coal Board. He begged the Mother of Parliaments for protection and was constantly ignored and rebuffed.' *Private Eye*, 16 May 1986
Edward Milne: Labour MP for Blyth 1960–74. 'Just before the February 1974 election he was ousted as Labour candidate following his persistence in trying to uncover Poulson-related scandals in the North East Regional Party.' *Daily Telegraph*, 26 March 1983.

the industry were focused on Mitchells and the struggle in which it was engaged in the 1960s and 1970s. They too will have been expected to learn a lesson.

I have no illusions. But if one has the capacity to throw even one small rock in the stream to impede the flow then one should do it. Perhaps even now, when the average Englishman's confidence and pride in the standards to which we have always thought this country subscribes have been undermined as one scandal after another has emerged, the climate may be right for a change. A change which will recognize and embrace those moral imperatives for which the law provides no substitute.

And maybe – who knows? – we may as a bonus one day get a real and effective inquiry into the construction industry.

Appendix

'Compete to Survive': an extract from the *Consulting Engineer*,
August 1971.

David Morrell firmly believes that the commercial success of
Mitchells, which is his prime objective, is founded not on the feather
bedding of negotiated contracts but on the sterner world of competitive tendering. The increase in overseas work from 24 per cent in 1968
and 1969 to 34 per cent in 1970 shows the success of his doctrine in the
face of international competition.

Commercial integrity
He is not afraid to speak his mind and his profound commercial
honesty has led him during the last year into a public debate on the
importance of competitive tendering on the economic health of the
country. Of the much publicized Anchor Project he says in his annual
report 'Last year, at a time when there was an extreme shortage of
heavy civil engineering work, we were bitterly disappointed when the
£28m Anchor Project for the British Steel Corporation was not
awarded to us. In the event it went to a contractor whose tender, on
the face of it, was higher, not only than ours, but of others that were
submitted.'

Lord Melchett, chairman of BSC, said after meeting Morrell, that
Morrell's views would help the Corporation in planning and control of
future projects. Morrell says in the company report that BSC have
made it clear that they are 'intent on promoting sound and responsible
contractural procedures'.

During this lonely period Morrell needed all the insularity and
internal strength for which he is noted. His disappointment was
aggravated by the political, public and commercial pressures which
were forced upon him, but he stood by his convictions. A conviction
that some negotiated contracts masquerade as competitive tenders and
that the client must often be more guilty than his professional adviser.
These negotiations, he maintains, create a double price structure
within the industry which tends to depress the truly competitive

market to sub-economic levels. A situation which is unhealthy to the whole industry.

Morrell is a big man, physically and mentally. In the autumn of last year he captained his 17m Bermuda rigged sloop *Sails of Dawn* across the Atlantic from Cowes to Barbados. He is passionately fond of sailing and his other interests of flying and the theatre have taken second place although he still flies his own Piper Aztec for business and pleasure.

Power lies with a few

Morrell feels that power lies in the hands of a few clients, and therefore they have an enormous potential for changing the system for the better. 'There is,' he said, 'at the present time, a tremendous amount of work which virtually falls within the personal gift of a handful of individuals. Reference is sometimes made to the apparently attractive idea of using the purchasing power of the public sector to impose new patterns. One would be happier if one could see flowing from these influences an automatic good. Unfortunately, there has been little evidence to date that we are making significant progress; rather the reverse. We must look foward to the time when, as I would see it, under the authority and leadership of the engineer, but in a spirit of mutual respect, we start to bring our total product more into line than we do at present with the expertise and resources which we collectively deploy.'

Public opening of tenders

Morrell has for years been an exponent of the public opening of tenders and fierce opposer to the negotiated contract which he sees acting against the interests of the economy. Of opening tenders he said, 'I have advocated the public opening of tenders for many years. Under the present practice, tender results are almost invariably known by a few soon after they are opened. They could be found out by more if those concerned were prepared to devote the time and trouble to the task. The aura of security is almost invariably more apparent than real and I would think nothing but good could come of doing away with a façade that has become completely discredited.'

A nice cosy enclave

Morrell's opposition to negotiated contracts goes back some years in his submission to Banwell in 1963 and he has continuously declared this opposition. Presumably he continues to promote these views as a member of the Civil Engineering Economic Development Committee and as a member of various committees of the Federation of Civil Engineering Contractors. Of the present situation he says, 'There have been occasions, well known within the industry, during the recent past when work has been negotiated at figures and on bases which are utterly unrealistic when compared to present-day competitive prices. There is no reason to believe that on most projects the clients' representatives, although perhaps a little naïve, have not acted in complete good faith. A certain abrasiveness is essential in the competitive area and I suggest it could be catastrophic to create anything that would be in the nature of a nice cosy enclave, wherein the interests of all the parties were so closely identified that it would be to the benefit of none of them to uproot inefficiency or incompetence wherever they found it.

'There has, however, been a change of climate which some would associate with the more relaxed standards that have developed in pace with the highly pressurized promotional campaigns that have been geared to the concept of negotiation. We have now reached the stage when all too often it is believed that the tendering process is a façade and the successful contractor is known before it is embarked upon. Whether this is right or not, we should so order our tendering procedures that such suspicions could not be entertained.

'There may indeed be projects where negotiated contracts are a fair way of spending public money but these are very rare, if only because of the difficulty in establishing reasonable criteria whereby a decision is made to negotiate and thereafter with whom to negotiate. The general question of negotiation, however, goes far deeper than this and in my mind strikes at the root of public interest. In the fifties, when contracting generally moved from a seller's to a buyer's market, the industry was faced with two alternatives, either to become more competitive or else to find some means of contracting out of the competitive climate. There followed a massive campaign to popularize the concept of negotiation, and particularly to make it respectable in the public sector.'

Disadvantages of negotiation

'The fundamental disadvantages of negotiation, which I set out in a report to Banwell in 1963, the validity of which has not in any way been impaired by the passage of time, are:

1 that it creates a double price structure and an unhealthy industry which is in nobody's interest;

269

2 that negotiated contracts frequently mask inadequate preparation and planning and therefore directly contribute to inefficiency;

3 that salesmanship and gimmickry are frequently a more important ingredient than constructional knowledge and that there must be a point where the proportion of negotiated work enables the less efficient to survive at the expense of others with the consequent decline in the efficiency of the industry generally;

4 that freedom from proper competition leads to payment of enhanced rates for labour and to the consequent undermining of the wage structure of the industry;

5 that by eliminating competition one destroys or impairs all the yardsticks that are a necessary adjunct to negotiation;

6 negotiated work is open to many abuses and it is the responsibility of the public sector not to assume that such abuses will not take place but to so order its affairs that in the years to come, no matter what changes occur, the temptation to abuse will either not be there or will be minimized.

'I think it is a tribute to the skill with which the protagonists of the negotiated contract have put forward their case that the counter arguments are so very seldom heard. It is true that there is inefficiency amongst medium contractors and large contractors too. This is something we share with every other industry and occupation. It is right that we should protect ourselves against incompetence but at the same time we should be wary about creating a climate where only the big can survive.'

There is no doubt that Morrell is determined to see justice done and he hopes that the declared attitudes of the present government will help. He says in his chairman's statement, 'it is my hope that from the publicity that has been given to this affair and from the reaction of the Corporation, there may stem a reversal of a process which I am convinced has been undermining the health of the industry. This hope is reinforced by recent statements from the Department of Trade and Industry indicating the government's determination to limit circumstances which may undermine the wage structure and possibly to convert the Monopolies Commission into a Commission for Competition. We in this company have always geared ourselves to a healthy competitive industry and we are convinced that in such an environment we will prosper.' With his determination Morrell is most probably right.

Chronology

1949 March — David Morrell joins Mitchell Construction Company as Chief Surveyor.

1953 May — DM appointed Assistant General Manager of MCC.

1954 January — DM appointed General Manager of MCC.
October — MCC awarded contract for Chapelcross.

1958 April — MCC Incorporated. DM acquires 20% of equity.

1959 September — MCC Northern Rhodesia established.

1961 January — Sir Duncan Anderson and Paton in private talk arrange appointment of Dubertret for preparation of geological report.

1962 23 March — MCC acquires Kinnear Moodie.
October — Geoffrey Rippon appoints Banwell Committee.

1963 16 April — DM submits paper to Banwell Committee.
20 June — MCC Holdings floated on London Stock Exchange.
July — MCC awarded main contract for Fawley Power Station.

1964 February — MCC commissions independent report on serious problems arising from ground conditions at Fawley.
June — MCC advises Rendel, Palmer & Tritton that, in their view, to continue deep excavations at Fawley without changes dictated by ground conditions would be to invite disaster.
16 July — Sir Christopher Hinton chairs meeting at Fawley and panel is appointed to consider whether MCC warnings are justified.
4 August — Fawley panel endorses MCC findings. MCC asked to make proposals which are adopted.
15 August — In accordance with plan MCC places over 10,000 cubic yards of concrete in one week – this pace maintained until 236,000 cubic yards placed.

271

1967	January	MCC awarded contract for new pipemill for Stewart and Lloyds at Hartlepool.
	April	Work started at site of pipemill.
1968	January	First pipe rolled at Hartlepool.
1969	25 May	NEDO Conference at Solihull under chairmanship of Sir Frederick Catherwood.
	September	MCC proposals for Anchor Steelworks submitted and well received.
	September	MCC advised that W.S. Atkins & Partners now appointed consultants for Anchor Steelworks and that they would be invited to re-submit proposals on basis of competitive tender.
1970	January	MCC invited to tender again for Anchor.
	26 March	MCC tender for Anchor despatched in the sum of £28 million.
	7 April	MCC learn that their tender figure is known to competitors.
	8 April	MCC asked to change tender to meet new requirements.
	11 April	MCC reluctant to change tender and seek verification of alleged ambiguity.
	13 April	MCC learn from press sources that all other tenders except McAlpine have been eliminated.
		Press advise that BSC thought there was no reason to let contract to lowest tender if there was only £200,000 or so in it.
	18 April	Following telephone call the previous night DM has a meeting with 'X'.
	23 April	MCC learn that McAlpine's general manager has told friend that they have been awarded Anchor contract.
	5 May	David Gardam QC advises MCC have tendered precisely in accordance with tender documents.
	12 May	DM asked if he would accept invitation to join Civil Engineering EDC.
	20 May	Dr Finniston, Deputy Chairman of BSC, advises DM that no decision has yet been taken on Anchor award.
	June	MCC invited to tender for Kariba.
	11 June	*Construction News* publishes details of tenders for Anchor.
	30 July	BSC announce that contract for Anchor has been placed with Robert McAlpine.
	3 August	BSC and W.S. Atkins hold press conference at Connaught Rooms.
	10 August	DM invited to join Civil Engineering EDC.
	1 October	MCC tender for Kariba despatched.
	28 October	DM has meeting with Lord Melchett.

272

1971	15 January	MCC notified of award of Kariba contract.
	March	Dubertret makes further report to Gibbs regarding geology at Kariba. Contents not disclosed to MCC.
	March	Davidson appointed general manager of KNBC.
	March	MCC starts work on site.
	April	Further detailed mappings of Kariba geology by the Department of Geological Survey of Zambia – results not disclosed to MCC.
	8 June	DM has first of series of meetings with McElroy, allegedly commissioned by *Sunday Times* to research construction industry.
	June	Matheson of Zambian Department of Geological Survey report, warning of dangerous conditions to be encountered at Kariba. Report not disclosed to MCC.
	August	Zambian Department of Geological Survey makes maps of geology prepared from observations of excavations being exposed. Maps not disclosed to MCC.
	August	Problems of bad rock start to manifest themselves at Kariba.
	September	DM appointed chairman of joint Building and Civil Engineering EDC working party to examine and report on public sector purchasing of construction.
	3 December	Gibbs' resident engineer notifies partner, Back, in London of dangerous rock falls at Kariba and need to seek safe solution. Back responds that rock falls 'may stabilize'.
	6 December	MCC give formal notice to Gibbs that the difficulties they are meeting could not be foreseen and claiming payment in accordance with terms of contract.
	8 December	Chairman of CAPCO, reproaching Zambia for failure to provide MCC with facilities as provided in the contract, reports to chairman of KNBC and to Zambian Minister of Power: 'It is clear that the contractor has the necessary organization, capacity and enthusiasm to meet his obligations under the contract.'
	21 December	Gibbs reject MCC submission that rock conditions at Kariba could not have been foreseen by experienced contractor.
1972	25 February	Letter from liaison group to president of FCEC expressing desire for change in conduct of Federation business.
	March	Work in machine hall stopped by Chief Mines Inspector as rock falls continue.
	April	Moratorium on plant repayments to World Bank introduced in lieu of payments to MCC for work done.

273

5–8 April	Harries and Back visit site to agree joint report on geology. Report agreed with resident engineer but Back refuses to sign.
19 April	First conference with Keith Goodfellow QC regarding anxieties caused by Kariba.
20 April	Meeting with David Montagu, chairman of Samuel Montagu.
20 April	First of series of meetings arranged by Montagu with Barker, general manager of the Midland Bank.
26 April	Meeting between members of liaison group and president, vice presidents and chairman of FCEC.
2 May	Andrew of Coopers and Lybrand visits DM at Bedford Square to discuss possibility of his firm undertaking an examination and report on MCC cash flow *vis-à-vis* future policy to be adopted by company.
3 May	DM informed by Paton that he would recommend to CAPCO an immediate payment on account of K1 million and would also put forward a proposal that the contract be reviewed in the light of conditions encountered.
9 May	Following FCEC dinner at Dorchester, DM accepts invitation to return with Sir Robin McAlpine to his Mayfair house for general discussion.
15 May	Following meetings with Andrew and Gilbertson, Coopers appointed following 2 May discussions.
18 May	Further report on Kariba geology prepared by Matheson, assisted by Kepje and Vrana of Zambian Department of Geological Survey: emphasizes dangerous conditions and reveals existence of earlier reports not previously disclosed to MCC.
24 May	Gibbs send drawings and instructions to site for installation of anchors to stabilize rock. RE points out that these amount to an admission of changed conditions and in consequence is instructed not to issue them to MCC.
25 May	McPherson killed in rock fall.
31 May	MCC advised that CAPCO do not agree that there are grounds for payment or for revisions of contract.
June	Professors Anderson and Shackleton visit Kariba independently to provide MCC with expert advice and make reports.
15–18 June	Wright visits Kariba.
15–25 June	DM to Kariba and Salisbury: meetings with Ward, Shepherd and Paton. Proposal for independent panel of inquiry agreed in principle.
1 July	Coopers start their assignment at MCC.
27 July	CAPCO advises KNBC that funds for payment of MCC are running out.

July	Constitution, terms of reference and procedures of panel of inquiry agreed. Panel appointed and embarks on inquiry.
20 August	Paton reveals foreknowledge of panel report – to be black on Gibbs' side and white on MCC's.
20 August	Paton suggests revision to contract to be based on reimbursement of costs with additions for overheads and management.
26 August	Panel reports its unanimous findings.
8 September	Paton to Ward and White lamenting Jones 'most unfortunate' admission to the independent panel.
29 September	Gibbs send telex to CAPCO detailing altered form of contract as agreed with MCC.
11 October	Gibbs send telex to CAPCO recommending press release and sending draft outlining problems encountered at Kariba and steps now taken to overcome them.
5 October	KNBC notify CAPCO that they reserve their position regarding the possibility of negligence on the part of CAPCO and of Gibbs.
25 October	CAPCO vetoes press release.
25 October	DM arrives in Lusaka to learn that a series of meetings has been convened between CAPCO, KNBC, the World Bank, Gibbs and MCC. DM receives telex from negotiators in London that Gibbs' representatives 'act like men conscious of something quite dramatic about to happen about which they wish to remain silent'.
27 October	Revised terms, different and less realistic than those already agreed and confirmed in September, are accepted by MCC in effort to resolve problems and incorporated in a document signed by Paton and DM.
28 October	Further repudiation of all earlier agreements in Lusaka including one signed on previous day. MCC given verbal ultimatum incorporating completely unacceptable terms. Talks terminated by the Zambians.
31 October	Coopers present their full report following their four-month investigation of MCC's financial controls.
27 November	Government of Zambia passed Statutory Instrument No. 243 removing Kariba site from the protection of Kariba North Bank Project (Safety and Health of Workers) Act 1971.
29 November	Meeting between Paton, Harding and Edney at which Paton is handed a prepared statement.
30 November –	DM to World Bank in Washington.
5 December	Assurance by Vice President Bell that he was impressing on Zambians the need and wisdom of agreement.
7 December	DM returns from World Bank.

8 December	Meeting Paton/Harding/DM at which Paton promises to issue certificate.
11 December	MCC learn that Paton has gone to Pakistan without issuing certificate. Paton's partner Norris states: 'We know you are entitled to additional payment: as to how long it takes us to decide how much I would not like to forecast.'
14 December	Meeting between DM, the brokers and the sureties to MCC Kariba performance bond (Prudential and Excess) at Bedford Square.
15 December	Moratorium on plant repayments ended and K168,000 deducted from November payment.
19 December	The first of a series of meetings convened by the Zambians and held at their High Commission in London.
20 December	Andrew of Coopers, having attended the first two sessions at Zambian High Commission, confirms to Mitchell holding company board meeting that he was confident that there would be an early payment of between £1 and £2m to MCC: he thought £1.8m realistic.
20 December	Gibbs send urgent message to Shepherd, CAPCO's general manager in Salisbury, urging him to come to London.
21 December	*The Times* reports on dealings in MCC shares including a 'big put option' effected on 18 December.
21 December	Contingency meeting at Samuel Montagu attended by Gillum, Hobson of Coopers, Wright and DM to consider steps to be taken if meetings at Zambian High Commission could not lead to meaningful payment.
21 December	Shepherd, CAPCO's general manager, arrives in London for behind-the-scenes meeting with Gibbs and Zambians.
21 December	Gibbs at partners' meeting consider possibility of 'expelling contractor on grounds of non-performance or insolvency' if MCC do not accept their conditions.
22 December	Shepherd of CAPCO returns to Salisbury. Atmosphere of meeting changes from one of cooperation and conciliation to confrontation.
27 December	Meeting at Zambian High Commission – MCC handed 'draft supplemental agreement', containing arbitrary and unacceptable terms that had no relation to previous agreements, together with 'deed of release'.
29 December	Andrew of Coopers, attending meeting at Zambian High Commission as representative of MCC team, informs meeting that for MCC to go on pumping money into Kariba would be suicidal and his firm could not recommend it. Meeting ends with departure of Zambians.

29 December	Paton advises Goodfellow that he was considering the issue of a certificate when the Zambians arrived and would now study and advise MCC of position.
1973 2 January	Paton advises no certificate will be issued.
2 January	Meeting at DTI attended by Bellamy, Foster, Paton and representative from DoE. Paton insists not one kwacha due to MCC. Foster advises DM to see Zambian High Commissioner Phiri.
2 January	DM has late-night meeting with Phiri at his home in London.
7 January	DM leaves for Lusaka with Mwambasi, Zambian Trade Commissioner in London.
8–13 January	DM in Lusaka but meetings disrupted by final closing of borders with Rhodesia. DM advised by Minister that only basis of agreement was that with which MCC had been confronted in London.
11 January	DM telephones UK and advises deputy Sneden that no further plant or personnel should be sent to Zambia.
January	Following return to London DM informed that Sneden may have made some progress with Gibbs in negotiations and agrees to defer action while Sneden makes further visit to Zambia.
19 January	Meeting between MCC board and financial advisers at Peterborough attended by Hobson of Coopers, Gillum of Samuel Montagu, Williams of Midland Bank, Goodfellow and Hardwick.
20 January	Sneden to Zambia in further abortive attempt to find solution.
23 January	DM writes to Vice President Bell at World Bank appealing again for intervention and detailing consequences if no solution found.
25 January	Gibbs issue 'Nil' certificate in respect of work done by MCC during December.
29 January	MCC advised that exchange control have withdrawn authority for their overdraft facilities in Zambia which must be repaid by 31 January.
29 January	Sneden returns to UK and reports unable to make progress.
30 January	MCC board meeting attended by Gillum of Samuel Montagu. Decision to ask for appointment of receiver. Gillum insists announcement to be delayed until close of business of Stock Exchange on 31 January.
31 January	a.m. Peppiat of Freshfields advises DM that he has had instructions from Washington to stop receivership. Gillum of Samuel Montagu insists 'too late'.

277

31 January	a.m. Collapse of MCC share price leads to suspension of dealings on Stock Exchange.
31 January	p.m. Appointment of Paul Shewell as receiver announced 3.30 p.m.
5 February	Shewell has conference with MCC's legal advisers regarding Peterborough Hospital arbitration.
15 March	DM has first meeting with Jordan and Cork at George Hotel, Stamford – following earlier talks between DM and Cork Gully representatives.
27 April	Jordan appointed liquidator at meeting of creditors at Chartered Insurance Institute.
10 July	KNBC calls upon each of sureties for payment under performance bond.
21 November	Barlow, Lyde & Gilbert draw attention to obvious conflict of interest and emphasize that Excess should have no access to reports submitted in relation to Gibbs' professional indemnity insurance but should abide by majority decisions of others.
3 December	Peterborough Hospital arbitration – award published.
1974 16 September	KNBC sues Prudential and Excess for payment under performance bond. (The first of 42 pleadings defining the position of the various parties and leading to the hearing on 14 March 1979 at which Mr Justice Donaldson fixed the trial date.)
1975 13 February	DM attends meeting with Jordan and Shewell at Cork Gully's office – the first discussion between DM and Shewell regarding affairs of MCC.
1977 26 July	Mr Justice Donaldson rejects application by KNBC to grant a stay in respect of MCC's counterclaim pending referral to arbitration in Zambia.
20 October	Allan Heyman QC instructed on behalf of Jordan to advise regarding possibility of action on grounds of negligence against Shewell.
7 November	Appeal by KNBC against Mr Justice Donaldson's decision dismissed by Lord Justice Ormrod and Lord Justice Roskill in Court of Appeal with costs against KNBC.
7 December	Jordan welcomes proposal by DM that he would meet a share of the costs in the action in return for an equal percentage of any net realization.
1978 7 April	DM learns that Excess underwriter J. Perry Mee is replaced by P.L. Smith.

7 April	Hardwick advises Smith of agreement reached in principle with Beale & Co. for a joint exercise of re-logging cores.
5 May	Committee of inspection approves DM proposal to share costs of action as put forward on 7 December 1977
5 June	Proposed joint inspection of rock cores by experts on either side vetoed by Barlow Lyde & Gilbert who advise underwriters that pressure has been brought to bear to prevent a similar examination by independent experts acting for KNBC.
29 June	Oppenheimer Nathan and Vandyk advise that participation of DM in Kariba proceedings on the basis proposed would be champertous.
9 August	Barlow, Lyde & Gilbert write to underwriters regretting that they have been unable to find any way of preventing case from going to trial – but report developments which might have 'heartening consequences': the plan to 'entice', which was not a conspiracy.
11 August	Meeting of ex-MCC senior executives at which DM meets Smith for first time.
19–25 August	Visit of Shackleton to Rhodesia to make detailed logs of cores – followed by visit to Geological Survey in Lusaka.
24 October	Meeting at Cork Gully office attended by all 'Mitchell' parties but including Smith and also Hewitt Woollacott & Chown and Engineering and Power Development Consultants Ltd representing Excess.
1979 22 January	Jordan writes DM expressing concern that Excess had apparently still not completed their review of their position.
24 January	Hardwick writes to DM saying that Excess had completed their review but the results were not known.
14 March	Mr Justice Donaldson fixes April 1981 trial date.
2 April	Haswell expresses willingness to act as expert for 'Mitchell' side.
6 June	DM advised that on insistence of Excess EPD appointed instead of Haswell.
18 July	EPD's first conference with counsel at which neither the Prudential nor liquidator were represented.
1 August	DM writes to Jordan and Haswell advising intention to withdraw from any further part in the proceedings.
19 October	Paul Morrell meets Jordan in London.
3–4 November	DM has meetings with Jordan in Singapore.
1980 3 January	Paul Morrell learns of EPD report and obtains copy.
8 January	DM learns in Sri Lanka that conference with counsel has been arranged for 10 January.

9 January
Paul Morrell advises Jordan that EPD report is misconceived and inept and should not be taken as a basis for any decisions.

10 January
Sureties and liquidator have conference with counsel to consider EPD report with EPD in attendance. Counsel concerned at effect of EPD's.findings and emphasizes the figures that are essential to him before he can give definitive advice.

17 January
Hardwick in discussions with Beale & Co. regarding terms of settlement.

21 January
Meeting Paul Morrell, Hardwick and EPD at which EPD accept that their report is wrong.

24 January
Meeting DM, Paul Morrell and Jordan at which concern was shared regarding the role of EPD and Hardwick.

28 January
Meeting at Cork Gully's office at which EPD present figures which are again shown to be quite wrong.

28 January
In view of EPD's performance, Jordan decides to instruct Davis Belfield & Everest to examine and report on contract including obtaining advice should they consider it necessary.

5 February
Meeting at Cork Gully's office at which EPD finally confirm the under-certification at Kariba was of the order of K6.398m.

2 April
Following meetings between Smith and underwriters to Gibbs' professional indemnity insurance and Hardwick with Beale & Co. representing KNBC, a meeting between some of the parties to consider terms of settlement. Mitchell Construction Holdings were not involved and Paul Morrell and Davis Belfield & Everest were not informed.

7 May
The secret settlement.

1 June
Amalgamation of Coopers and Lybrand and Cork Gully announced.

1982 2 June
Liquidator writes to creditors advising them that the settlement provided a sum of approximately £1m payable to him as liquidator.

1985 27 March
Extraordinary General Meeting of shareholders of Mitchell Construction Holdings at Chartered Insurance Institute.

20 April
DM, now aware that funds to pay MCC had been running out as early as July 1972, approaches Dr Brian Mawhinney, MP for Peterborough, asking him to inquire from HMG, as guarantor to the World Bank loans to Zambia, how bridging finance was arranged with which to

pay Yugoslav contractors until 14 August 1974 when new loan arrangements were included.

29 July Letter Timothy Raison, Minister of Overseas Development, to Brian Mawhinney – suggests no bridging finance necessary as World Bank funds available.

26 September In response to further inquiry Raison advises Mawhinney that IBRB (World Bank) funds were available throughout the project and that recourse to financing other than IBRD 'was apparently not required'.

2 December Raison to Mawhinney – again in response to further inquiry – 'IBRD loan funds were available for both the foreign and the local costs throughout the life of the project'.

1986 13 January Raison to Mawhinney – in response to DM's statement that the Minister's letter did not conform to the facts as DM understood them and, furthermore, that provision of IBRD funds for local (i.e. civil engineering) costs would involve a major departure from World Bank principle and practice – states that funds for local costs were always available but admits that they had to come from CAPCO.

9 March Raison to Mawhinney (DM having drawn attention once again to the fact that CAPCO had no funds) – suggests DM should apply to World Bank for any further information.

24 June World Bank inform DM that all information has been given to HMG and they have nothing to add.

11 December Letter from Shewell finally refusing to make available papers relating to the company's affairs during period when he acted as receiver and manager, on the grounds that he believed action was being contemplated against him.

1987 5 January Following further correspondence directed at securing an answer to DM's initial query, Christopher Patten (Raison's replacement as Minister for Overseas Development) writes to Mawhinney insisting that HMG had no financial obligation in respect of the Kariba North Bank Power Station and regrets that the Overseas Development Administration were not in a position to provide answers regarding the financing of local costs.

20 March DM, having learned of a number of payments made by HMG in respect of Kariba and having asked for an explanation, Patten advises Mawhinney that 'as it appears from his letters that Mr Morrell has known about the agreement under which these payments were made all

281

	along [a wrong assumption] nothing further would be gained by seeking to answer his questions'.
1 June	Hardwick letter finally refusing to let Mitchell Construction Holdings see Kariba settlement to which it is allegedly a party.

Index

283